SUICIDE – THE ULTIMATE REJECTION?

SUICIDE – THE ULTIMATE REJECTION?
A PSYCHO-SOCIAL STUDY

Colin Pritchard

Open University Press
Buckingham • Philadelphia

Open University Press
Celtic Court
22 Ballmoor
Buckingham
MK18 1XW

and
1900 Frost Road, Suite 101
Bristol, PA 19007, USA

First Published 1995
Reprinted 1996

A catalogue record of this book is available from the British Library

ISBN   0 335 19033 2 (hb)   0 335 19032 4 (pb)

Library of Congress Cataloging-in-Publication Data
Pritchard, Colin. 1936–
    Suicide – the ultimate rejection?: a psycho-social study / Colin
Pritchard.
        p.   cm.
    Includes bibliographical references and index.
    ISBN 0–335–19033–2. — ISBN 0–335–19032–4 (pbk.)
    1. Suicide.   2. Suicide—Prevention.   3. Suicide—Sociological
aspects.   4. Suicide victims—Family relationships.   5. Suicide—
Statistics.   I. Title.
HV6545. P/5 1995
362.2'8—dc20   94–43417
                                                                              CIP

Typeset by Graphicraft Typesetters Ltd, Hong Kong
Printed in Great Britain by St Edmundsbury Press Ltd,
Bury St Edmunds, Suffolk

CONTENTS

ACKNOWLEDGEMENTS

I am heavily indebted to many professional and academic colleagues. Some of my academic debts will be evident from the bibliography, which is extensive and intended to serve as a resource and an exemplar of interdisciplinary relevance.

I owe much to many students' commitment and vocation, which refurbish my own. I am grateful for their questions, which stimulate the necessary research and practice consideration: from the Universities of Leeds, Bath, Hong Kong Poly-technic, Curtin, Monash, Sydney and, above all, the University of Southampton.

I have learned much from individuals and families who have allowed me the privilege of entry into their lives which is acknowledged by donating half the royalties of this book to the National Schizophrenia Fellowship. To preserve their privacy they cannot be named, but their example of overcoming adversity is a constant encouragement. All the illustrative examples drawn from practice have of course been anonymized to ensure individual confidentiality.

To the many colleagues who have contributed to my academic development and extended my practice understanding, I offer sincerest thanks, even though I have not always been as good a student as I might have been. They include the late Elizabeth Barraclough, Louise Bruce, Elizabeth Irvine, Maria Farrow, Marian Hamilton, Max Hamilton, Alice May Harrison, Peter Noakes and Peter Sedgwick. Happily I can still express my appreciation to: Ron Baker, Brian Barraclough, Peter Boss (Melbourne), Anne Buchanan, Alan Butler, Eric Button, Joe Campling, Isobelle Card, Peter Coleman, Deborah Clooney, Malcolm Cox, Ian Diamond, Martin Davies, Tony Gale, Jane and James Gibbons, Colin Gordon, Karl Gorniak (Munich), Gabor Heggesi (Budapest), Margaret Hamilton, Tim Holt, Arthur Hunt, Peter Huxley, Jim Iffe (Perth), Kenan Irmak (Marburg), Ray Jones, Michael Kerfoot, Kay Kay Ku (Hong Kong), Malcolm Lacy, Bernard Lau and Jenny Mac (Hong Kong), Clive Marsland, Vera Mehta (Vienna), Jean Nursten, Joe Oliver, Phyllida Parsloe, Silvia Pasti (Bucharest), Geof Pearson, Werner Andreas Petrick (Toblach), Raymond Plant, Jackie Powell, Herschel Prins, Stewart Rees (Sydney),

Ken Reid (Michigan), Eric Sainsbury, Daphne Shepherd, Francis Sheldon, Chris Shilling, Ursula and Paul-Walter Stuff (Attendorn), Richard Taylor, Chris Thompson, Noel Timms, Peter Wadsworth, Eric Walker, Richard Williams and Derek Williamson.

In the preparation of the book, special thanks are due to: June Tilling for her professional patience; colleagues from the Open University Press; Joan Malherbe for her forbearance; Alan Pearson for his meticulous proofreading; and Nick Evans for his invaluable editorial assistance.

Finally, to Beryl, whose professional commitment and dedication are a constant inspiration, but most of all for her love, humour, friendship and incredible tolerance for more than thirty years.

LIST OF FIGURES AND TABLES

CHAPTER 1

INTRODUCTION

Following the suicide of a seventeen-year-old man, his grieving family were left desolate after a funeral in which he was interred in unhallowed ground. The echoes of Ophelia's funeral from Shakespeare's *Hamlet* are obvious yet the burial occurred in a European Community country, Greece, in 1992 and highlights the interrelationship of personal and family tragedies with social, political, religious and legal attitudes to the phenomenon of suicide. The young man apparently felt rejected because of an unrequited love, and had impulsively killed himself. His grieving family felt rejected by his apparent disregard for their feelings, while the shocked local community expressed its ambivalence in attending the funeral, which was held outside the village cemetery, *en masse*.

Suicide is a human phenomenon, found throughout recorded history. It was noted in biblical times within the Jewish and Christian faiths. It is mentioned in the *Bhagavad Gita* within the Hindu faith, in classical Greece and Rome, and later throughout the middle ages, when the reaction to the heresy of suicide was severe hostility from the universal Church, whose later fathers railed against the canonical sin of despair.

Suicide occurs in every culture, not only in the Western developed world, but also in India, China and, despite severe theological prohibitions, Islam. It has attracted many myths of national stereotyping and, as will be shown, assumptions often held by English-speaking people about suicide in Japan and Sweden are very questionable.

There is another form of myth, that of 'beautiful' deaths, which often surrounds the end of young people in apparently idealistic suicides. This is best epitomized by the famous painting by Henry Wallis (which is now in the Tate Gallery) of the death of the young poet Chatterton in 1770. He was barely eighteen when he poisoned himself in his London garret. The painting shows a slender young man, in apparently peaceful deep repose, with the early morning light coming through an open window, which partly reveals detail half-hidden in shadow. The educated viewer can guess that the open box full of notepaper, which on closer scrutiny is seen to be all torn, was the result of Chatterton destroying his work. The picture echoes Keats's line that he was 'not dead but slept', and that his death was a reflection of his life, suggesting the sentimental notion that he had died for his art, that life was too brutal for such a sensitive soul to continue breathing the unartistic air of an industrializing, brutal, non-aesthetic world.

The reality was more harsh. Chatterton died of despair and in poverty, because he was rejected by those to whom he promised, and by whom he had been promised, so much. Throughout our exploration of suicide we return to this recurrent theme of rejection and rejecting. So very often in the suicide predicament, we find that there is a subjective experience of the victim feeling repudiated by those around him or her, be they a particular individual, family, community or circumstance, which shatters his or her hold on the value of life. Those close to the victim can equally feel forsaken and rebuffed. How could it be that their loved one apparently felt such little regard for them, and could jettison life, evidently disregarding the grief and loss imposed upon a shattered and confused family? This is an interactive hurt, where all concerned are victims, for few can be neutral in the presence of suicidal behaviour. It is for this reason that we see suicide as the ultimate psychological and social rejection. We eschew the Chatterton vision of suicide as being sugary and sentimental. It is an artificial and elevated notion of self-death, for, cruelly, the physical reality is of a vomit-choked face, of the hideous distortions of a twisted rope, of the grotesque multiple fractures of a shattered body, of a stinking bloated cadaver whose rotting remains are thrown back by a rejecting sea.

However, it will be argued that suicide is not an obscure or specialist area of academic social or psychological or psychiatric study, but has a relevance to all those in the health and social community fields, policy-makers and citizens alike. Indeed, the extent of suicide reflects the level of cohesion in a society, and can be taken as an indicator of the well-being of that society, as it impinges upon its individual members.

Where is the evidence for such a sweeping statement? It lies in the simple contrast between the political and media concern over the tragedies of child abuse and neglect deaths, and the degree to which societies around the world commit resources to homicide as opposed to suicide. Suicide is not only a major psycho-social problem for those directly involved, but is in resource and impact terms far more serious than *all* kinds of homicide. For example, based upon World Health Organization data (WHO 1973–94), in 1992 there were 4,628 suicides in the UK, a rate of 121 per million males. This is more than ten times the homicide rate, which includes all the terrorism-related deaths in Northern Ireland. In the United States, from the latest figures available, 30,232 people died from suicide in a year, more than 500 a week; this gives a male rate per million of 199, compared with a homicide rate of 144. It must be remembered that the American murder rate is the highest in the Western developed world. In Australia, male suicide exceeded homicide by 210 to 29 per million, more than seven to one, and in 1990 and 1991 there were more suicides in Northern Ireland than all the 'troubles' deaths put together, which was the case for six of the past eight years.

The other major media concern is deaths from child abuse. In the United Kingdom, which has had the greatest reduction in child abuse deaths in the Western world over the past twenty years, there were more than eighty suicides a week, compared with just one murder of a child under fourteen per week. Incidentally, twenty years ago the rate was 2.4 per week, and while the gap between child abuse deaths and suicide would not be as wide in the USA, Australia or New Zealand, suicide is still a far more frequent tragedy than child murder.

However, because of media focus, it would probably be true to say that if you asked any community-based professional, whether general practitioner, social worker or health visitor, where lay his or her greatest professional anxiety, it would probably centre on the ethical and professional dilemmas and complexities of child abuse. This is in spite of recent research showing that more than 10 per cent of all young adults who were probation and social service department clients had been involved in some form of suicidal behaviour (Hudson *et al.* 1993; Pritchard *et al.* 1993). In terms of human costs and demands upon service resources, suicide is the second highest cause of death in young people in every developed Western country. Associated with death by suicide are the so-called 'attempted suicides', and depending upon age group, 'attempted suicides' range in number from forty to one hundred for every actual death. They are the most frequent cause of acute medical admission for young adult females, and the second most frequent for young adult males. Consequently, suicidal behaviour places enormous strains upon health and community services.

At the same time, without exception, in every country, suicide is not neutral in its impact. It sucks people, families and professionals alike, into a vortex of confused and ambivalent emotions, and there is evidence that it leaves scars upon all survivors.

Suicide is most often associated with mental illness, and this simple concept, which has long been known as a 'psychiatric emergency', will be explored later. The suicide level among the mentally ill is eighty to ninety times that of the general population, and thus there is a notion of a degree of morbidity attached to mental illness. While this is true, two new social and health problems are emerging, giving an additional twist to the complexities of suicide. There is a link between unemployment and suicide that cannot be gainsaid, and the worsening trends in unemployment for younger people of both genders is proving to be an almost intractable problem, which may have a further impact upon suicide rates. At the same time the insidious growth of HIV infection, and later AIDS, over the next decade is likely to attract further suicide, giving further impetus to the sense of urgency.

It is not all bad news, however, for we will explore evidence, based upon interdisciplinary research, which demonstrates that an integrated approach can make major inroads into some of the causal factors of suicide. This optimism is supported from what some might consider an unlikely source, namely Britain's Department of Health. In an innovative and seminal document, the British

Government laid down a range of health targets for the nation (DOH 1992). This followed the World Health Organization's aspirations for the world by the end of the millennium, but uniquely the Secretary of State for Health, reasserting the principle of prevention as a foundation for the NHS, gave targets to the British health and community services to reduce deaths, not only from coronary heart disease, lung cancers and AIDS, but also those associated with mental illness. This is a logical twinning of the Durkheimian ideas of social cohesion and measures of accountability of outcome of professional service. It has been suggested that this British initiative will quickly be followed in other Western countries for, just as infant mortality rates are often seen as an indicator of the degree of the health of the nation, it is being suggested that suicide will become a paradoxical indicator of the effectiveness of health and social community services. Thus, from the outset the issue of suicide not only has ethical, religious, legal, personal, social and medical complexities; it will, it is believed, be at the centre of the political debate about the health of the nation and society. It is suspected that we cannot avoid controversy, not least because there is so much yet unclear and unknown, but implicit in governments' aspirations to improve health is the acknowledgement that the annual toll from suicide is unacceptably high and probably unnecessary.

We are haunted by the obscene eighteenth-century metamorphosis of the lonely suicide of Thomas Chatterton from a dismal, despairing misery to a 'beautiful' myth, which denies the reality of the brutality of arsenic poisoning, following an artistic, personal and social rejection. The death of the modern young Greek is prescient: he was rejected by his lover; in turn he rejects life and his family, who experience the twist in the vortex of suicide, as they face ostracism and rejection from those around them. Truly, suicide is 'the ultimate rejection'.

Measuring rates of suicide

The definition of suicide is at first sight deceptively simple. Suicide occurs when a person dies by his or her own hand. In British, Australasian and American law, a coroner's court determines a suicide verdict, exactly as a criminal court determines whether a person is guilty or not guilty. This is based upon the need to have both an *actus rheas* (a guilty act, the behaviour) and, crucially in specifically determining suicide, a *mens rheas* (the guilty intent). In effect the question the court must decide is not only whether the person killed himself or herself, but whether he or she *intended* to. Consequently, if you find a dead man alone in a room with a weapon in his hand, or an unbiased witness who may have seen him shoot himself, clearly the act was unquestionable: the *actus rheas* is established. But was this decisive unequivocal outcome intended, or was it an accident? This problem continues to bedevil the issue of counting and measuring suicides, as many have claimed (Chambers and Harvey 1989) that courts are often influenced in their decisions by a reluctance to record suicide, not only because sometimes there are real uncertainties, but often, where possible, to spare the feelings of families who still experience the stigma surrounding the event. Therefore, it is argued, not only are suicides likely to be under-reported, but there may well be unresolved uncertainties in the minds of both family survivors and the professional staff who may have been involved. Incidentally, not only may courts seek to temper the tragedy, there may also be an unconscious subtle desire on the part of others involved to prefer this uncertainty, rather than face the exploration of who 'rejected' whom. Certainly Chambers and Harvey (1988, 1989) and others, such as Kolmos and Bach (1987) and Kleck (1988), have tried to determine whether the true suicide rate is much higher than the official statistics suggest, and this is an area of continuing controversy. What the uncertainty around the suicide verdict does, which eventually leads, via the count, to the national rate, is to highlight the complexity of deciding what is suicide.

In Britain and Australasia in particular, the most important piece of *evidence* that decides the suicide verdict usually centres on the issue of intent. This is determined by whether there was some form of communication, either verbal or, traditionally, in a 'suicide note'. Increasingly over the years, courts have accepted what might be described as tangential indications from the deceased when they have expressed their intent to other people, such as relatives and professionals, who may be in a position to have some idea about the deceased person's state of mind. There has been some suggestion that suicides are sometimes hidden in what appear to be accidents; conversely, there is confusion about purpose, and whether the death and circumstances were a coincident misadventure. Some deaths are officially categorized as 'undetermined deaths'. These are recorded where no one knows the cause of death, or the decision has not yet been made. Nevertheless, violent deaths within the 'undetermined' category do occur more often in people who have had or are having a mental illness (Roy 1986; Fremouw *et al.* 1990), but we do not know whether these *were* covert suicides or whether, because of the distress, disruption and distraction associated with mental illness, sufferers are more likely to die from such injuries anyway. Such complexities can even reach the national media and arouse a whole range of conjecture. This occurred in the so-called 'Marconi suicide deaths'. The editor of a computer journal, Tony Collins, noted what appeared to be an unexpected cluster of suicides over a relatively short period of time. He found himself engaged in organizing a number of obituaries concerned with scientists working in the electronics industry. There was a wave of speculation about the reasons for this, from covert espionage operations, through some destabilizing effect of exposure to electronics, to increased stress in reaction to a shrinking arms industry; or was it just a simple statistical fluke? The events drew the media attention of the English-speaking world, and Collins's book *Open Verdict* (1990) was appropriately titled, and highlighted just how easily speculation can arise in the not-so-simple decision of whether a person died from suicide or not. Consequently, when we make national and international comparisons of suicide rates, we have to take into account methods of recording. And broadly, it is true to say that the English-speaking countries have similar systems, though not exactly the same, but there is greater variation in Western and Eastern Europe.

Some authorities have raised questions about the accuracy of national suicide rates (Kolmos and Bach 1987; O'Carroll 1989). However, on balance, research into annual national figures has demonstrated that there is a reasonable reliability in the figures (Holding and Barraclough 1978; Sainsbury 1983; Kolmos and Bach 1987; Kleck 1988; Speechy and Stavarky 1991), not least because any inherent errors appear to be consistent over time *within* the same culture. Thus while it is accepted that many coroners, especially when dealing with the difficult issue of adolescent suicide, will want to minimize the anguish of the family, careful analysis has shown that even in this area the figures are reasonably stable (Males 1991). In any international comparison, therefore, we draw upon the World Health Organization annual mortality statistics, which are reasonably reliable because they are based upon intranational data over time. However, to compare suicide between countries it is better first to examine any changes *within* a country's rate (e.g. the Anglo-Welsh male rate for 1973 was 94 per million; by 1992 this had risen to 121 per million, in effect a *rise* of 29 per cent over the period). Over this period, Sweden's male and female suicide rates were always higher than Britain's. However, if we examine the Swedish male rate (which in 1973 was 295 per million, but by 1990 had fallen to 241, which is an effective *reduction* of 12 per cent), the initial impression changes dramatically. This is the main rationale for making an internal comparison of a country's mortality over time before contrasting it with another country. Incidentally, Sweden is one of only two countries to have a reduction in male suicide over the period (Germany is the other), which may well be influenced by better employment situations and welfare systems (Pritchard 1995a, b). Moreover, we do not make a direct cross-national comparison, because there *might* be key differences in recording methods; but comparing a country's rate with itself over time will account for any recording variations. Thus emerged the surprising fact, counter to the media image, about Swedish suicide, which at first sight appears more serious than it is in England and Wales, which *may* be only partially true; but of greater practice and policy significance is that, over the past twenty years, British male suicide has worsened considerably. However, there are gender complexities, not least because there are major changes occurring, which may not yet be 'completed'; so women's deaths will be examined separately.

What is in this book?

It will be argued that suicide not only is the most intense, extreme consequence of *personal* psycho-social distress, but can also be an indicator of environmental factors that compound the potential for personal anguish. It will also be argued that Durkheim's great insight that a nation's suicide rate is indicative of the cohesiveness of that society is borne out by modern international research.

This book has emerged from more than twenty years of research and teaching mental health to medical, psychiatric and social work students. The author was taught by one of Britain's most eminent psychiatric researchers, Max Hamilton, that if one teaches a practice, one must continue to have a practice link, in order to avoid sounding like a textbook. Thus, via a small, independent and free mental health practice, I am still aware of the *practitioner's* anxiety, uncertainty, confusion and anger at the personal and social injustices which so often confound people's lives. I hope, therefore, that the text is not too far from the front-line reality, where life is seldom as organized and tidy as it sometimes appears in professional literature, which seems to ignore the messy apprehensions that come from trying to 'catch the quicksilver' of someone else's life, as it progresses through calms, crises and emergencies.

However, we do seek to match empathy and analysis, as empathy alone can be a shared chaos, while analysis without empathy is coldly sterile. Consequently we draw upon the social and behavioural sciences, modern clinical psychiatry and not least literature, both classical and contemporary, in seeking to offer an integrated approach to practice. The interdisciplinary nature of effective mental health intervention is stressed, as so often the topic is compartmentalized from either a theoretical or a disciplinary perspective: behaviourists versus ego-dynamic; pharmacological versus psycho-social counselling; psychiatrist versus approved social worker.

There are a number of particular features to the book. First, in our exploration of the causes contributing to suicide, we will schematically explore what is described as stress as opposed to psychiatric suicide, but in particular, albeit briefly, examine the new intriguing bio-physiological research, which may have implications for assessment of risk levels and/or the possible treatment of particular situations. At all times we will seek to match the research evidence with experience, emphasizing that all practice must be client-specific, in time and place. Therefore at all times we are conscious that the best practice *art* is always based upon the best available *science*.

Second, there will be a challenge to the somewhat sentimental, if not self-indulgent, approach to suicide taken by some social scientists who have seldom, if ever, had to confront the outcome of an individual family tragedy. While suicide in the last analysis is an intensely personal act, the social ramifications, and how society impinges upon individuals in actual or potentially vulnerable situations, are always an important consideration. And though no one needs to court controversy when exploring issues related to suicide, almost inevitably contentions will arise, not least between those who wish to paint in broad sociological brush-strokes and those of the single anti-statistical case analysis.

Third, the book has an international cross-cultural dimension as we examine changes in suicide in all developed countries over the past twenty years. In addition there is an urgent need to examine and understand the variations of suicide in the multi-ethnic societies of Western Europe, North America and Australasia.

Fourth, the idea that suicide is 'the ultimate rejection' is both an assertion and a question, as suicidal behaviour is essentially interactive, impacting upon the sufferer, his or her immediate family and the wider society. Hence comes the psycho-social ambiguity in the suicidal constellation, as rejection is experienced by the sufferers themselves, their families and society in an often angry, confused search for the scapegoat upon whom to cast the blame.

Fifth, we take a very positive approach to the prediction and prevention of suicidal behaviour, while not denying the difficulty. It is believed that there is sufficient research evidence that, based upon an optimal integrated treatment approach, we can repudiate the pessimism that often surrounds suicide and can actively begin to reduce the dreadful toll.

Sixth, a particular focus will be upon the bereaved families of the sufferers, who often require specific help in their own right, which, unlike in North America, is rarely given in Britain.

Finally, but not least, there is a brief exploration of the ethical and practical dilemmas surrounding suicide, which parallel the issues of euthanasia. The interface of the two issues is examined, asking the question as to when if ever can there be a 'rational' suicide, and a justification for 'assisted suicide'. In the new world of 'cost counting', the author's former confidence in professionals' primary objective of client or patient care has been severely undermined, and one fears a slippery slope where the rationale for decisions is determined by factors other than patient care. This may or may not be unjust to the new leaders of Britain's National Health Service, but time will tell. It is hoped that this book will make some contribution to clarifying those fraught and anxious moments when professional, family and sufferers alike, face the crisis of acute distress and despair. Inevitably we have to partialize and atomize these complex issues, but I would remind readers of the truism that the reality of individuals' lives is the totality of their experience, both physical and psycho-social. This includes their history, the socio-economic context in which they act out their lives, and their unique cognitive perceptions of their experience. This book tries to weave together 'knowledge-insights' drawn not only from practice and empirical research but also from the history and literature of our culture. We begin this psycho-social study of suicide, the ultimate rejection, with a historical and cultural exploration of Western society.

CHAPTER 2

SUICIDE IN HISTORY AND LITERATURE: SOCIAL AND CULTURAL VARIATIONS

Suicide, or self-killing, has been known throughout the whole of recorded history and has been a phenomenon in every cultural and social setting. What has changed over the centuries are philosophical, social and legal attitudes towards suicide. Former attitudes still reverberate, creating confused and ambivalent echoes which continue to plague modern humanity. However, to understand societies', other people's and our own attitudes to suicide, subconscious and overt, we need to combine insights gained from literature and philosophy with the more precise understanding provided by practice-related empirical research.

It might be argued that to understand the sources of modern attitudes to suicide, we only need to explore the seventeenth- and eighteenth-century philosophers, such as Locke, Hume and Kant, especially the last, whose ideas on suicide showed a continuity with classical authors such as Aquinas, Aristotle and Plato. But as a practising psychiatric social worker and empirical researcher, I believe that there are major advantages in understanding the psychology and sociology of suicide, via a brief look at some Western literature, both classic and modern. It is argued that to gain the most authentic psychological understanding of another's mind involved in the suicidal constellation, we need to turn to the great poets, who best illuminate human phenomena, including something of a person's despair and experience of the ultimate rejection of the world and self.

Classical and religious responses to suicide

Within the Judaeo-Christian tradition, there are eleven instances of suicide described in the Bible's Old Testament and one in the New Testament. Perhaps the most famous death in the former is the suicide of King Saul following his defeat by the Philistines, heard in David's lament, 'how are the mighty fallen'. Saul had sought the assistance of his bodyguard to help him kill himself. The soldier was horrified at the sacrilegious notion of killing his anointed king, and turned the sword upon himself. Saul, apparently aided by such an example, then followed suit.

Brian Barraclough (1990), a world-leading researcher, significantly demonstrates that in neither the Old nor the New Testament are there any overt negative statements made about suicides; they are simply reported without any comment whatsoever. Perhaps the most famous of all suicides, and the only one in the New Testament, that of Judas Iscariot, is referred to in two of the gospels, and without any judgemental reflection of any kind. Saul's death would today be described as being in the classic Roman tradition, though it preceded Rome by almost a thousand years. Traditionally, in Hebraic times, suicide was considered mainly to be related to some form of madness or 'frenzy'. There is, however, an honourable exception made of the first century mass suicide by the Jewish defenders of Masada, who killed first their families and then themselves, rather than fall into the hands of the conquering Roman Emperor Vespasian. This tragedy still evokes an ambivalent admiration, but similar tragedies in modern times, such as the apparent mass suicide by a religious cult in Latin America, cause some degree of moral disquiet, not least because in post-biblical times there are clear Christian and Islamic sanctions against suicide.

It appears that the overt prohibition against suicide was first formerly pronounced by Saint Augustine (AD 345–430), who in his *City of God* described the action as a 'mortal sin'. From around this time the Christian Church began to express increasing concern about suicide as a form of false martyrdom. The fifth-century heresy of the Donatists was seen as an affront to God, and the self-slaughter was an act of despair, which was both a denial and a rejection of the potential mercy and salvation of God. Within a little more than 100 years, the Council of Bragga (AD 566) prohibited masses to be said for the souls of those dying by suicide and the comfort for them of a Christian burial in hallowed ground. This sanction lasted for many years within the Christian Episcopalian tradition, and Wymer (1986) reports that the last recorded 'unhallowed' burial in Britain occurred as late as 1823. Sadly this reflects the recent report, in 1992, of the young Greek man being buried outside church ground. The accumulative impact of such attitudes to suicide must have played some part in the distress, shame and stigma which still surround the issue. The *cri de coeur* of Laertes at the funeral of his sister Ophelia gives us a sense of the anguish that was, and is still, felt and his condemnation of the 'churlish priest', who was reluctant to give full rites because her death 'was doubtful', is but one of many examples of the paradox and ambivalence of persisting early attitudes. Yet even this rejecting orthodox response went side-by-side with occasional willingness to be understanding, seen in a speech by Marcus Andronicus: 'be not barbarous. The Greeks upon advice did bury Ajax, that slew himself' (*Titus Andronicus*, I.i).

Suicide was not always condemned by the early and medieval church when, for example, following some sexual assault, such as rape, the victim took a 'virtuous' or honourable way out. She could then claim the sympathy and the forgiveness of her society and family, in both Roman and Christian times. This is reflected in the deaths of Lucrece and a number of lesser-known martyrs whose reputations and virtue had been besmirched. This demonstrates another element in the mixed emotions surrounding suicide, found in the apparent rationale for such extreme action, which absolved them from the customary rejecting anathema.

The Christian Churches' response to suicide influenced not only canon but also statutory law, though it is interesting to note that even in the fifteenth century, when there were severe sanctions against suicide, such as forfeiture of property, loss of absolution and entering Dante's Third Circle of Hell, exceptions were made if the person was considered to be deranged. Typical of the times, was the intercession of compassionate clerics that led the soldier King Edward III to establish the sanctuary for lunatics in the Bedlam Hospital, founded in 1347. This was a most progressive and humanitarian act, reflected in the Chaucerian Knight's and Nun's tales: they knew the 'melancholy' humour which created such dangerous physical and spiritual fear and anxiety. Nevertheless, even today in the Roman Church, suicide remains a cardinal sin, though clearly there is a vastly better understanding and clemency than in yesteryear. The 'offence' still appears to lie in the person's rejection of hope, and the moral dilemma inherent in the phenomenon is contained in the old German word for suicide, *Selbstmord*, self-murder.

This dilemma about intent and rationality will be explored further, but suicide is still stigmatized both socially and professionally (Fremouw *et al.* 1990; Usher 1991) which may partly account for the ambivalence surrounding euthanasia, another form of 'self-killing' that appears to be differentiated from suicide only by assumed aetiology and rationality. Nevertheless, it must be remembered that in English and Welsh law it is still an indictable offence to assist in procuring either suicide or euthanasia. This is also the case in the USA, as seen in the sermons of the so-called Doctor Death, Dr Kervochian, who advertises such assistance and is currently going through the New York State Court of Appeal.

The theological objection to suicide centres on the notion that despair means the rejection of God's grace (Thomas Aquinas, 1225–74). It also strikes a very modern chord, in that Aquinian objections to self-murder included the distress, hurt and deep sense of rejection felt by the survivors, i.e. the victim's family, group, tribe or society. Another example of ambivalence and double standards is the brutal way in which Simon de Montfort (1208–65) father of the first English parliament in 1258, tarnished his repute in his vicious oppression of the Albigensian 'heresy', which he partly justified by their heretical acceptance of suicide. As Barraclough (1990) later showed, in neither the Judaic nor Christian parts of the Bible are there any direct injunctions against suicide. However, this is not the case in the Islamic tradition, which continues to be a major influence upon many Islamic people.

There are three quite specific sanctions expressed in the Koran against self-killing. The Prophet Mohammed, who pre-dates Dante by almost seven centuries, also assigns suicides to the third or lower levels of Hell. The impact of this injunction still has considerable force in Islamic countries, and it may be one reason why, with the exception of Jordan and Turkey, there is virtually *no* recorded suicide in the national statistics of the Islamic nations. Such abhorrence and the corresponding horror of suicide has very important practice and clinical significance in multi-ethnic communities. This results in the need for practitioners to consider carefully the potential implications when working with people of the Islamic faith, or with those who hold the more traditional values of the Christian Church. We will return to these practice issues later.

In respect of the broad Hindu faith, while the notion of 'altruistic' suicide appears acceptable in the tradition, there is a taboo against suicide, particularly among men. Again the ambivalence emerges from the rationale for the suicide, which has profound gender differences. There are other variations from the Western profile of suicide, which may well account for the differential patterns of suicide found among people from Asian and Islamic countries. For example, unlike in the Eurocentric societies, there is an honourable Hindu tradition associated with bereaved women committing suicide. This may be a factor in the finding that the suicide rate among women from the Hindu tradition in Britain, appears to be almost twice the rate of men from the same ethnic background (Soni Raleigh et al. 1990). This is virtually the exact opposite of most Western-orientated societies, including Japan. Again, these are points to which we will return when discussing suicide and ethnicity.

The classic Greek–Roman attitude, often described as the 'honourable' course of action, was described in Homeric times, from around 700 BC onwards. Particularly celebrated examples were Cleopatra, who preferred death to 'riding in Young Octavian's triumph', or the Emperor Vitellius following his defeat by Galba, a response which has echoes in other cultures, such as the Japanese samurai tradition.

Perhaps the most famous Greek suicide is that of Socrates, who, even to many of his own time, was most unjustly persecuted by the anti-intellectuals of his day, when Athen's rulers, in a time of decline, sought a scapegoat. Yet even here, Socrates is said to have disapproved of self-slaughter, and his taking of hemlock was seen as a public duty, to spite the 'injustice' he had been legally condemned to by the *demos* and society of his day. Plato, and later Aristotle, 'agreed' with Thomas Aquinas that suicide deprives the community and family of the person's potential creativity and, in this sense, the suicide's rejection of life, family and city is therefore unjust.

Homer tells of the suicide of Ajax, which is perhaps the first unequivocal recorded death related to psychological derangement, and is different from the majority of 'honourable' exits in subsequent classical literature. Men and women were equally recognized as heroic in this area. For example, Sophocles records Antigone's death, who finds herself pinned on the horns of the dilemma of responding to two diametrically opposed moral imperatives. Antigone defied civil law by giving honourable burial to her brother, who was a traitor to the city state, but she obeyed the laws of propriety and family kinship by her rejection of the city's immutable dictat.

Other Greek women's deaths, like those of Jocasta and Phaedra, have one thing in common, sexual impropriety. Jocasta was the mother and inadvertent wife of Oedipus, and learning of her breaking the sacred taboo of incest, killed herself. Phaedra fell in love and wished to marry her stepson Hippolytus, which came very close to breaking the fearsome taboo, yet both women are seen as partial victims of an unjust fate. Suffice it to say that, in all these Greek cases, there was an element of ambiguity and ambivalence.

It might be fair to say that Roman suicides had a good press via the genius of Plutarch, Tacitus, Juvenal and the Renaissance writers. Again it was ambivalent, as Macbeth, trapped by Burnham Wood with no way out, sneeringly says: 'Why, should I play the Roman fool, and die on mine own sword?' Seneca (first century AD), sometimes described as a philosopher, was perhaps the most prominent of the self-publicists, though perhaps we have been overly influenced by the scepticism expressed by the moderns Eliot and Graves. Seneca's death can be seen in the light of a free man's rejection of tyranny in his ringing 'You enquire the road to freedom? You shall find it in every vein in your body.' This is very grand. The Victorians, in particular, admired the nobility of these Romans who in the face of adversity, rather than bearing apparent shame and degradation, killed themselves, exemplified by Brutus and Cassius following their failure in the civil war with Octavian and Mark Antony. Women do not go unrecognized, as Cleopatra, with Antony, repeated the gesture to the admiration of succeeding generations.

Lucrece reflects a number of later Christian slayings, and was absorbed into the Christian calendar. She died by her own hand after being ravished, while Petronius, the probable author of the Satiricon, died under mild protest, although he was scurrilous about the antics of Nero. Nevertheless, the arbiter of elegance made his death appear to be almost in good taste. Many of these and other suicides recorded by Tacitus, Plutonius and Plutarch were political, in that the emperors of the day, rather than executing political opponents for 'treason', could save their heirs and successors from extreme economic catastrophe by offering them the honourable option of suicide. Nevertheless, as with the Greeks, the feeling of ambivalence about suicide, though muted, continued as suicides were buried with their right hands chopped off. Yet Gibbon, in recording the deaths of Roman emperors such as Nero and in particular Vitellius, illustrated his admiration when he said of the viscerally challenged Vitellius, 'nothing in his life so became him as his ending', in a life in which honour had figured little other than at the end. Such was the 'Roman' way.

The beginnings of 'modern' attitudes

We will focus upon three nearly contemporaneous people from the late sixteenth and early seventeenth centuries; William Shakespeare (1564–1616), John Donne (1571–1631), both poets and playwrights, and Robert Burton (1577–1640), another Midlander, who was both cleric and physician, being the author of *The Anatomy of Melancholy*.

Burton's text was published in 1621, and exudes an outstanding sympathetic humanitarianism, as he was compassionate and tolerant, and even dared humour, in a search for understanding of the frailties in all of us. Burton saw that melancholy 'is an inbred malady in every one of us'. In the spirit of Jesus of Nazareth,

Burton had an empathy and oneness with sufferers of deep despair. In his treatment regime, which still merits a look, he brought together the best of science in his day and the humility to learn from earlier ages through their literature, poetry and history, and empowered his patients by an active acceptance of common humanity reflected in this ringing declaration:

But see the Madman rage downright
With furious looks, a ghastly sight.
Naked in chains bound doth he lie,
And roars amain, he knows not why.
Observe him: for as in a glass
Thine angry portraiture it was.
His picture keep still in thy presence:
Twixt him and thee there's no difference.
(Robert Burton 1621, The Anatomy of Melancholy)

The last line, which accepts a common humanity with the deranged, is breathtaking in its tolerance and equality, as even today professionals in the mental health services have a tendency sometimes to distance themselves from their clients. It should be remembered that Burton lived at a time when witches were still believed in and learned treatises were written by no less a personage than the king, James I. Not surprisingly, therefore, they were still persecuted, and as Usher (1991) and Roy Porter (1992) remind us, the mentally ill were often targets for all sorts of scapegoating horror, not least being accused of witchcraft. Yet Burton sought a humanitarian and integrated approach in his effort to understand his fellow human beings. It is this humanity which still speaks to us over the centuries, even though much of his science is redundant. We probably do not come across another great humanitarian in the field of mental disorder until we meet the Quaker Samuel Tuke, founder of the York Retreat, almost 200 years later.

Robert Burton probably did not know John Donne (1571–1631), though they may have shared something close to the experience of depression or melancholy, as Donne would have agreed with Burton's statement that 'every man is the greatest enemy unto himself'. Donne was the author of the original, and at the time infamous, book, *Biathanatos*. This was a thesis which explored the nature of self-killing in a relatively non-judgemental and accepting way. He saw suicide as a paradox and sought, in some cases, to justify the action, which was dangerously against the prevailing orthodox ecclesiastical and judicial view of the times. It must be remembered that it was not until the early nineteenth century that the most punitive laws (involving loss of property or even death) against declared atheists were allowed to lapse, so that the great scholar Edward Gibbon was still very careful about being considered a non-believer. It is noteworthy that it is not until 1635, four years after the death of Donne, that Sir Thomas Browne, another in the tradition of medical poet, first used the word suicide. He was also the first, rather naughtily, to say that 'charity begins at home'. Browne, like Burton and Donne, probably had some experience of melancholy when he wrote 'we all labour against our own cure; for death is the cure of all diseases', but he saw life much more positively when he said 'the long habit of living indisposes us for dying'.

Donne, however, who was recognized as a great poet and playwright in his own time, and was Dean of St Paul's, was more influential because he was part of the establishment. He had emerged from a Roman Catholic background, but with the arch-Protestant, Martin Luther, worried that his occasional low spirits either came from the devil or were an affront to God. Wymer (1986), in his seminal analysis of Jacobean attitudes to suicide, places Donne at the very centre of the evolving progressive approach, arguing that 'Donne undermines every traditional argument against suicide (whether regarded as an act against nature, reason or God) – and that Donne makes out a coherent and consistent case against any absolute prohibition on suicide.' Indeed, Donne inferred that Jesus of Nazareth, by his voluntary sacrifice, committed suicide *de facto*. This is a very daring and progressive position to take, perhaps even today. Thus it may be argued that Donne started the essential and necessary work of dissecting out from canonical and secular law the prohibitions and some of the stigma and terrors of suicide. This finds echoes in Arthur Koestler's outraged response to the horror of totalitarianism, be they from left or right, which made him one of the ornaments of the twentieth century. Nevertheless, Koestler, along with his partner, elected to die. Some may feel that the linking of Donne with Koestler is extreme, but it seems to me appropriate to trace parallels in self-killing, which are described as suicide and sometimes as euthanasia.

Donne's *Biathanatos* loosely translates as life and death, *bia* meaning living, *Thanatos* being the name of the god of death. While the title is very concise, the monograph had a very substantial subtitle, which was theologically very significant: 'A declaration that the paradox or thesis, that self homicide is not so naturally sin, that it may never be otherwise.' It had been thought by some that this first English book on suicide might have been a double parody. Yet bearing in mind Donne's Roman Catholic background, his evolving views on suicide, possibly emboldened by his awareness of Montaigne's essay on the subject, were nevertheless, at the time, a brave thing to publish, not least because he shows what Alvarez (1971) almost sees as a qualification, that Donne had actively contemplated, if not attempted, suicide, which was anathema to his contemporaries. Donne had described a man who was saved from drowning, and confessed that 'I have often such a sickly inclination', which appears to be one of the spurs for him to explore the topic, for he tells the reader: 'when so ever any affliction assails me, methinks I have the keys of my prison in mine own hand and no remedy presents itself so soon to my heart, as mine own sword'. It would have been theologically and politically safer to have quoted Seneca.

Donne went on to explore the death of Jesus of Nazareth, and he argued that, because Jesus had a *choice*, his death was altruistic, that he was making a sacrifice for others, as sometimes does the good soldier who accepts the duty of the 'lost cause', justified as an act of sacrifice for the benefit of his comrades. So Jesus' sacrifice was also a self-death, a form of suicide.

One can pick out in Donne common themes with the Shakespearean suicides, which merit closer scrutiny. There was a recognition that 'ecstasy' or 'madness' was one acceptable cause for self-killing. It is suggested, however, that the interactive theme of rejection of the victim by the world, and of the world by the victim, is discernible in most of the plays, as each character projects his or her experiences of being rejected or rejecting. For example, Gloucester, in *King Lear*, the lovers in *Antony and Cleopatra*, Brutus and Cassius in *Julius Caesar* and Lady Macbeth, all actively reject the consequence of their situation and, in reject-ing the world, die. Conversely, other characters feel they are rejected: Ophelia is apparently spurned by her lover Hamlet; Romeo is left behind by the apparent death of Juliet, while she in turn feels deserted and rejected by his death; Othello is similar to Ophelia, in that he feels that he has been rejected by Desdemona's apparent infidelity; finally, the young Prince Arthur, in *King John*, is driven to desperate acts by apparently being rejected by all around him.

This dual interactive concept of rejection will be found to a greater or lesser extent in most aspects of suicide. It was graphically exemplified in an eighty-year-old man who had learnt of his diagnosis of terminal cancer. 'Mr Adams' tried to drown himself but was rescued and returned home to his very loving and supportive wife. Three days after the event he confessed to her his intent. In response to her distress he said, 'I was not leaving you, I was leaving the pain.' Her response was, 'How could you think of deliberately leaving me behind?' She then fell into a severe depressive mood, which required a considerable degree of counselling support for her to seek to resolve this profound sense of being rejected by her partner of more than fifty years.

In a search to understand suicidal situations, some, such as Alvarez (1971), deny or belittle efforts to categorize, measure and assess the risk of suicide, arguing, with some *partial* truth, that such an approach atomizes the individual, and rightly pointing out, as Maris *et al.* (1992) acknowledge, that there is little success in precise prediction of individual situations. Conversely, without efforts to understand, every situation becomes random, whereas, as will be seen later, there are a number of identified factors which can help the professional, the family and the sufferer to comprehend something of the risks being run.

There is a longstanding tradition in the humane services of an emphasis upon the personal and the individual, in a search for a specific empathy and under-standing. This 'qualitative' approach can lead to denial of the 'quantitative', as if an empirical approach based upon a series of studies is a disavowal of the indi-vidual, or we turn the person into a detached statistic. It is a feature of our approach that an essential synthesis is sought, because 'analysis' enumeration without 'empathy' is sterile and depersonalizing, but 'empathy' without 'analysis' can lead to confusion and chaos, as all are sucked up into the maelstrom of the crisis and existential despair.

It cannot be gainsaid that to consider ending one's own life must be as profoundly distressing as, or perhaps on occasions even more so than, the distress of family and relatives. Hence this is always an area fraught with emotional tension, which is so admirably shown by dramatists, throughout the ages, who counterpoise the great ethical and emotional themes of human life (Wymer 1986). From the earliest times it was recognized that people might be at risk from them-selves, and their friends would need to 'follow them swiftly and hinder them from what this ecstasy may now provoke them to' (Gonzalo in *The Tempest* III.iii). Shakespeare explored some of the key elements in mental illness during Macbeth's discussion with the physician about his wife's melancholy, when he asked: 'Canst thou minister to a mind diseased, pluck from the memory the rooted sorrow, raise from the brain the written troubles, and with some sweet oblivious antidote cleanse the stuffed bosom of that perilous stuff which weighs heavy upon the heart.' The Doctor had early conjected that she 'more needs the divine, than the physician'. Yet in Macbeth's review we see the themes of stressful events and the way illness impacts itself upon the mind and the personality of the sufferer, and the search for 'some sweet oblivious antidote', which can also be alluringly dangerous and tantalizingly elusive.

In a seminal text, Rowland Wymer (1986) examined suicide in the literature of the seventeenth century. He approached the subject from a historical literary exploration of Jacobean drama, rather than as a psychologist, to expose the 'problematic status of suicide and its relationship to despair' of the day. Wymer argues that the subject 'provided inexhaustible opportunities for writers wishing to generate different kinds of ethical complication and emotional effects'. The themes relevant to Jacobean times are identified in his chapter headings: Suicide, despair and the drama; Retribution; Temptation and affliction; Repentance, expiation and honour; Death for love; Historicism and Roman deaths. These were the major contemporary preoccupations in late Tudor and Stuart times, which produced some of the greatest glories of English literature. Wymer looks at the tensions, contradictions and paradoxes in human life as expressed in drama. I use these to gain some greater psychological and empathetic understanding, and turn without any apology to the greatest psychologically authentic dramatist of all time, William Shakespeare.

In parenthesis it is acknowledged that literary critics with a wider socio-political perspective, such as Eagleton (1983) and Dollimore and Sinfield (1985), rightly place Shakespeare within the socio-political context of his time, and it may be argued that, as a playwright to the Elizabethan and Jacobean Courts, he was part of the 'propaganda' machine of the establishment. Certainly, he reiterated the calumnious libels against Richard III, thus reinforcing the glory of the Tudors. Moreover, despite his own probable leanings to the old religion, he was content to make snide remarks against 'Popish plots', even in the unlikely vehicle of *Titus Andronicus*, set in Roman Republican times. Yet for all this, Shakespeare, like Shostakovich, who also laboured under a totalitarian regime, was able to impose questions in his work when he has Richard III saying of his wooing of Anne of Warwick: 'was ever woman in this humour wooed, was ever woman in this humour won?' In Tudor myths, Anne was a Richardian victim, though in truth she had been a life-long family friend. Perhaps in his historical plays, in spite of all the 'political' pressures, Shakespeare demonstrates his allegiance to the psychological authenticity of his art; for, example the poet's sympathy in Richard's reflection, 'shine out fair sun – that I may see my shadow as I pass – and descant on my own deformity.'

Be that as it may, Shakespeare's claim upon us is that he allows us to enter the world and ethos of others, in a genuinely empathetic way. In his thirty-five plays and two narrative poems, there are ten clear instances where suicide plays an important part in the action. This does not include numerous references in other plays to suicide and its dangers. For example, in one of his comedies, he has Leonato say: 'the ecstasy has so much overborne her it is feared that she will do a desperate outrage upon herself' (*Much Ado About Nothing* II.iii). The stereotypical Tudor arch-villain, Richard III, contemplates the threat of suicide in response to the statutory guilt he should feel, which threatens the soul: 'Lest I revenge, what myself upon myself – guilty, guilty! I shall despair. There is not a creature loves me and if I die no soul shall pity me.' His mother, the Dowager Duchess of York, says to his face: 'a grievous burden was thy birth to me, tetchy and wayward was thy infancy, thy school days frightful, desperate, wild and furious'. We cannot help but think: what better description is there of a rejecting mother than this? Let us leave the Roman plays on one side, as suicide there appears to be a response to a combination of stoicism, pride and avoiding the triumph of the adversary, such as in *Julius Caesar* and *Antony and Cleopatra*. Two British queens die in response to despair, interestingly both off-stage: Imogen in *Cymbeline* and the queen in *Macbeth*.

The Hamlet soliloquy, in which he contemplates suicide, can still send shivers down the spine as we hear his response to the rejection felt in bereavement, apparently not shared by his mother:

> Oh that this too solid flesh would melt, thaw and resolve itself into a dew! Or that the Everlasting had not fixed His canon 'gainst self-slaughter! Oh God! Oh God! How weary, stale, flat, and unprofitable seem to me all the uses of this world!
>
> (*Hamlet* I.ii)

Following his realization of murder, and rejection by an incestuous mother for an uncle 'not fit', all the contradictory emotions arise of honour, dishonour, attractive oblivion, religious scruples and prohibitions:

> To be, or not to be, that is the question:– Whether 'tis nobler in the mind to suffer the slings and arrows of outrageous fortune; Or take up arms against a sea of troubles, And, by opposing, end them? . . . To die, – to sleep; – To sleep! – Perchance to dream; ay, there's the rub; for in that sleep of death what dreams may come, when we have shuffled off this mortal coil. . . . Who would bear the whips and scorns of time, the oppressor's wrong, the proud man's contumely, the pangs of despised love, the law's delay, the insolence of office, and the spurns that patient merit of the unworthy takes, When he might his quietus make with a bare bodkin?
>
> (*Hamlet* III.i)

Rejection, rejection and rejection.

In *King Lear*, Gloucester reacts to the torture and blindness imposed upon him by actively planning his suicide, though some today may call this euthanasia. Yet *all* these 'honourable' characters feared that they were being *led astray* by some 'ecstasy', which at the time was seen as some form of derangement. Thus in the shadows of seemingly rational and noble response lurked the fear that they were not 'in my perfect mind' (Lear), or were tempted by the devil or madness. There are contemporary echoes in the writings and lives of Sylvia Plath and Jill Tweedie.

In the narrative poem *The Rape of Lucrece*, Lucrece's response to the extreme of sexual abuse perhaps belongs to the Roman theme, but it would be easy to romanticize, if not sentimentalize. Wymer's description of the deaths of Romeo and Juliet as 'death for love' ignores the angry adolescent impulsivity, in which the passion of the moment can lead to such drastic outcomes. There is a dangerous allure in accepting what appears to be an almost noble desperation, which leads to an impulsivity of fatal consequence. It is the genius of Shakespeare to make us see the world through the immediacy of teenage people.

However, *Romeo and Juliet* would hardly have been credible if their activities had been performed by older people. This is not 'ageist' but the recognition that the relevance and acceptance of behaviour is often age-related, and if those young people had been a little less rash, they might well have enjoyed a reunion that would have led to comfortable domesticity.

One death, often not recognized as suicide, is found in the lesser-known play *King John*: the demise of the adolescent Arthur, nephew to King John. The young Prince Arthur is imprisoned by the villainous John in a high tower. The key issue is, the young Arthur was flying from an intolerable position, rather than wanting to die. He half realizes that he is risking death, which appears almost to be attractive, and in Arthur's soliloquy (IV.iii) he argues that, as justice is on his side, God will protect him. Therefore, while contemplating hurling himself from the castle wall, he says 'good ground be pitiful and hurt me not', and he moves between planning his subsequent escape, after jumping, and the fear he feels 'as good to die and go, as die and stay'. He leaps and is killed. Those of us who have worked with adolescents and young adults know this impulsive *flying from* the 'intolerable' all too well, which tragically can lead to 'unintended' running into oblivion.

At first sight, Othello might also belong to Wymer's 'dying for love', for he killed Desdemona because he thought she had betrayed him, he was 'one that loved not wisely but too well' and, amazingly but authentically, claims to be 'one not easily jealous, but being wrought perplexed in the extreme'. He did not truly understand the extent of his *paranoid* jealousy, failing to appreciate just how easily aroused it was, to travel along a continuum to dangerous and obsessional abnormality (White and Mullen 1989).

The interest that Shakespeare's tragedies have for us is that with the exception of *Othello*, *Macbeth* and *Hamlet*, all the suicides he portrays have a degree of understandable, albeit regrettable, rationality about them, and may be described as 'stress related' (Pritchard 1994a). The despair and depression in *Hamlet*, and of Lady Macbeth, come close to the derangement of ecstasy and madness, as, we would claim, do those of Othello. These belong to the 'psychiatric related suicide' and, as will be demonstrated later, suicide is far more often associated with mental disorder and mental illness than with stress factors, though of course the two overlap and interact. How, therefore, can we claim Shakespeare as authentic, or is the assertion that suicide is predominantly associated with psychiatric factors false? It is argued that Shakespeare, like Burton and Donne, shows that many people, many within the range of 'normality', experience some element of rejection, depression and despair in their own lives; thus they have the experience and imagination to reflect on people in similar circumstances who took the step of ultimate rejection, suicide. However, the nature of psychosis is qualitatively and essentially different from what might be described as an extreme but normal state. Thus Shakespeare's wonderful observation of the demented Lear is both evocative and authentic, yet his lunatic character 'poor Tom', while reflecting the social experience, is clearly a person who is acting or indeed counterfeiting the phenomenon of 'feigned ecstasies' (*Titus Andronicus* IV.iv), as Edgar behaves as people believe the psychotic or madman acts. Is it not singular that of the many hundreds and thousands of people who have experienced the trauma of schizophrenic psychosis, so few have actually been able to describe that experience other than in an allegory and metaphor? Nevertheless, Roy Porter (1992) parades for us some of the exceptions who over the ages have been able to describe something of the feeling of the emotional and social vortex of the psychotic experiences, classically Daniel Schreber.

Perhaps the most immediate can be seen in some of the paintings of Van Gogh, yet it is reiterated that so few people have been able to share their psychotic experience with others in an intelligible way because it lies essentially outside our usual experience, even for Shakespeare. There are parallels in the overtly physiological field, as is seen in people who suffer from neurological diseases. Many have great difficulty in describing the sensations they experience, (apart from indicating the loss of control), and what they are *actually* physically feeling, because the neurological disruption is so far outside the usual experience of people that often all they can do is to explain them by simile. It is for this reason, it is argued, that Shakespeare's examples of suicide teach us much. His silence on those few occasions when 'madness' which we would recognize as schizophrenia dominates, shows that few, if any, of the poets can speak of the psychotic experience. A book destined to be a classic, Roy Porter's anthology of 'madness' in literature, finds the few exceptions who can make intelligible the vortex of psychosis. In the chilling silent withdrawal to the 'comfort of madness', we come close to the horde of the conscious vortex peopled with: 'moping melancholia, demoniac frenzy – shrieks and shouts unholy' (Milton).

Current attitudes and dilemmas

It is hoped that this rather discursive review of history, culture and literature indicates two recurrent themes: first, the ambivalence and ambiguity which continue to surround suicide; second, that suicide can be a reaction to stress, related to disease and illness, and a rejective interaction of an accumulation of factors. Unlike in previous times, suicide can be discussed relatively easily today, even within the mass media of the late twentieth century. For example, in the worldwide magazine *Time* there have been three major articles concerning suicide, which while acknowledging dilemmas, were mainly concerned with where

firm baselines should be drawn, accepting without question the 'obvious' rationality of such actions in many situations. Yet a little more than 100 years ago,
Robert Louis Stevenson, in what was considered to be a horrendous book, *The
Suicide Club*, found himself almost at the extreme end of the use of language,
because he could not describe in sufficiently villainous terms the leader of this
'devilish' club.

Conversely, modern poets and novelists have almost celebrated suicide, and
though it is acknowledged that this may be somewhat controversial, Alvarez,
Burns, Sexton and Plath have attracted sympathy and understanding for the
suicide experience, but inadvertently may have obscured something of the
horror, sadness and despair of the ultimate rejection. Alvarez (1971), in his classic
synthesis of literature, personal experience and search for meaning, despised the
'number counters' and empiricists who would seek to measure the torment of
experience in trying to analyse the human emotions. We have some sympathy,
for almost self-evidently the poet can best describe, though the scientist can best
define, human activity. Moreover, there are limits and dangers in extrapolating
from one's own personal experience, a lesson that professionals cannot ignore; yet
I fear that there is beginning to be an almost candy floss Romeo and Juliet vision
of suicide. This is not the reality of physical corruption, of the total end to which
the ultimate rejection leads; the personal 'final solution' can be messy, bloody,
foul and, worse, unnecessary. It is hoped that we can demonstrate that there is
sound science upon which to build our practice art, that empathy and the understanding of people in distress is pre-eminently central to any effective form of
intervention, and is not a denial of their personal rights, but a defence against
unwarranted stress. But we need to understand that even the most apparently
rational self-rejection may have other underlying causes, which invalidates that
overt rationality. This is not to defend the piety of Edgar, who at the end of *King
Lear* says: 'men must endure their going hence, even as their coming hither'. Nor
are we an ally of the 'churlish priest' who smugly felt that he had been over-
generous to the suspect Ophelia. Our approach is based upon the humility of
recognizing that often *we do not know* and, in such desperate situations, we should
always seek to offer the person in distress a second chance, based upon the best
evidence available. In the words of the psychiatrist and existential philosopher
Karl Jaspers, 'Illness *we can treat*, to life we can only appeal.' But we must always
guard against inadvertent rejection of those in extremitus, caused by our being
absorbed in their or society's 'rejecting desperation'. At the same time, in both
law and professional ethics, we can be called upon to account for our actions,
often in the midst of the hurly-burly of practice, having to make judgements,
often with incomplete information and resources.

A case example

Let us explore a case example, to highlight difficulties in determining the best
course of action within the perennial situation of limited data and resources. The
situation in this instance is not about suicide, but the dilemma associated with

what to do with a homicide, who is possibly mentally ill. The reader is invited to share in an exercise, which is offered to mental health students, to judge in which mainland European city the following event took place, in which year, and to say what would they recommend.

The case is relatively straightforward. The local magistrate had written to the president about what action should follow a case of matricide where the person being looked after was, at the time of the 'crime', in the community. The president's reply was as follows:

> If you have ascertained that Paul is so insane that he is permanently mad and thus that he was incapable of reasoning when he killed his mother, and did not kill her with the pretence of being mad, you need not concern yourself with the question how he should be punished, *as insanity itself is punishment enough.*
>
> At the same time he should be kept in close custody, if you think it advisable. This need not be done by way of punishment, as much as for his own and his neighbours' security. If, however, as often happens, he has intervals of sanity, you must investigate whether he committed his crime on one of these occasions and thus has no claim to mercy on the grounds of mental infirmity. If this is so, refer the case to us, so that we may consider whether he should be punished in accordance with the enormity of the crime − if he did in fact commit it in a rational interval.
>
> But since we learn by letter from you that his position in respect of place and treatment is such that he is in the hands of friends, even, in fact, confined to his own house, your proper course is to summon those in charge of him at the time and to enquire how they were so remiss, and then to pronounce on each case separately, according to whether there is any excuse or aggravation for their negligence.
>
> The object of keepers of the insane is not merely to stop them from harming themselves, but from destroying others; and if this happens there is some justification for casting the blame for it on those who were somewhat negligent in their duties.
>
> (Based upon a translation by A. Birley)

Succinctly this brings together assessment, intervention, moral and legal issues of personal responsibility, ideas about the impact and duration of mental illness, and finally the dilemma of community versus residential care, of control versus care and the responsibility of professionals to individuals and societal protection.

Have you decided on the country, president and time? The phrase 'insanity itself is punishment enough' displays great understanding and compassion and it is not surprising that the 'president' was the 'philosopher emperor', Marcus Aurelius (AD 121–180). And Marcus' letter was written in the second century AD when he was Chief Magistrate. What is so attractive about the answer is that it highlights the inherent dilemmas concerning the issue of care versus control, when dealing with a would-be suicide owing to ecstasy or derangement or, in modern terms, mental illness. These issues are perennial and have to be faced. It might be noted for later discussion that here was a chief executive who did not include among the issues for consideration 'cost', boundaries or administrative convenience.

It is worthwhile dissecting Marcus Aurelius' thesis, which will prove to be an exemplary analysis of the key interactive control/care issues. In the first paragraph, Marcus is concerned with whether there was an adequate assessment and diagnosis, differentiating between mental illness or a pretence of being mad, preceding by 1,400 years Shakespeare, who says: 'his feigned ecstasy shall be no shelter for these outrages' (*Titus Andronicus* IV.iv). Yet clearly in classical days, at the height of the medieval period and in Shakespearean times, as well as today, there is an acceptance that the guilty act has to be accompanied by a guilty intent. Consequently someone who was mentally ill could not be held responsible for what was still a legal crime of self-murder.

The second paragraph concerns safety and, if necessary, 'close custody', not 'done by way of punishment as much as for his own and his neighbours' security'. In a remarkable third paragraph, we see the dilemma of care in the community; if it fails, then the authorities seek to find someone who is responsible. The Emperor Marcus, like every politician, will always welcome discretion and minimal use of restriction by both family and professionals, especially the latter, until something goes wrong.

Let us remember the effects of what was originally a very humane but legally orientated mental health act, the Lunacy Act of 1890, not repealed until 1959. Everything was concerned with restriction, ostensibly in the name of protection and care for the patient and the community. The effect, however, was the most repressive of regimes, emerging from the most compassionate underlying rationale. This was inadvertently exploited by the 'big nurse' in Ken Kesey's *One Flew Over the Cuckoo's Nest*. Over time, she had became a monstrous user of Orwellian double-speak, transposing 'care' into pure 'control'. Marcus Aurelius' letter reflects this perpetual conflict of rights when we need to control, but as 'therapists' we need to care, even though the balance is so often difficult, if not impossible, to attain.

Finally, the third and last paragraphs present staff, and to a lesser extent families, with the stark reality that the responsibilities of those looking after the mentally ill exceed their concern with the primacy of the patient. Irrespective of the situation, authority will always seek to determine who was 'so remiss', 'negligent in their duties', and whether there is some 'justification' for casting blame, and ignoring the lack of resources, adequate training or post-qualifying training (Pritchard 1992c). Such a 'modern' response to a policy situation 'gone wrong' should not surprise us, for literature and history remind us of the continuity of human experience.

It has been contended that the very progressive institution of targets in *The Health of the Nation* (Department of Health 1992), which focuses upon preventing death by suicide, was implying a vote of confidence in the potential abilities of the community, health and psychiatric services. It contained, however, an Aurelian sting in the tail, because if the professionals 'fail' we will be indicted, exemplified in complaints about 'social' rather than 'health' care costs for the elderly. The former are charged: 'it is the doctors who are responsible', says the Minister of State Mr Bovis, 'not politicians' (BBC Radio 4, 11 August 1994). This is breath-taking effrontery, and fails to point out that the 'responsible' doctors are oper-ating a politically determined policy. It may well be that, with an increasingly better informed laity, it will not only be the state that asks: 'who was so remiss?'

Interestingly, a recent American text (Fremouw *et al.* 1990) gave considerable consideration in both its preface and first chapter to clinicians' legal responsibil-ities in defending themselves against claims of negligence should a psychiatrically ill person die from suicide. It will be intriguing to see what evolves in Britain in the next decade.

Durkheim

For the final strand in this historical review of the complex attitudes surrounding suicide, we turn to the great French sociologist, Emile Durkheim. While Montaigne, from Catholic France, had earlier shown sympathy, Durkheim, the father of modern sociology, saw the study of suicide as a case example of how society interacts with individuals, and how individual actions reflect something of the nature and structure of their societies. Durkheim was the first modern 'topologist' of suicide, as he saw that within the single action there could be many strands. First was the notion of rational, and altruistic suicide, reflecting the Romans, Montaigne and Donne. Then he saw 'vengeful' suicide, which was almost a psychological expression, the 'chaotic', which some would attribute to mental illness, and finally and of greatest interest the 'anomic'. It is here that suicide is seen almost as indicative of the degree to which there is cohesion or dis-cohesion in a society, a concept which has a degree of broad acceptance (Berrios and Monaghan 1990). This is not the place to discuss in detail Durkheim's ideas, as some have been overtaken by socio-historical changes. The importance of Durkheim is that he supplies the missing conceptual element in our psycho-logical understanding of suicide, namely the social. Here there is a wonderful convergence between the sociologist Emile Durkheim, and the metaphysical poet John Donne. The latter, in one of his sermons, wrote: 'No man is an island, entire of itself; every man is a piece of a continent, a part of the main. Any man's death diminishes us' because he saw himself involved in humankind. Donne also wrote, 'Never send to know for whom the bell tolls, it tolls for thee.'

Before Durkheim, self-slaughter was an offence against God, mankind or the state, or was the result of 'ecstasy', 'passion derangement' or possession. It was always seen as a singular personal act. Durkheim fills out Donne's embryonic social understanding, by showing that the nature and ethos of a society can have a profound impression upon its members. It is for this reason that we seek to integrate the highly personal, individual and specific situation, and to place it within the wider social context, under the title 'psycho-social'. For we recognize that those involved in suicidal behaviour are not only rejecting their plight, but may well be responding to their experience of some longstanding social and therefore psychological rejection by others, be they family, society or indeed professionals (e.g. they have been intolerably labelled 'lunatic'). To consider suicide without the socio-economic factors would be to view suicide as having only one dimension, namely the personal. It may well be that there are such things as rational, sensible, logical suicides, but the case that there are social dimensions is made from an unexpected source in *The Health of the Nation*. The Department's approach implicitly accepts that some deaths, such as by suicide, are preventable, and that those who die could have been saved. In Aurelian terms, therefore, we ought to determine 'who is to blame'.

This leaves us with further dilemmas when we seek to decide whether to use active intervention, which controls because we care, but risks disempowering the citizen, so that we, to paraphrase James Baldwin, become not part of the solution, but part of the problem.

With the personal decriminalization of suicide, indeed its secularization, we might say that at this point in history, suicide is hardly a controversy. However, suicide's 'sister', euthanasia, the desire for a 'good death', is quickly becoming a related issue, as it overlaps with suicide. In essence, suicide is a personal matter; euthanasia depends upon the passive or active cooperation of another. At this point, we need only briefly to outline some of the issues, because the boundaries between suicide and euthanasia can become very blurred.

The suicide–euthanasia axis

In 1993 the eminent journalist Jill Tweedie, in an interview with her fellow journalist Polly Toynbee (*Guardian*, 14 September 1993), explored the impact upon her and her partner of the news that she had motor neurone disease, a disease whose symptoms are especially horrible. Death often occurs within three years, although it can take longer, and the disease is associated with increasing deterioration of the person's mental condition and motor abilities. In other words, people rapidly become helpless and, in particular, may have difficulty in swallowing. Jill Tweedie, on learning the news, is reported as saying, 'I don't want to be uplifted or uplifting, I just want to go on being me.'

In the article that Toynbee writes she recalls Dylan Thomas, who shared the anger of his father at his encroaching demise. Thomas wrote: 'Do not go gentle into that good night, Old age should burn and rave at close of day; Rage, rage against the dying of the light.' Few would quarrel with a person who understands the fate awaiting her if she explores the possibility of taking control of her life, by considering practising suicide or euthanasia. There is good research evidence to support this assertion (Mermelstein and Lesko 1992); for example, people with early cancer may *contemplate* suicide or the 'right' of active assistance from staff. Toynbee in a most sensitive way contrasted the impact of this cruel diagnosis with the death of her own husband, who while only having a short illness, nevertheless elected 'not to know' that he was terminally ill. Emotions are powerful, and anger at injustice and being victimized is understandable. Toynbee wrote that Tweedie would decide in her own good time, and take her appropriate action, but implied that the sufferer would not passively wait for domination by the disease.

From the opposite camp, as it were, Christopher Howse (1993) wrote an article in the *Daily Telegraph* that did not let this approach go unchallenged. In 'The selfishness of self-slaughter – self-killing is wrong' he rehearsed the traditional Platonic–Christian view that we do not own our lives, and therefore cannot discard or reset our body, 'even if it causes atrocious pain'. Suicide is wrong, even after laying aside the traditional views of hell and damnation, because self-slaughter 'is a betrayal of fellow terminal sufferers'. Howse gave examples of cancer, AIDS and other neurological disasters. He reiterated Allah and Aquinas, and gave an example of a man who faced blindness as an adult. He had contemplated suicide but realized that 'he must have been stark mad', because on reflection he appreciated that there are many examples of very happy people who have been blind all their lives. Howse acknowledged that there are hard cases, but 'it is hard cases which make bad laws', and the argument against killing ourselves is the same as against murdering other people, or against abusing children. He argued that there is a standard which cannot be breached. Suicide is a selfish act apart from anything else, and often an aggressive one.

It would seem from these two examples that towards the end of the twentieth century, in the issue of suicide we can still discern the echoes of Hamlet's famous soliloquy but, as will be seen later, there are crucial differences in the attitude you or I may take to an actual or hypothetical suicide or euthanasia.

'Professional' as opposed to 'private' responsibility and suicide

In respect of either suicide or euthanasia, the adult has certain moral responsibilities, irrespective of the law *expressly* forbidding 'assisted' suicide or euthanasia. However, as citizens and individual people in our own right, and then as professionals from the social and health care services, some may find the same person holding alternative positions in different roles.

Some readers would intuitively ally themselves with Jill Tweedie, others with Howse, but for *practitioners*, irrespective of current law, it is believed that there can be no principled position to hold other than to seek to prevent suicide, enabling the sufferer to reconsider and have a second chance. As an individual citizen however, the author, at least in theory under the circumstances involved, has *total* sympathy with Jill Tweedie, in terms of both personal suicide and euthanasia in the face of motor neurone disease.

It would seem reasonable in these circumstances to end my or a member of my family's life, and motor neurone disease would be the worst exemplar of such a hideous hypothetical circumstance. Yet, in Jill Tweedie's recently published autobiography (1993), we learn that she made a very serious suicide attempt, and on recovery was 'saved' only by the inertia of her depression from making a second bid. Yet she later achieved tremendous personal fulfilment, and made a major contribution to the fuller emancipation of women. This was assisted by the impertinence of some professionals who helped her through her misery. Surely we must always offer another chance.

This was not always the position the author held, and some outstanding professionals believe that, for some people, suicide is almost inevitable and can be a blessing for the sufferer. Many of us know cases where after valiantly fighting against intractable mental illness, often with numerous successful interventions by caring professionals, people are overwhelmed by their misery and learn how to circumvent the best professional plans, and finally die. There often follows a sense that they are now at peace. However, two cases that directly involved the author totally shattered this undoubtedly humanitarian and progressive position.

'Mrs Baker' was nearly seventy and had been diagnosed as terminally ill with a painful cancer, with a possible six to nine months to live. Within the last half-year her son had been sent to prison for embezzling the family business, which she brought with her into the marriage. Within the same week, her only daughter had been killed in a road accident. This highly intelligent, self-reliant, aware woman took the most elaborate precautions and chose a very effective way to end her life. By a remarkable fluke she was discovered and was compulsorily admitted to the psychiatric unit. The consultant insisted that Mrs Baker must be willing to undertake a course of anti-depressant treatment, plus intensive psycho-social support for a specified period. If she agreed to this then she would be discharged within three weeks; if she failed to give these assurances, she would be detained under the mental health legislation. Some of us felt outraged, and protested at what appeared to be a cruel, callous, insensitive imposition. Nevertheless, Mrs Baker, albeit reluctantly, agreed to the coercion and followed the prescribed course of treatment, including the 'compulsory' support, which as she generously recognized was imposed upon all by the consultant. Six months later she wrote to the consultant thanking him for saving her life, even though she knew she probably had less than two or three months to live. But she wrote, 'Life is precious and I must have been mad, thank you for daring to be right.' Mrs Baker died peacefully, slightly less than three months later, and to his infinite credit the consultant was very supportive to the staff.

The second case involved 'Mr Cole', aged sixty, who appeared to be suffering from a progressive senility of the Alzheimer's type. It was particularly tragic because Mr Cole had been the cornerstone of a very happy family, a man who was one of 'nature's gentlemen', an ideal family person, highly respected by neighbours and the bank for which he worked. Within six months there was a total personality change and this previously gentle, caring man had become a six-foot, fourteen-stone, irascible bully, who appeared to be seriously mentally impaired. The family supported Mr Cole in a most heroic manner, in particular his wife and their two daughters and sons-in-law. Indeed it was only following urging from the support services that they reluctantly agreed to brief respite care. It was a measure of their devotion that when Mr Cole, who apart from physical appearances virtually no longer resembled their father, expressed dislike of being an inpatient, they took him home, despite the fact that he had been extremely violent on three occasions against the slightly built Mrs Cole, to the extent that the professionals began to fear for Mrs Cole's safety. After eleven months of further deterioration, Mrs Cole was prevailed upon, albeit reluctantly, to have an evening away from home. Mr Cole was on very heavy doses of tranquillizers to ensure he slept well. However, on her return she found that he had taken a massive overdose of a whole cocktail of drugs, complicated by an ensuing gastric perforation from which he might have bled to death. He was admitted at midnight and underwent emergency surgery for repair of a perforated ulcer. The son-in-law remonstrated with the social worker, who was a key worker for the family, that we were prolonging both Mr Cole's and his family's agony, and it must be admitted that the social worker felt as the son-in-law did, since Mr Cole was expected to live barely another three to six months. Both son and social worker felt that Mr Cole had been denied the last opportunity to demonstrate his affection to his family. However, after six months, instead of further deterioration and death, there were signs of improvement and over the next nine months Mr Cole made a remarkable recovery. Today there is still some evidence of minor neurological impairment, but he has successfully completed his undergraduate education!

If Mr Cole had died, all who knew the case would have said *pax vobiscum*, he is at peace. But all the experts involved with the family, including various specialist professors, two consultants, a GP and a psychiatric social worker, would have been wrong.

The cases of Mrs Baker and Mr Cole taught this practitioner that, no matter how hopeless or helpless a situation is, we as *professionals*, irrespective of our own personal beliefs, have no duty other than to continue to offer our services. Consequently we reject the advice of the Earl of Kent upon the collapse of Lear, when he said: 'Vex not his ghost – let him pass for he hates him that on the rough rack of this world would stretch him out longer.' No matter how apparently rational the grounds for suicide are, as professionals we must continue to offer our client the privilege of the second chance, and no matter how apparently hopeless the situation, we have to 'dare to be right'. This might possibly be considered to be a controversial and somewhat absolutist position. It is hoped that it is not, but rather a position learnt from practice and the need for real humility, for responding to each situation on its merits, because so often we do not know.

Within our title, 'the ultimate rejection', there is an implication that suicide is not just an end for the sufferer, but can also be a beginning of new distress for the survivors. Arguments will be explored concerning the overlap of suicide and euthanasia, and it is hoped that the reader will consider some of the real practice dilemmas inherent in a current situation in which technology, structure and knowledge are changing, and have changed, so quickly that we need to be willing to reconsider whether we too are inadvertently becoming part of our client's ultimate rejection.

It would seem that in order to provide an optimal service that respects fully the dignity of the individual, our 'practice art', be it social work, nursing, medicine or clerical, must be based upon the best available scientific knowledge on how to offer client-specific intervention. Without that form of analysis our empathy may truly be chaotic. It is to some of the science-based material that we now turn.

CHAPTER 3

DEFINING SUICIDE 1: PSYCHIATRIC AND SUBSTANCE ABUSE FACTORS

In our review of the historical and cultural antecedents of suicide we leaned heavily on classical writers and poets. Such an approach would have the approval of Alvarez (1974), who was dismissive of those, whom he called 'self-styled experts', whose approach seemed to emphasize the statistical, de-humanized sociological and the detached and atomized biological view of human beings. On the other hand, there is a need for an antithesis of the 'romantic agony' which poetically sanitized young deaths, ignoring tragedies in middle and elder years. In Shelley's poem *Adonais* we find: 'Peace, peace, he is not dead, he doth not sleep, he hath awakened from the dream of life. He lives, he wakes – 'tis death is dead not he; mourn not for Adonais.' This echoes 'that monstrous lie' (Owen) which echoes annually at the Cenotaph in the Orwellian double-speak phrase of: 'They shall grow not old as we that are left grow old; . . . We will remember them.' If this brings comfort, fine; but, both at the Cenotaph and in the romantic dirges surrounding Chatterton's death, the real brutality, crudeness and often sheer mess of suicide is ignored. It is fear that makes it too easy to romanticize suicide. In order to seek balance and avoid polemic and the other extremes of sensationalism, we turn to international empirical research to begin our exploration, which hopes to contribute to the prevention or reduction of suicidal behaviour.

As will be seen, the studies come mainly from researchers who present the very opposite of the detached laboratory images of the insular social scientist. They often come from practice, such as psychiatric social workers, clinical psychologists and psychiatrists, and continue to seek a better understanding of the tragedies in people's lives, in order to contribute to providing wider choice for people who reach such levels of desperation. We do not, however, seek to transform this difficult topic into a dry academic thesis full of statistics, but to draw upon material which reflects the best in psychiatric social work, clinical psychology and psychiatry, where the practice art is developed through advances in the scientific underpinning of that art.

The need for a 'science'-based practice: lessons from practice 'when the theory did not fit'

It may be helpful to summarize our approach. It is believed that the majority of suicides are related to mental disorder, which is influenced by interactive biological, psychological and social factors. At this stage we are only considering suicide proper, i.e. not 'suicidal behaviour' or 'attempted suicide', which will be seen as having a different, but overlapping, profile. In addition, we seek to integrate the scientific with the intuitive insights of literature and what Karl Popper called the metaphysics of Freud, recognizing that the best of current knowledge is not exclusive, but asserting that without an enquiring 'scientific' base, we are in danger of quackery, rigid unchallenged orthodoxy or current 'fashionism'; that is why science is important.

Science and research are about rethinking, re-examining and analysing, if at all possible, in a non-biased, non-prejudged and open-ended way. It was argued earlier that analysis (science) without empathy is sterile, but equally empathy (art and practice) without science is chaos and stasis. Tennyson put it beautifully: 'The old order changeth, yielding place to new, . . . Lest one good custom should corrupt the world.' The rationale for the need for a science-informed practice emerged from the experience of some real and acute practical dilemmas. This was exemplified in the diagnosis and treatment of 'childhood autism'.

Leon Kanner, a very warm, caring and humane child psychiatrist, of international reputation, provided a model for understanding childhood autism in the late 1950s that remained the model for more than thirty years. Regrettably, some practitioners have not yet learned of the limits of this approach.

Childhood autism, sometimes described as childhood schizophrenia, typically involved a child who had none of the physical stigmas often found with mental handicap or learning disabilities, such as with Down's Syndrome. Frequently these children were particularly handsome, and with islets of special skills or talent, yet they appeared to have a profound learning disability. These special skills at the time suggested that the children did not have a learning disability, but perhaps suffered from some psychological state. A particularly good presentation of this was seen in the famous and moving story of *Rain Man*, starring Dustin Hoffman and Tom Cruise. It may be remembered that the now grown-up autistic man Raymond had a very limited psycho-social repertoire, but had a special skill, a genius for memorizing numbers.

Kanner (1943) had noted that the parents of such children, having exhausted the then available services, often protested that their children were not 'mentally retarded', emphasizing that their children were different. Kanner commented that often these parents were also apparently cold and detached, and he, being strongly influenced by the ego-dynamic ethos of the times, described such parents as 'refrigerator parents'. He postulated a failure of bonding between child and parent, owing to the parent's coldness, which appeared to impair the child's ability to develop relationships. This ran alongside the notion of 'schizophregenic parents', i.e. parents causing schizophrenia. The key feature of autism, which is still observed today, is the inability of the child, or later adolescent, to learn to respond to other human beings, as he or she has difficulty in differentiating emotionally between animate and inanimate objects, including other people.

The notion of 'schizophregenic parents' took very strong hold in the 1960s and early 1970s, emerging into popular culture in the film *Family Life*, as parents were seen to be a contributing root cause of their children's later schizophrenia. Here adolescent turbulence was thought to lead on to depression, schizophrenia and indeed suicide, because of the parents' unfeeling and unsympathetic response to their children. The writings of various ego–dynamic authors, such as Lidtz, Bateson and Wynne, were combined and popularized, some might say inadvertently plagiarized, by Ronald D. Laing, who was famous in the anti-psychiatric movement. Most readers will be in sympathy with people with a mental disorder, no matter what their view of the origin of that disorder, as people suffer not only the distress of the disorder but also the stigmatized, disadvantaged and exploited situation afforded to them in society. Thus it was easy to make the link between cold, unfeeling, harsh, psychologically tyrannical parents and childhood autism and/or distressed adolescents, leading to mental disorder and suicide. Place such a victim within the context of a dehumanizing capitalist system, said the 1960s anti-psychiatry protagonists, where the person's 'real self' was subjected to brutal and insidious conditioning to become a conforming person, and not surprisingly there followed the break-down of the person, who was then labelled schizophrenic.

Thus, at the extreme, parents and families were seen to be inadvertent political tools of the dominant ideological system, which is accepted as being exploitative and alienating (Pritchard and Taylor 1978). The emotional appeal of such a linkage was, and perhaps still is, very real, because few can doubt that there is an interaction between cultural and family value systems and the political norms of the day, with each probably reinforcing the other. Thus it was easy for some practitioners in effect to blame parents for their children's, adolescents' or young adults' mental disorder. Childhood autism was thought to be the very epitome of such early hostile psycho-social conditioning, and made an easy target. How true was all this, for despite the attractive appeal of global Marxian sociology and neo-Freudian psychology, where was the evidence?

The author first began to have doubts about such an influential and seductive thesis when working with parents of an autistic child, who were making desperate efforts to improve the quality of the child's life. Significantly, 'Mr and Mrs Drake' knew more about the theoretical and practical issues surrounding autism than the practitioner did, which can be very disconcerting, if not embarrassing! They confronted the worker with questions about his views on whether they were 'refrigerator parents'. It was self-evident that in respect of their other children they were not. This, of course, did not invalidate the theory because it could be that the negative problems of the family were only being projected upon the scapegoated 'ill' person. However, not only did Mr and Mrs Drake assert that they loved their child, but their efforts on the child's behalf were heroic. When staff shared the child's day and experienced the regular kicks and bites, without any apparent provocation, we began to appreciate some of the demands and stresses *he* placed upon the parents. The sociological concept of reification was almost made flesh.

It was appreciated that the parents meant it when they said, 'the only way to cope with "John" is to be detached'. Otherwise they became extremely distressed by their feelings of being rejected *by the child* they loved. This raised a question: were these parents, who in every other respect were warm, outgoing, friendly and intelligent people, but undoubtedly showed a detached, weary cautiousness with their autistic child, the cause of their child's problem? Or was their response to his lack of development a *reaction* to the child's difficulties? Such questions are very relevant, not only with regard to child autism, but also with people who may have depression or are in a schizophrenic state. It would seem logical that people who live side-by-side may not, as the neo-Freudians inferred, be pathogenic for their family member, but rather be showing a defensive response, since the only way to deal with the disruption brought about by the child or young adult is to adopt a neutral and detached awareness. Perhaps it would sometimes be better if we put the notion of a 'no fault' clause into interpersonal relationships?

One of the difficulties facing people in interpreting another person's behaviour without 'training' will be to interpret that person's behaviour in the light of their own experience. Professionals, however, are equally likely to interpret that person's behaviour in the *light of the dominant theories* of the day, and here we agree with Alvarez that we sometimes seek to fit the person to the theory, and not the reverse; we should ask, how relevant is the theoretical model we use in *this* case? The dilemma is that sometimes a theory is appropriate and accurate for one client, but not the next, or indeed for the same client at a different time or in a different situation. This important question, or insight, learned from direct work with sufferers, is no more than that, namely a questioning of the appropriateness of a theory in particular circumstances concerning childhood autism.

This reminded the author that sometimes even the 'great' recognize the limits of their theories. Sigmund Freud believed that one day his model would be superseded by a better explanation, and possibly a psychology with a physiological base (Freud 1933), but that has been forgotten as his metaphysic became a movement.

Recent work on childhood autism, in the mid- and late 1980s, such as that by Gilberg (1992) in Sweden and Professor Sir Michael Rutter and colleagues (1994) in Britain, have transformed our understanding of childhood autism. It is now being reclassified as a 'disorder of communication', which has essentially an organic base of some neurological impairment. Thus Mr and Mrs Drake had understood that their child had developmental difficulties from the day of his birth. They had sought an emotional response from him, and when this was not forthcoming, the questions and doubts they raised had been turned aside by the then experts, and were used as 'evidence' to validate observations which were assumed as 'causal' when in fact they were *reactive*. Unsubstantiated theories can damage our health! The rest reflected the history of so many families of people with mental disorder, be it childhood autism or schizophrenia. Mainly, they were blamed and stigmatized, and the 'treatment' goals were aimed at them. This is not to say that environment and families, which are perhaps one of the most important environmental influences, have no impact upon family members; clearly they do, but we should recognize that there is a two-way process. If, as with childhood autism, it finally proves to be that the depressive disorders and schizophrenia have substantial constitutional predispositions, as many believe they have (Mann and Arango 1992; Rende *et al.* 1993), then the emotional response from the client, impacting upon the family, may well create a self-damaging reaction; conversely, a negative emotional environment from the family might trigger the potentially vulnerable person's break-down, and further reinforce the negative family response. Thus, in practice, we need to consider all factors within this interactive model, which is why we favour the bio-psycho-social *integrated* model of understanding, responding to and treating mental disorder. While recognizing the limits of current knowledge, we turn to current empirical work for more precise guidance, though without deserting the invaluable intuitive and practice experience. In the search for a continued integration, in the service of the specific person, in his or her unique situation, we seek to reduce the factors and stressors that may lead people to the 'ultimate rejection'.

It needs to be emphasized that suicide and what is usually called 'attempted suicide' are very significant and different processes. At this stage we are only discussing *actual* suicide, and referring to studies that have examined people who have died by their own hand. There are important differences between suicide and suicidal behaviour, or what has been called 'parasuicide' (Kreitman 1978). More recently, 'parasuicide' has been described as 'deliberate self-harm' (DHSS 1984), which moves the focus away from assumed partial or actual intent. Parasuicide or 'deliberate self-harm' will be considered separately at the end of this chapter.

Contributory causes of suicide

The single factor most often associated with suicide is mental illness, mainly depression. The figures range from 40 to 80 per cent of all actual deaths (Fremouw *et al.* 1990). In a very important text, Barraclough and Hughes (1987) reviewed epidemiological studies on suicide, and produced a classic survey on 100 consecutive deaths. They found that almost 70 per cent of the people dying had severe depression, and a further 10 per cent had psychiatric-related problems. In the country with the highest rate of recorded suicide in the world, Hungary, Arato *et al.* (1988) repeated the earlier Barraclough work, following through the first 200 consecutive suicides in Budapest. It should be noted that the Hungarian suicide rate is usually four times the British level, which Arato believes is partly because of a lack of psychiatric resources (Arato *et al.* 1990). The importance of the Budapest study was that within six months there were already 200 completed suicides, which was a far shorter time than the Barraclough sample study required, but the Hungarians also found that 80–90 per cent of fatalities had some form of mental illness, predominantly depression.

Others have confirmed that the main type of disorder is depression (Marttunen *et al.* 1991; Maris *et al.* 1992) and, irrespective of other factors, such as age and gender (Kreitman 1988), mode of death (Heim and Lester 1991), a range of psycho-social factors (Allebeck 1988; Rich *et al.* 1989) or even socio-economic factors (Platt 1988; Platt *et al.* 1992), depression was the prevailing affective and cognitive theme.

We will later explore the cognitive and emotional elements in depression, particularly hopelessness (Beck *et al.* 1990; Beck and Steer 1991), but it is the frequency of depression, and other mental illness, which leads us to suggest a different formulation from the traditional suicide and/or attempted suicide. We would replace this older division with predominantly *psychiatric-related suicide*, to be juxtaposed with what we would describe as mainly *stress-related suicide*, which, as will be shown, in non-recessionary times appears to account for between 10 and 20 per cent of all suicides in Britain.

We emphasize the notion of non-recessionary times because it does appear in the majority of Western countries that the association of psychiatric disorder with suicide appears to be relatively stable over time. For example, it was noted that in the 1960s and early 1970s there was no internationally significant correlation between changes in suicide levels and unemployment rates, but this changed significantly in the 1980s and early 1990s (Platt 1984, 1988; Pritchard 1990, 1992a, 1995a; Platt *et al.* 1992). This is not to say that there is no interrelationship between psychiatric- and stress-related suicide, but it is believed that it is helpful to the practitioner at first to differentiate between the two, and then to recognize that either may lead to suicidal behaviour and that they compound each other.

A typical situation is where a person with recurrent schizophrenia becomes 'reactively' depressed, i.e. stressed about his or her situation, and responds with suicidal behaviour activity (Cheng *et al.* 1990; Cohen *et al.* 1990). On the other hand, a person who has had a previous depression episode, but still lives a fully competent life, is suddenly made more vulnerable by unexpected unemployment and therefore exposed to all the misery and self-doubt that is so often the response of most people, particularly with long-term joblessness (Warr and Jackson 1988). To understand fully the link between suicide and mental disorder, we need to review, albeit briefly, the main cognitive and experiential themes in the mental disorders.

Influence of mental illness upon suicidal behaviour

Unipolar affective disorder (depression)

The mental disorder usually called 'depression' is now described as 'unipolar affective disorder' (WHO 1993). One may still see in textbooks and occasionally in research papers the term 'endogenous depression', which schematically was useful to differentiate a profound disorder of mood that had no apparent basis in reality and emerged from within the person. This was the opposite to 'reactive depression', which appeared to be in *response* to a 'stress' situation, of either a short or a long duration.

The term depression is of course problematic, in that a low mood, or sometimes a feeling of emotional glumness, of being 'out of sorts' or 'fed up', is a frequent experience of many people. In this sense it is 'normal' and many people

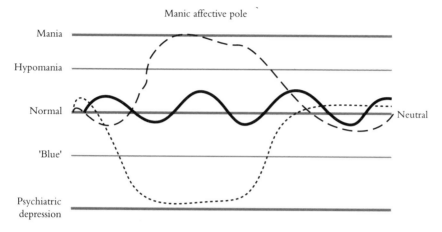

Figure 1 Differentiating bipolar affective disorders: the range of 'normal' and 'abnormal' moods.

can feel 'depressed' without having depression. There is another side to this coin, where a person can feel particularly well, 'on a high' or with a pervasive feeling of well being. This can be the experience of a large number of people without it being felt, thought or observed as a problem or a disorder. A person simply feels 'in a good mood'. Yet imagine that this 'good mood' was magnified and exaggerated to an extreme; it would be then seen to be excessive and 'manic'. The disorder is simply at the extreme ends of the mood continuum. It is a useful concept that the extreme *disorder of mood* that is profoundly low and moves to the depressive side of the continuum is depression. The opposite pole, the ecstatic and exciting mood, swings to the other end of the affective disorder and into mania.

Unipolar affective disorder only seems to disturb one end of the mood/affective continuum, whereas the bipolar disorder may include the manic side of the disorder of mood. Figure 1 illustrates the range of mood, both ordinary and problematic.

One other pair of concepts still found in the literature is 'psychosis' and 'neurosis'. Traditionally psychosis meant a disorder of the mind that was characterized by a lack of awareness or insight, with disturbances of thought with no apparent basis in reality. Unipolar affective disorder, or 'psychiatric depression', a term we prefer, would fall into the 'psychotic' category, as a profound disturbance of mood which has no basis in reality, though clearly external factors can either trigger or negatively compound the individual's situation.

'Neurosis' concerns psychic distress that has an apparent root in past or current stressful events, or in which the level of psychological disturbance does not cut off the person from being aware of or having insight into his or her situation. Thus 'reactive' (we prefer the term 'stress-related') depression would fall into the 'neurosis' category. However, experienced practitioners know that even though insight and awareness may be present in some sufferers, the experience can be very severe and, at the extreme, a precipitant towards suicide.

People are not like textbooks, which is a recurrent theme. Perhaps one of the reasons why the terms psychosis and neurosis are used less nowadays is their imprecision, as sometimes people with quite clear psychiatric depression are aware that they are ill, or someone with schizophrenia appreciates that 'my voices are back', even though he or she experiences the cognitive reality of the content of the voices. Conversely, while someone with a 'neurotic' state has no disorder of perception, his or her cognitive situation seems to demonstrate that there is little or no insight.

'Psychiatric' depression is associated with suicide, and important as it is, this is not the place to discuss in too great detail the likely aetiology of 'unipolar affective disorder' or psychiatric depression. There is, however, significant evidence to show that changes in the biochemistry of an affected person do occur, though whether this in itself is reactive or causal still remains uncertain. There is also some evidence that psychiatric depression is familial, in that it runs in families, even in adopted-away children. This strongly suggests that there is a genetic component in a significant number of sufferers, who are found to have first- or second-degree relatives who also suffer from some affective disorder (Winokur *et al.* 1994). What this simply means is that some people are more susceptible than others to psychiatric depression; the *majority* of people with psychiatric depression, or schizophrenia, do not have a first-degree relative with the condition.

Topography of unipolar affective disorder

There follows a useful checklist of unipolar affective disorder symptoms, which aims to help understanding of why some people in the midst of this terrible psychic distress contemplate and sometimes act upon the idea of taking their own lives.

The impact of unipolar affective disorder is one of profound mood change, where the sufferer experiences the deepest misery and sadness. During this state, the person appears to be unable to shed the psychic 'grief', even in the presence of overwhelming evidence as to why his or her profound feelings of dejection are unwarranted. This is not to suggest for a moment that we should ignore the reality of the experience to the person; rather we should acknowledge the sub-' jective truth of his or her despair. However, even within the depressive mood, it is important for counsellors, therapists and social workers to offer a positive response in an effort to reach sufferers, in the midst of their misery, to remind them that someone understands and is concerned.

The following symptomatic experiential themes may be useful for understanding the severely depressed person:

1 *Mood*. There is a profound disturbance of mood, which is one of prevailing sadness and misery.
2 *Cognition*. There is an important disturbance of cognition, so that everything

around them is interpreted dismally: 'how weary, stale, flat and unprofitable this world seems to me' (*Hamlet*). Some authorities believe that in very severe psychiatric depression this melancholic cognition can almost appear delusional. Sufferers can believe that they are hateful, worthless and, at the extreme, that they are already dead and are responsible for all the ills of the world.

3 *Energy*. There are very often tell-tale changes in mood and energy, usually expressed as 'diurnal variation', in which the mood is especially low in the early morning hours, with relative lightening of the misery in the afternoon. Very often this might be the first sign that a person is entering a unipolar affective disorder state.

4 *Sleep*. There is a disturbance of sleep, where it is quite usual for the person to be able to sleep almost as soon as going to bed, but with very early waking, sometimes accompanied by quite dreadful changes of mood.

5 *Appetite*. There is a loss of appetite, and an apparently linked weight loss. For some sufferers this loss of appetite is an early signal, though, equally, it could easily be interpreted as a reaction to apparent lack of energy and cognitive misery.

6 *Accumulative affect*. The above are accompanied by a prevailing sense of worthlessness, and not infrequently a sense of guilt and blaming, allied with a feeling of helplessness. Nothing they can do can change things and, crucially, there is a feeling of hopelessness. 'Mr Evans' once described his depression as 'psychic hell – everything was black, even my thoughts pained me', which is often experienced and translated by observers as profound anomic despair. Not surprisingly, medieval theologists were critical of such people, who were in this state because they could not accept the offer of comfort and the potential grace of God, and in this sense they were denying the efficacy of their religion. In others the therapists felt rejected, and this is especially powerful when we seek in good will to reach the person in his or her misery. According to Dante, above the entrance to Hades was the legend 'All hope abandon, ye who enter here.' These words may have little emotional meaning unless you pause for a moment, and realistically ask yourself how you would feel if you truly believed that you were guilty, worthless, ineffectual and helpless, and that you truly had *nothing to hope for*. You are abandoned, rejected, beyond 'salvation', and do not merit help, even if it is dimly perceived to be available. Not surprisingly, we would all echo Milton's classic phrase, 'hence loathed melancholy, blackened midnight born amongst horrid shapes and sights unholy', and we would have entered 'psychic hell' as we 'abandoned hope'.

7 *Ego and self-esteem*. Another symptom which is important when one is trying to develop a rapport with the person is the frequent catastrophic collapse of self-esteem and self-image. This is differentiated from the disturbance of cognition, within which it might logically be subsumed. The total self-rejection, sense of desolation and even degradation, linked to the profound sense of worthlessness, guilt and helplessness, becomes a numbing despair. This is superbly described by the poet King David: 'I am a worm and no man' (Psalm 22). 'Mr Evans' once described his experience: 'I knew I was nothing, nothing to the uttermost, it was as if I had become a black hole.' Such utter dejection and

the sense of rejection is often the cognitive fuel for self-slaughter and, in ego-dynamic terms, a shrinking of the ego, which is a vital dimension for understanding the person and his or her possible behaviour. This 'unmanning' collapse of self-esteem was felt by Prince Arjuna in the *Bhagavad Gita*: 'In the dark night of my soul I feel desolation. In my self-pity I see not the way of righteousness'. Not surprisingly, such experiences totally immobilize the sufferer, who sees 'no way out'.

This form of 'psychiatric depression' or 'affective disorder' can be objectively measured using clinical rating scales such as those of Hamilton, validated in the 1960s. The Hamilton Clinical Rating Scale for Depression has been standardized and used throughout the Western world. Most important, in terms of treatment, as well as in demonstrating the validity of the phenomenon, is the fact that the scales are used to show changes in the mood of the person following different kinds of intervention, including double-blind anti-depressant drug trials (e.g. Angst *et al.* 1993).

While the above checklist attempts to describe the observed patterns in the disorder, it is crucial to remember that the illness, like all illnesses, is uniquely experienced and forms a distinctive manifestation, in that the condition is being presented and mediated through an individual's life, with all the personal history, strengths and weaknesses of his or her particular psycho-social situation. Thus, psychiatric depression will always have a *personal and specific* meaning, to both the sufferer and the family. And it is this meaning that the social worker or counsellor must understand and address.

Form versus content: the medical model, its value and limits

It is useful for understanding psychiatric disorder to differentiate between the 'form' of the condition and its 'content'. Figure 2 shows this in the form of a box, with boundaries being the form; within this structure is the content. To understand the person and the situation, one needs to comprehend the content of that person's life, which is encased by the form or pattern of his or her depression or other psychiatric disorder, such as schizophrenia.

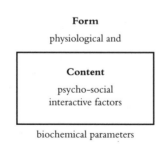

Form

physiological and

Content

psycho-social
interactive factors

biochemical parameters

Figure 2 'Form' versus 'content'.

The form

The concept of form is analogous to the major components in the disease process. This 'medical model' is often derided by some writers, who frankly appear to be so detached that one suspects they have never met a person with profound mental disorder, or been in an emergency situation where one fears for the sufferer or others. Yet one suspects that if they themselves were ill with some acute abdominal pain, they would hope that the 'medical model' would be utilized, while the content, the psycho-social element of their lives, might have a lower priority. The example is worth exploring.

Is the abdominal pain caused by 'appendicitis', a 'social' excess of drink or food badly prepared by ill-educated staff, who as victims of poverty contaminate their customers? The first self-evidently requires medical help, though because of the speed of the NHS reaction to appendicitis; in the second, the biggest negative impact upon the person might be to lose his or her job, i.e. a negative social consequence. In the last, the sufferer might need the 'medical model' approach even more quickly, as people die from salmonella, even though it has a 'social' cause.

In essence the medical model rests upon knowledge of the structure (anatomy) and function (physiology) of the body. Any injury, poisoning or disease creates a *process*, which will, depending upon the type, affect the structure or the functioning of that body. Depending upon which organs are affected, there will be a predictable and known pathology *processes*. Thus, for example, the presence of tuberculous bacilli in the lungs will cause congestion, breathlessness, weight loss, etc. and, if unrelieved, secondary damage to the lungs, which can lead to further damage and at the extreme, death. The TB example is useful because it is not necessarily the presence of the tuberculous bacilli, but rather the state of the person when the infection occurs, that is important. Tuberculosis is often a disease of poverty, and poor people are much more likely to have lower resistance, as seen in the re-emergence of the disease in both the UK and the USA (Brudney and Dobkin 1991). On the other hand, some people appear constitutionally more susceptible to lung infections, which is a good example of the *interaction* between physiology and the environment of the person.

It is similar with mental disorder, in which on balance, it is suggested, underlying causes will have a significant bio-physiological component, exacerbated by the environment, or triggered by particular stresses, possibly at a particular time. This may affront some critics but nothing is more sterile than the old-fashioned debate about *either* nurture or nature, as sociologists rediscover the physical body (Shilling 1993) and geneticists the extra-biological in a quiet acceptance that 'cancer is essentially an environmental disease' (Bodmer 1988) – it is all inter-related and interactive.

The potential weakness of the medical model is that it only perceives the person as an organism, and in that sense as passive in terms of either environment or treatment. The inappropriate use of the model denies the vitality of the interactive process, where the individual and environment affect and sometimes shape each other. At worst, the medical model ignores all those behavioural, attitudinal and choice-shaping factors found in the accumulative influences of the historico-socio-psycho-economic experience (Pritchard and Taylor 1978).

The human experience is unquestionably a composite of history, sociology and political times. Any medicine or 'therapy' that ignores such factors fails to offer a truly 'patient-/client-specific' professional service.

The content

The content is very familiar to those from the social and behavioural sciences and consists of the important individual and family elements that make up the meaning of our lives, in terms of events, roles and relationships, and their interaction. From such processes we impose meanings on our lives within specific interrelationships of people, roles and events that are important to us. The best way to explain this is by an example. A depression occurring in a young adult will have a different meaning to a sufferer and his or her family than one occurring in a mature adult who is responsible for children, or in an older person, who because of bereavement and age finds himself or herself isolated.

Crucial in the suicide dimension is when the psychiatric depression is compounded by real elements in people's lives, so that not only do they appear profoundly sad and see little grounds for optimism, but the social rejection often accompanying unemployment or old age, for example, can accentuate their depressed state. Nevertheless, it is important for psychiatrists, social workers, counsellors and all family members to understand the *interrelationship* of 'form' and 'content' in the experience of the disorder. Consequently, professionals seeking to intervene must not forget the *specific meaning* that the situation will have for the sufferer and his or her family about their shared experience of depression.

This lesson was learned from 'Mr Franks', a very successful businessman, who appeared to the world to be omnicompetent. Mr Franks gave the author a lift, and in the course of the journey mentioned that his wife had been successfully treated some years ago for depression. In passing I mentioned that it must have been difficult for him at the time. Mr Franks suddenly became very distressed because it emerged that this was the *first* time that recognition had been given that this very successful person might also have felt vulnerable. 'I thought the end of the world had come – I did not know she was ill, I thought our marriage was on the rocks and I didn't know why.' He had had a very distressing and confused six months, and a crisis occurred when Mrs Franks overdosed: 'It was almost a relief to realize she was ill and it was not us that were wrong.' The apparent meaning of this slow, insidious, psychiatric depression was a failing marriage, which could not have been further from the truth. Incidentally, it was also a reminder that the impact of mental illness is no respecter of persons and can be as devastating to the middle as other social classes.

'Stress-related' (reactive) depression

We need briefly to consider what one could see as a less severe form of depression where, in one sense, all that we have discussed is experienced as a lesser form of misery and depression. However, this is too simplistic a view. For example, in the classic form of 'stress-related' (reactive) depression, the profound grief following a key bereavement, many of the feelings and the deep sense of misery can be completely overwhelming. Indeed, Freud's superb observations led him to conjecture that psychiatric depression was linked to 'mourning and melancholia', which arose from actual or symbolic profound bereavement and loss. The importance of stress-related depression is that it can be associated with both suicide and suicidal behaviour, especially in younger adults, which can cross ethnic boundaries (Barraclough and Hughes 1987; Brent *et al.* 1993; Adams *et al.* 1994; Kingsbury 1994).

What differentiates stress-related from psychiatric depression, or unipolar affective disorder, is an apparent trigger, predisposition or external stress that leads to a responsive misery, as shown in the following psycho-social topography.

1 *Mood.* A sense of misery and sadness, but in response to an apparently negative appearance or situation.
2 *Reactive process.* There is a total picture that is often similar to the profound grief following bereavement, which includes loss, hurt, shock, protest and questioning why. Usually, and this is often the crucial practical differentiation, the person can be diverted and aroused from his or her state of misery, as, for example, in bereavement, even if only temporarily.
3 *Psycho-physiological reaction.* If depression is unrelieved, secondary symptoms can arise, which may confuse, e.g. there may be a degree of reactive sleep or weight disturbance. On closer examination, however, it is clear that these came after the event.
4 *Trigger reaction.* Typically there is a trigger event or process in the person's life which precipitates the depressive reaction, e.g. divorce, physical trauma, unemployment, etc. One important feature is that reactive depression can be secondary to other mental disorders which can complicate the assessment. In particular, if a person finds themselves in a repetitive, negative, non-win situation, such as suffering from recurrent episodes of schizophrenia, a depressive reaction is not uncommon, and over the years can be a quite fatal complication.

Alternative explanations for affective disorder

Perhaps it should be mentioned here that in both unipolar affective disorder or psychiatric depression and stress-related depression, there are differential assessments which need to be considered. For example, the person may have an underlying physical disorder, such as hyperthyroidism, a severe and peculiar response to influenza, early dementia, drug or alcohol misuse, and the diagnosis of these is of course a problem to the psychiatrist. Nevertheless, community-based therapists should always be aware of the link between physical illness and a depressive mood response. It is a matter of continued sadness to the author that one hears time and time again that someone from the mental health field 'missed' an organic problem. This mainly occurs because of 'tunnel' vision, which we may equally complain of in physicians and surgeons who behave as if people were only their organs, and their families or social situations did not exist. Community mental health workers are not, and should not try to be, medical doctors, but with an open mind, and willingness to be alert to clients' 'complaints', they may often be a referral source for the medical practitioner, thus improving liaison with family doctors. There is evidence that middle-class professionals can have difficulties in communicating with clients and patients, as acknowledged in the Patients' Charter (1992), often because the doctor can spend so little time with the person. Who has a better opportunity than the social worker to listen?

A former 'socially orientated' gynaecologist, 'Dr Grant', used to say that as a third of all 'working-class women over the age of forty have a minor but chronic gynaecological condition', he would expect the social worker to refer the women, 'because the social worker is trained to listen – to women who often don't have the words to express what they are feeling'. And as Brown *et al.* (1990) have shown, working-class women often have the poorest access to public services, which compounds their poor self-esteem. Incidentally, this 'diffidence' about talking to professionals in areas of such 'sensitivity' is not new, but is part of a wider sexism, seen at the death of Queen Victoria: it was found that she had a prolapsed uterus, which must have given her trouble for over twenty years (St Aubyn 1993); interesting and unexpected confirmation of Dr Grant's thesis.

Mania (bipolar affective disorder)

The other 'pole' of affective disorder is mania. Sometimes mania occurs without a depressive phase of the illness (see Figure 1), though a substantial number of sufferers experience both extremes of the affective illness; hence the term 'manic-depressive' disorder. We need only briefly to consider mania, which might be described as the very antithesis of unipolar affective disorder. However, the two conditions can, with differing emphasis, coincide in the same person. The pattern is often that the sufferer, following a short bout of psychiatric depression, swings into mania, or vice versa. It is during this swing period that suicide can be a risk, as the despair is contrasted with the recent ecstasy.

Schematically, bouts of mania proceed along the following lines.

1 *Mood.* There is an incredible disturbance of mood, to one of great elation and on to ecstasy.
2 *Cognition.* A cognitive disturbance leads the person to become a super-optimist, with tremendous speed of thought and distracted concentration. A combination of manic mood and cognition appears to overwhelm the sufferer's awareness so that he or she lacks insight and appears psychotic. Indeed, sufferers can be so 'speeded up' they may appear delusional and even hallucinatory. But unlike in depression, when everything is bad, in mania 'everything is for the best in the best of all possible worlds', making Dr Pangloss from *Candide* appear a super-pessimist.
3 *Energy.* There can be diurnal variation and disturbance of sleep, in that the person *apparently* never tires, and does not appear to require sleep. This is a singular feature in mania. The sufferer's energy appears boundless: 'They mount as with wings of eagles, they run and grow not weary' (David). This can be

frightening to those around them, not least in conjuring up Milton's 'demoniac frenzy', but the extent of this energy is dangerously deceptive.

4 *Physical.* Appetite and weight loss appear to be because of over-activity and can be a complication of mania, particularly in the absence of sleep. If untreated, this can lead to physical collapse and, before effective tranquillizers were available, death could occur from exhaustion. In reality, while the subjective experience is one of boundless energy, physical collapse will be inevitable, and sudden, unless the person can be slowed down sufficiently to recover.

5 *Self-esteem.* There is a colossal inflation of self-esteem, as if the world has become a capital I, with an overwhelming sense of well-being and excitement, which can even be delusional: 'I am God'. One awkward complication may sometimes occur if the person in mania becomes frustrated. He or she can have an angry response, though practice suggests that as he or she is easily distracted, the classic injunction to 'stay cool' is a good one.

With modern sedatives, mania is relatively easy to treat, and some practitioners may never see a full-blown mania, because once it has happened, the person and/ or those around him or her can recognize the early symptoms and intervention can be sought. Prognosis is actually very good, including complete recovery, though the problems often lie in the psycho-social impact of the disorder. Moreover, if this disorder becomes recurrent or cyclical, it can be very demoralizing for all concerned, with 'reactive' stress as a script.

Hypomania

Hypomania appears to be a scaled-down version of fully blown mania, though in reality it can often be more problematic for families and others, because the person is not so obviously out of touch with reality. If the 'subdued' mania is not fully appreciated it can lead to all sorts of psycho-social difficulties; for example, in an expansive mood of well-being, the person might donate overly generous sums to charity, neighbours or startled strangers. In another example, 'Mrs Hays' goes on a shopping spree, and incurs debts she cannot meet. Sometimes it is difficult to convince sceptical sales people that the jolly, friendly Mrs Hays is really ill, not least because 'she seemed to be in such a good mood, she cheered us all up'.

Mania is not often associated with suicide, but it can be in certain circumstances, especially for some bipolar sufferers. If they experience a manic or mild manic attack, followed by depression, the contrast can be almost catastrophic. Suicide becomes more frequently associated with the manic side of affective disorder, if the recurrent bouts of manic-depression undermine the sufferer's 'reason for living'. Mrs Hays found her commitment eroded when she found herself unsupported: 'I didn't want to give up, but I can't take any more of the ups and downs, the uncertainties – and feeling such a fool when I try to take things back.' The sufferer, Mrs Hays, was now unsupported, and her morale was eroded and overwhelmed.

The schizophrenias

Schizophrenia is probably the most traumatic and extreme form of mental disorder, though approximately a third of all patients who suffer from one attack make a complete recovery and never have further episodes (Gibbons 1983). It has to be acknowledged, however, that a further third do have recurrent attacks and a final third of such sufferers are often left with some noticeable degree of longstanding social and psychological impairment. Consequently we need to examine schizophrenia because, after depression, it is clearly the most frequent mental illness that has links with deliberate self-harm and suicide, though we can only deal with it briefly.

Suicide appears to impact at the two extremes. In the acute stage a very small minority can engage in suicidal behaviour, in response to delusional ideas; these include beliefs that they are being persecuted or are being taken over by persons or powers outside their control, or, very disturbingly, their 'voice' tells them to self-destruct. At the other end of the continuum are those who appear to have long-term chronic schizophrenia, with recurring episodes that impair their personality, and almost certainly create a stress/reactive type of depression, undermining their ability to cope (Cohen *et al.* 1990; Murphy and Wetzel 1990).

'Mrs Irons' had three severe episodes of schizophrenia in a twelve-year period, each bout lasting for almost three months. After a very disturbed first month there was a marked improvement and she made a complete recovery, being able to return to a professional job. The illness had placed a considerable strain upon her marriage, which had broken down six months before the last episode. In a valedictory letter of appreciation to her psychiatrist she said, 'As there's no guarantee it won't happen again – I simply cannot face the possibility of another attack without "Alan" [husband] – thank you for your kind calmness over the years.'

Schizophrenia is a syndrome found throughout all cultures. Improved intercultural comparisons used in the Diagnostic Statistical Manual 4 and the International Classification of Diseases 1992 clearly demonstrate that the syndrome occurs in every continent of the world. It is now freely acknowledged that its aetiology is multi-causal (Hughes 1991; Pilgrim and Rogers 1993). In addition, as will be seen from our discussion of form and content, the meaning to people of the impact of the illness is not only idiosyncratic but very culture-specific. For example, the popular idea of a common delusion is to think that one is Napoleon. This is highly unlikely in Britain. Much more common in the late twentieth century are people who believe that Winston Churchill has spoken to them, but much more frequent are beliefs that they are being spoken to by the monarch or God. Being culturally specific, delusional ideas will often include the most up-to-date technical developments, such as being controlled by TV or radio waves, or influenced by spaceships. We read of people in the nineteenth century feeling they were controlled by electricity; today it can be the voices of Venusians or computer gremlins. There are examples of people from the Hindu tradition believing that the god Khali is telling them what they must do, and examples of people belonging to the Islamic tradition hearing the Prophet or the angel Shatan direct their thoughts. Nevertheless, the pattern of the syndrome appears to be well recognized throughout the world (WHO 1993), and in all its cultural variations it essentially appears as a disorder of ideas, with delusions and hallucinatory states.

There are a number of 'first-rank' or 'cardinal' symptoms, which are detailed in the following topography.

1 *Disorder of thought.* Sometimes this includes 'thought stopping', a sense that their thoughts are being disrupted, speeded up or slowed down. Sometimes they believe that thoughts which don't belong to them are being inserted into their minds, or that their thoughts are being broadcast and can be heard by other people. This has major implications for client–therapist communication.

2 *Disorders of volition.* Sufferers believe that their will is being affected, and/or experience it, in that they lack a sense of purpose, feel inert, are purely reactive or have an overwhelming feeling of passivity, which they feel is because of external agents that control or influence them.

3 *Disorder of mood and perception* can be seen in the classic incongruity, where the sufferer appears to reverse the appropriate emotional response, such as laughing at a sad situation. Sometimes there can be a quite marked oscillation of mood, sometimes described as labile, which is reminiscent of manic–depression, where laughing is followed immediately by distressed crying. In view of the disorder of thought, however, it is easy to see how mood and perception can be disturbed.

4 *Primary hallucination/delusion.* Many authorities believe that the presence of hallucinations is a prerequisite for confirmation of the diagnosis of schizophrenia. Hallucination simply means a disorder of one of the five senses.

(a) The most common are auditory hallucinations, namely hearing a noise, specific voices or sounds. Sometimes these voices take on a recurring pattern, very often hostile, and not surprisingly can create considerable distress, particularly if they are accusatory. It is very important to remember that the person actually hears the voice in his or her head, which of course is a very disturbing phenomenon.

(b) Visual disturbances used to be considered rare or possibly a response to some physiological change or toxic substance, such as drugs, classically LSD, though they do occur, but much more rarely than people think. On the other hand, sufferers often describe how things look very special and different, with both visual and auditory experiences appearing modified. Everyday objects can appear to be surrounded by an unreal penumbra, which the sufferer often invests with a very poignant meaning. This may at first be an attractive experience, but then is often confusing. Sufferers feel that the visual or auditory sensation has some great 'psychical' significance, creating a degree of emotional excitement because of an inferred message behind the heightened visual or auditory sensations. For some sufferers this can *feel* visionary, but it is often accompanied by a growing sense of frustration because the 'promised' meaning is unrealized. For some sufferers, visual changes can be an early warning that they are entering a period of illness, leaving them confused and sometimes feeling bereft.

(c) Disturbance of olfactory sensation (smell) is not common but does occur. However, there can be an overlap with a possible organic disturbance, such as occurs in early warnings of the onset of an epileptic seizure. On the other hand, olfactory changes do happen in schizophrenia without known epileptiform EEG or symptoms.

(d) Hallucinations of taste, like olfactory hallucinations, do occur, but not often. Self-evidently they are easily associated by the sufferer with some malign influence, fear or belief they are being poisoned.

(e) Hallucinations of sensation or touch are associated with delusions of infestation. There is also a link with the relatively rare *folie à deux* – which is a 'shared psychotic state' in which the 'ill' person has a dominating relationship with the other partner, and can pose particularly difficult problems in assessment and treatment, with the complication of suicide not being unknown (Barton 1995).

Delusions concern a belief and, as already intimated, are culture- and time-specific so that ideas about X-rays, television rays and aliens from outer space are common now, while it would have been witches and demons in earlier times. It would be easy to see delusions as almost a form of imposition of meaning to explain the disturbed sensory hallucinations, and we are reminded of the classic 'Though this be madness, yet there is method in't' (*Hamlet* II.ii). It is important to remember, however, that the experiences are believed to be real, and of course will evoke some form of emotional response.

In brief, the best way to understand schizophrenia is to see it as primarily a *disorder of thought*. This should alert the therapist to the need to take the greatest care in seeking to communicate with the sufferer. What does this primary disorder of thought mean? Figuratively speaking, it is as if the sufferer's 'two-way radio' of ordinary communication – I hear you (receive) and respond (broadcast) – has been disturbed, so that the message received will perhaps be somewhat garbled but, even if it is not, the attempt to answer may be 'transmitted' in a distorted way.

In parenthesis we take it as self-evident, not just because it is a duty in the Mental Health Act, that any person suffering from mental disorder has to be interviewed in an appropriate manner, in terms not only of age, gender and culture, but also of his or her individual psycho-social situation. It is believed that all professionals, when meeting members of the public, have the *responsibility* for the communication, not the client.

In some textbooks, notions of types or patterns or schizophrenia are outlined. These are probably associated with the age of onset. For convenience we will briefly review these classic typologies.

1 *Simple schizophrenia* occurs between the ages of sixteen and twenty. Most noteworthy is that the sufferer's affect is flattened, and the formerly normally developing adolescent's psycho-social functioning at first slows down and then deteriorates; in effect there is a halting of psycho-social maturity. Frequently, the first major complaint is that the person stays in bed all day, appears

uninterested and has a lowered libido; the last also occurs in the presence of physical illness and, very significantly, drug misuse. Note well that while 'normal' adolescents may 'lie abed' often, this is matched by youthful energy: caressing the dawn and then having the energy to 'hear the chimes at midnight' without any lack of libido. This is not so in simple schizophrenia, which is characterized by the person obviously under-performing both intellectually and socially. One of the founders of modern clinical psychiatry, Manfred Bleuler, first described the syndrome as dementia praecox, i.e. dementia in the young, as it appeared to be a form of mental deterioration. It may be that this pattern of the illness shows an early onset, which disrupts the developing personality. It has, regrettably, probably the poorest prognosis of all patterns of schizophrenia.

2 *Hebephrenia*, whose onset occurs from twenty to twenty-five, is very often florid in onset. It comes on very quickly, usually after only a week or so of prodromal feelings, where the person begins to feel inexplicably uneasy, perhaps agitated or rather quiet and withdrawn. Other people recognize that, a week or two before the acute attack, the sufferer was 'a little off it'. Suddenly one gets hallucinations, disorders of thought, and not infrequently quite bizarre delusions and erratic behaviour. Nevertheless, despite the apparent extreme of the disorder, which may even be thought to be manic, there appears to be a very good prognosis, not infrequently with only one lifetime attack.

3 *Katatonia*. The phrase katatonia is still used in some texts and describes a pattern of schizophrenia which is an extreme state rather than a 'type' itself. In effect the term means an autonomic state, and the person is extremely disturbed by the disorder of his or her thought, volition and cognition. He or she is severely withdrawn, in an almost statuesque state, with an apparently total collapse of personal volition. In extreme cases the person may imitate either the actions or words of another person, which is known as echopraxia and echolalia, respectively. It is beginning to be appreciated that this autonomic zombie-like response *might* have been strongly institutionally induced in some of the old back wards of the former mental hospitals. The condition is now so infrequent as to be symptomatic of either a very serious attack of schizophrenia or the extreme psycho-social deprivation that was often associated with the large institutions of the nineteenth century, with echoes of Big Injun in Kesey's *One Flew Over the Cuckoo's Nest*. However, there is a growing opinion that there are essentially two types of schizophrenia: type I, with acute and active symptoms; type II, which is more subdued and moves more easily into 'chronicity' (Gibbons 1983). This debate is not fully concluded, reflecting yet again that there is still much to learn about the phenomena.

4 *Paranoid states*. The final pattern, called paranoia, usually has a more delayed onset, in the late thirties or early forties. This typology appears to be a well-defined pattern of schizophrenia. The person feels a prevailing sense of persecution, sometimes encapsulated in delusional ideas, so that he or she can often function perfectly well within limits, but suddenly 'the' idea triggers off a stream of associated suspicious ideas, called 'ideas of reference'. Some situations can occur when the sufferer hears or sees something on television or radio or in a newspaper which has for him or her a special and personal meaning.

While this form of schizophrenia is associated with potential violence against others, as sufferers seek to protect themselves from their 'persecutors', it can also lead to suicide. The person seeks, in desperation, to escape from the worst imaginable persecution: voices within saying that he or she is excrement and should die.

There seems to be little doubt that there are bio-psycho-social factors in the causation of schizophrenia, and growing evidence suggests that the stronger and more classic the symptoms, the stronger the constitutional endowment. Nevertheless, even among young people with two parents classified as having schizophrenia, only a third develop the syndrome. However, there is a much closer concordance between monozygotic (identical) twins than between dizygotic (non-identical) twins, even among twins who were separated at birth, which points to a biological element (Rosenthal and Kelty 1978). This shows that the interactive mechanisms of 'nurture and nature' are not fully understood, and there is more to know. What is important for the therapist is that such disturbed behaviour in a family member almost inevitably will create a reaction; it is not, as was once thought, that families cause the primary disorder. Nevertheless, Falloon's (1985) work clearly indicates beyond any measure of doubt that the family and immediate environment play an important part in the extent to which a person copes with schizophrenia, and the risk of further break-down. It is sufficient to say here that it seems reasonable to suggest that a person with schizophrenia has a constitutional predisposition that may be triggered or exacerbated by stress in his or her psycho-social circumstances. What should not be forgotten is that the vast majority of people with a long-term mental disorder, be it schizophrenia or depression, but particularly schizophrenia, rely predominantly upon household members, other relations and families, who are the most important persons in any mental health work (Gibbons *et al.* 1984). Thus, in terms of ideas of 'rejection', families, despite pressures and sometimes hostile professionals, endure the most and still continue to provide the single largest support network the mentally ill person is likely to have.

While suicide, it must be remembered, is probably more often a reaction to chronic and probably unsupported schizophrenia (Cheng *et al.* 1990; Cohen *et al.* 1990), the growing evidence of biochemical disorder cannot be gainsaid, though whether it is causal or reactive is still not completely determined. Despite some of the problems of side-effects, in the acute state of the syndrome psychotropic drugs are vital, not only for people with schizophrenia, but also for those with psychiatric depression. Unless the very severe psychic pain is controlled and diminished, the person's morale is gravely undermined, which, it is believed, is a key factor in why the mentally ill are so vulnerable to suicide (Paraskavias *et al.* 1993).

Some bio-physiological pointers to suicide and its possible link with mental disorder

There is a longstanding division between ideas of 'nature' and 'nurture' in the causation of mental illness (Hamilton 1976). Over the years, there has been a growing recognition of a fundamental truth, that genetics interacts with environment, and environment with genetic predisposition, in a whole range of human activity (Bodmer and McKie 1994; Jones 1994). Nothing is more sterile than over-emphasizing either nature or nurture, for the very essence of classic Darwinism concerns the interaction between the two. The evidence is clear: all organisms interact with their environment; human physiology is as important to behaviour as psycho-social stimuli are to bio-physiological functioning. We should rid ourselves of the Descartian 'dualism' and see the person in totality, which includes all interactive bio-physio-psycho-social elements.

As biochemistry becomes more sophisticated and measurements become more exact and reliable, not only have the biochemical changes related to affective disorders and the schizophrenias been demonstrated, but, over the past few years, there has been a growing appreciation of biochemical changes related to eventual suicides (e.g. Bourgeois 1991; Golden *et al.* 1991; Montgomery 1993). Cheetham *et al.* (1991) provide a valuable review of post-mortem studies of levels of neurotransmitters in the brains of deceased people who have been involved with either depression or suicide. They show there are associations with different metabolic levels of some, such as serotonin, but while there are very promising results, the picture is as yet unclear or sometimes contradictory. As Cheetham *et al.* remind us, depressed persons who have committed suicide may well not be representative of depressed patients in general, and there is a lack of consistency in the results. There are a number of problems. For example, are the variations found in the levels of serotonin causal, or influenced by previous treatments, or owing to the experience of depression or even the trauma of the suicide event? We just do not know. Cheetham's modest and careful review pays close attention to problematic methodological questions: for example, will a violent death create a different biochemical reaction from that of a quiet death; an accident, a fight, hanging or jumping from a building, as opposed to a large overdose where the person is relatively calmer? For non-specialists and specialists alike this becomes confusing, as it appears that different neurotransmitters in the different parts of the brain may or may not be associated with not only depression, and resultant suicide, but also the degree of impulsivity (Bourgeois 1991) or aggression (Golden *et al.* 1991).

What does appear to be undoubtedly emerging, is a consensus that there are biochemical changes, but whether they are pre- or post-action is unknown. We need to maintain an open mind. While we should not forget that the financial incentives for organizations in the drug industry are enormous, it is clear that the plethora of papers published on serotonin over the past years reflects a massive interest and investment in this area of research. Thus, in view of biochemical links with treatment that deals with symptomatology (Berrios 1990), this is an area of research that *might* promise improved prediction and/or intervention in the next century. We shall have to wait and see, though our prediction would be that as we know more, it is likely that we will see an even greater realization that the individual person, within the context of his or her own biochemical and psycho-social situation, will continue to react uniquely, which will continue to demand a person-specific intervention and treatment programme.

Substance misuse (alcohol and drugs)

Another component in psychiatric-related suicide is substance abuse, of alcohol and drugs. Some may believe that these are not psychiatric conditions *per se*. Rather they are problems of living, though in respect of alcoholism in particular, with its familial and probably genetic component and its association with depression (Berrios 1990), it seems that there are good practice grounds for it to be included in the psychiatric category. There is also growing evidence that drug-dependent people are partially 'self-medicating', as it were, to ease the psychic and sometimes social pain of their situation (Murphy and Wetzel 1990; Janlert and Hammarstrom 1992; Mendleson and Rich 1993). Of course, some drugs are sufficiently mood and perception changing as to be considered as being in the medico-psychiatric field; for example, LSD is particularly dangerous, and there is some evidence that the persistent, frequent and long-term use of cannabis leads to clear psychotic states in a minority of cases (Andreasson *et al.* 1990).

Certainly alcohol, and its initial apparent stimulus, or rather disinhibition, effect, is physiologically and psychologically a depressant and certainly both alcohol and drugs can impair judgement. Experience would suggest that the presence of either alcohol or mood-affecting drugs induces or compounds impulsive behaviour, which in particular circumstances can lead to death. 'Mr James' gave us all a considerable amount of anxiety, for in an effort to cope with a sexual orientation that *he* could not accept as a 'fundamental Christian' ('I'm the worst kind of sinner, I know it's wrong'), he would 'lapse', become depressed and then 'freak out' in an alcoholic binge. In the midst of remorse and self-hate, he would impulsively take massive overdoses, where only luck avoided the resultant vomiting leading to his death. What alarmed the therapist was the almost deliberate Russian roulette he would play, 'to see if God had forgiven me'.

In respect of drugs and suicide, an interesting study from Sweden (Allebeck and Allgulander 1990) merits brief discussion because it reviewed 50,000 young national servicemen, following up this essentially 'normal', i.e. non-patient, cohort over a thirteen-year period. It must be remembered that such a longitudinal sample, by definition, would have already 'filtered' out those older adolescents and young men who were not then fit enough to be accepted for national service. The review showed that a psychiatric diagnosis in later life was significantly linked to subsequent suicidal behaviour, which was at a far higher rate than in those without mental illness diagnosis. In particular, later suicidal activity was found to be linked to personality disorder, and especially drug dependence.

Among a patient sample, Beck and Steer (1989), using the internationally recognized Hamilton Scale and the Beck Depression Inventory, Suicidal Intent Scale and Hopelessness Scale (on which there is more later), found that alcoholism was the strongest predictor of eventual suicide over a five-year period. When linked with other factors, such as unemployment, alcohol compounded the risk in terms of both actual suicide and the Suicidal Intent Scale.

In Britain, Hawton and Fagg (1988) found that the use of long-term hypnotics was strongly linked to eventual suicide in a cohort of people previously involved in deliberate self-harm. This matches similar work by Cullberg *et al.* (1988), though they linked drugs and alcohol, which are very often misused together, with suicide, often coming at the end of a long social deterioration associated with alcohol and drug misuse. The association of drugs and alcohol with suicide and other problems emerges in a number of very prestigious studies (Yeo and Yeo 1993), and is confirmed in later work by Britain's leading 'suicidologists', Hawton *et al.* (1993).

The clincher on the dangers of alcohol potentiating the problematic came from an ingenious study by Wasserman *et al.* (1994). They analysed suicide and crimes of violence in the republics of the former Soviet Union following the five-year period of severe restrictions on the sale of alcohol. There was a very strong correlation across all the republics between reduced mortality rates and lowered alcohol consumption. (This is not an anti-drink section by the way. The merits of good wine, red in particular, have been known throughout history. The problem is classically, do not drink to excess (Sournia 1990).)

We appear to be on safe ground to say that the presence of alcohol or mood and perception changing drugs *potentially* worsens any negative psycho-social situation and, irrespective of intent, increases the risk of damage or death to the person.

Personality disorder (psychopathy)

The concept of personality disorders or psychopathy has long been associated with controversy. Indeed, some psychiatrists would exclude the problem from the responsibility of clinical psychiatry, though both the International Classification of Diseases and DSM 3 place the 'complex' within the psychiatric field. It has to be acknowledged that there can be a misuse of the diagnostic category, and traditionally it was said that if the psychiatrist did not like the male patient, he was described as a 'psychopath'; if the psychiatrist disliked a female patient, she was described as 'hysteric'. There is some evidence to show that the background and personality of the psychiatrist can lead to what might be described as more punitive diagnosis and subsequent treatment (see Butler and Pritchard 1990). In the late 1970s and early 1980s, this could be associated with ethnic prejudice or a lack of an understanding of psycho-social phenomena in ethnic minorities by psychiatry, which was accused of institutional racism (Fernando 1988). However, there is growing evidence that, with improved clinical psychiatric training, such trends are being diminished (Perkins and Moodley 1993; McGovern *et al.* 1994).

This being said, however, there can be no doubt that the phenomenon of 'personality disorder/psychopathy' does exist in a patterned way and is often present in people who have a longstanding history of a lack of engagement with other people, and of self-disruptive and destructive behaviour. This often damages both themselves and others, and is associated with both types of suicidal behaviour, including suicide (Linehan *et al.* 1987, 1993; Allebeck and Allgulander 1990). Whether there is an overlap between personality disorders and child abuse or neglect is debatable, but we will explore this in the next chapter when we examine problems of adolescence, and the interface between child neglect and abuse, including sexual abuse and subsequent suicidal behaviour (Casey 1991; Bayatpour *et al.* 1992; Yeo and Yeo 1993).

Suicide and the forensic dimension

At this stage it is perhaps worth commenting upon the phenomenon known as murder-followed-by-suicide syndrome. This is where the assailant extends the violence from the victim to himself or herself, and not uncommonly this involves mental disorder. In Britain almost a fifth of murderers die from suicide, and a similar finding comes from recent work in Australia (Easteal 1994). In practice one might find these fortunately relatively rare but tragic circumstances within some profound depressions. People can have an almost delusional quality to their cognition, a fear of impending doom. Therefore, in an act of distorted protection, they damage their loved ones, not infrequently their child, to save them from the terrible fate which is to come.

In the presence of paranoia, it is again relatively rare, though there is still a risk, for deluded sufferers to damage the people they were protecting, seeing them at the centre of their persecution, and then to involve themselves in suicide. This is a good illustration that, when there is depression, or a feeling of oppression, aggression may not be far behind. It should be stressed that these are rare circumstances, but most clinicians would agree the need to be *particularly* cautious in the presence of paranoia, because this group disproportionately appears among patients in special hospitals. However, the situation has to be put into proper perspective.

Extrapolating from materials supplied by the Medical Director of the Special Hospitals (Barker 1993) and based upon the Department of Health (1992) figures on prevalence of schizophrenia, our calculations show that at most there would be between 120 and 160 murders per million people with schizophrenia, which is between about 30 and 40 deaths per annum. This could be juxtaposed against the 184 deaths per million number of registered road vehicles, and from a simple statistical comparison, the average citizen is *more* at risk from motor vehicles and car drivers than from the mentally ill. However, self-evidently the *families* of sufferers, particularly from paranoia, and those who may work with them are proportionately at greater risk because they are more often involved with such sufferers. If the road death comparison is not reassuring, we can calculate the number of people with depression and look at the suicide rate: 4,800 deaths per annum. The extent of *self*-damage by the mentally ill turns out to be between 8,000 and 10,000 per million depressed people. These figures are a crude mathematical calculation, but illustrate the truism that the mentally ill are far more dangerous to themselves than ever they are to other people.

A recent study by Benezech and Bourgeois (1992) from France raises an interesting perspective. In analysing a year of murders followed by suicide, they found that depression, rather than mania or paranoia, was the dominant theme among the murders. This should be set alongside the work of Wilson and Daly (1994) who explored the psycho-social antecedents of murders. They found that amidst a range of mental health problems, the murderers, mainly but not exclusively men, had killed their spouses or partners *more* frequently *after* an estrangement than when living with them. A significant proportion of these men followed up their assaults with suicidal behaviour.

Such cases are of course at the extreme, but the association between offending behaviour and mental disorders is increasingly being accepted. In different samples of probation clients, more than a third were found to have a mental health problem, and more than 10 per cent had been involved in deliberate self-harm (Hudson *et al.* 1993; Pritchard *et al.* 1993). The work of Gunn *et al.* (1991), who found substantial levels of psychiatric illness among prison inmates, goes some way to explain the significantly higher level of suicide among prisoners and forensic psychiatric patients (Dooley 1990; Johnson *et al.* 1993). Here we have yet another factor to complicate life for the busy non-specialist professional.

CHAPTER 4

DEFINING SUICIDE 2: OTHER CONTRIBUTORY PSYCHO-SOCIAL FACTORS

Deliberate self-harm (attempted suicide) as a factor contributing to actual suicide

Perhaps the most complex issue facing anyone concerned with suicidal behaviour centres on the problems of intent, motivation and affect. Was the person truly seeking oblivion and death, but the self-damaging behaviour was not lethal, or others intervened to halt the process? This is described as 'attempted suicide', 'parasuicide' or 'deliberate self-harm'. However, very often we do not know what the person intended, and often he or she is uncertain and ambivalent. Conversely, people who are angry with themselves, a parent or spouse inappropriately behave to show their sense of desperation in a self-damaging and apparently 'self-killing' way, but in no way do they *wish* to die. Rather, this is a form of reaction to the situation and is flight from an aversive situation. Tragically, on occasions such behaviour proves to be lethal, or an expected intervention does not materialize, and the person dies. Attempted suicide, or deliberate self-harm (DSH), is an important factor associated with eventual suicide but, as will be seen later, it is a different phenomenon.

This 'separateness' of DSH merits further discussion, but we will consider the behaviour only in *relation to actual suicide* at this stage. In practical terms, therefore, there is an overlap of 'suicidal' behaviours, though there are clear distinctive features, illustrated in a wide range of research, to show that people who kill themselves are statistically a distinct group from those who involve themselves in other forms of apparently suicidal behaviour (Barraclough and Hughes 1987). In many individual situations such distinctions are of little comfort to the distressed family or bemused professional trying to make sense of the current crisis.

This ambiguity about 'intent' is one reason why Kreitman and Phillips (1969) coined the expression 'parasuicide'. They recognized that motivation and intent were often ambiguous, and that the meaning for the person might be very different from that for other people. The behaviour could range from a carefully planned but low-lethality method to a sudden, impulsive, self-damaging response, with only a minor trigger, which ends in death.

The problem with the term 'parasuicide' is that it implies an intended partial destination or direction, apparently related to death. Therefore, despite its clumsiness, we prefer the Department of Health's designation, 'deliberate self-harm'. DSH suggests nothing about intent or motivation, but simply states that the person has damaged himself or herself. This is not to minimize DSH, which should give cause for concern, because no matter how 'accepting' the professional is, it should not be forgotten that DSH is a highly abnormal and extreme action, albeit sometimes understandable.

The importance of DSH is the frequency with which *previous DSH incidents are linked to completed suicide*, as demonstrated by important work by Hawton and colleagues (1993). In young adults (fifteen to twenty-four years old), the ratio of previous DSH to actual suicide ranged from 1.2 to 4.4, with a mean odds ratio of 2.3. It should be noted, however, that these were young adults, and DSH occurs far more frequently among the under thirties and, in particular, women. So while men currently kill themselves at approximately three times the rate of women, DSH occurs twice as often among females as men, especially among younger women (DHSS 1984; Barraclough and Hughes 1987; Cullberg *et al.* 1988; Brittlebank *et al.* 1990).

It would appear that the younger the person the greater is the ratio of DSH to completed suicide, approximately 80 to 1 in the under-twenties and 40 to 1 in under-thirties. In the case of elderly people, however, the ratio is down to 4 to 1, which reflects the possible mental state of older people, but more importantly their competence and possible access to lethal methods, and the greater likelihood of their living alone or being isolated (Henderson 1989; Platt *et al.* 1992).

However, as Barraclough and Hughes (1987) point out, despite the apparent similarity between the results on suicides and people with psychiatric depression, a key differentiation is that people who had died were ten times more likely to have had a previous DSH episode than those with only depression. However, the authors go on to highlight that a key feature is the social antecedents of people who go on to kill themselves, as opposed to either depression or DSH.

Our focus at this stage is on the association of DSH with eventual suicide. The DSH process in its own right will be examined in the next chapter, and contrasts between the two phenomena will be explored to assist the practitioner in making informed judgements as to the type and urgency of intervention.

Lethality

This may be a good point at which to discuss the wide range of methods that people use to damage themselves and kill themselves.

Method is often associated with gender, and the more macho, assertive methodologies are linked with men. For example, in Western Europe hanging, drowning and the use of car exhausts have a predominance of male perpetrators, whereas self-poisoning is more frequently, though of course not exclusively, associated with women.

Age is an important determinant, younger people of both genders more often resorting to available drugs. Sadly there have been case examples, explored in the popular media, of adolescents in distress overdosing on paracetamol. They have no firm motivation to die but tragically the behaviour results in painful liver damage and, not infrequently, eventual death. McClure (1987) explored methods used in Great Britain, and highlighted this gender divide, but also noticed that extreme and unusual methods were more often associated with severe psychotic behaviour; for example, the use of band saws (Clark *et al.* 1989). Of course, the easy availability of guns in the United States goes a long way to account for the relatively high level of suicide in that country. This and other factors partly account for Canada and the USA having male youth suicide rates (in fifteen to twenty-four year olds) among the worst in the developed world over the past twenty years (Pritchard 1990, 1992a, 1993a, 1993c). Crucially, the availability of lethal means is one reason why farm workers in Britain have a higher rate of death by firearms; and doctors and nurses have above average rates of suicide, predominantly through the lethal use of prescribed dangerous drugs. Classically, for British women before the 1970s, coal gas, which was so easily available in kitchens, was the most 'popular' method (Sylvia Plath so died, for example). The reduction and cessation of domestic coal gas supply was an important factor in the fall in female suicides from the 1970s onwards (Kreitman 1988). A recent analysis showed a link between the availability of lethal methods in West Germany and changes in the suicide rate (Wiedenmann and Weyerer 1994). There are cultural variations in lethality. For example, it was found in Singapore that parasuicide was associated with drug overdose, whereas suicides' *most* frequent method was jumping from tall buildings, unlike in Britain (McClure 1987), because in Singapore skyscrapers are a major architectural feature (Peng and Choo 1990).

Psychological features

Bearing in mind the likely emotional experience of someone with depression and/or schizophrenia, there will probably be an overarching sense of distress and tension. However, these psychological features are important indicators for 'stress-related' suicide, not just that associated with psychiatric disorder. Low self-esteem can be an important feature, as can ideas of unworthiness and a sense of hopelessness (Beck 1988; Beck and Steer 1991; Beck *et al.* 1993a), which often undermine people's sense of morale and leave them feeling out of control of their own lives (Howe *et al.* 1993). In the practical situation, it is important to understand the meaning of these experiences to the person as he or she tries to make sense of his or her life situation. While a sense of despair and depression may be prevailing, Beck's and others' recent work suggests that a sense of hopelessness may well be the superordinate construct, which marks a difference between later misery and suicidal activity.

A very valuable model of the psychological concomitant of suicide was developed by Edwin Schneideman (1985), which he described as the 'cubic model of suicide'. Using a content analysis of over 5,000 suicide notes, Schneideman extrapolated major themes from the personal tragedies of people who left a record of their intent and action. It must be remembered that a considerable number of people assumed to have died by their own hand often do not leave 'notes', and O'Donnell (1994), looking at deaths on the London Underground (in 1985 and 1989), found that only 15 per cent had left a communication, and argued that these had provided little insight into the causes of suicide as subjectively perceived. Yet a 'note' or some form of acceptable communication is a very important factor in British coroners coming to a decision of a suicide verdict. Nevertheless, the weakness of O'Donnell's position is that the use of the 'underground' as a method of suicide is extreme, and people killing themselves in this way may or may not be representative of the majority of suicides. We would interpret suicide on the underground as more likely to contain a higher proportion of people with a schizophrenic illness or a high degree of impulsivity.

While these qualifications need to be borne in mind when we are considering the origins of Schneideman's work, its value is that it is towards the 'qualitative' end of the research continuum, rather than the empirical, though it merits both consideration by the practitioner and evaluation from the researcher. He describes three broad themes.

1 *Perturbation.* By this he means psychic pain or extreme stress. There is a notional 1 to 5 range, with 5 being the most dangerous.
2 *Psychological constriction.* With this condition the person believes that there are *no other options*, psychological or social, in resolving his or her severe perturbation. Again a 1 to 5 scale is used, with 5 showing that the person is convinced 'there is no other way out'.
3 *Penchant for action.* There needs to be a penchant for action, or at least impulsivity. Under the Schneideman interactive 'cubic model of suicide', a person may be in extreme perturbation, feeling totally at a loss, with no options or alternative 'way out', *but* without sufficient energy to act, the person is left immobilized.

Regrettably, Schneideman, who is one of America's most eminent suicidologists, has not gone on to link these themes with any intent or prediction model (e.g. those of Beck or Lettieri). Nor has he any place for the social-psychological, but the strength of the model is the insight it gives into interactive themes, and the emphasis placed upon understanding the distress of the sufferer, which is so important when we consider the development of a sustaining and protective rapport.

There is research which shows that violence in relationships can be a trigger for suicide, though recently there have been some inconclusive findings. It appears that men who perpetrate a violent act, or psychological violence, then go on to damage or kill themselves. Conversely, women tend to be the *recipients* of such psychological and physical violence, which seems to confirm low self-esteem, ending in self-damage and sometimes death (Fischer *et al.* 1993). Certainly this theme is seen in the well-known link between suicide that is preceded by murder, in which the man is more often the assailant, and the fact that some people's violence seems to overwhelm their coping styles, leading to suicide (Kotler *et al.* 1993; Easteal 1994).

Post-bereavement stress can be an important factor, and has long been linked with suicide and deliberate self-harm. This is a complex interaction, but it appears that around the first and second anniversaries of the demise of a key relationship, the survivor's chances of becoming involved in suicidal behaviour rise considerably (Gibbons 1978; Shepherd and Barraclough 1978). In particular, a negative post-bereavement response is often found as an important trigger in elderly suicides whose partners have now left them isolated and vulnerable.

When these psychological factors are compounded by psychiatric depression and/or schizophrenia, the person can have a real sense of being rejected. This is the cognitive response to being bereaved, a sense of unworthiness, low self-esteem, a sense of hopelessness and being a recipient of another person's psycho-physical violence. This theme of rejection is two-way, however, so that sometimes the sufferer can be rejecting, albeit in anger and distress, his or her partner, family and community. Sometimes, of course, this 'rejection' by the sufferer can be part of the illness: he or she feels unworthy of offers of help; or there is the double bind of the sufferer who rejects family because of earlier feelings of rejection, where neither side can cross the emotional chain of mutual hurt.

Because of the strong association of mental illness with suicide, most people will experience the effects of prejudice and discrimination against the mentally ill, and even professionals can be influenced by our culture's prejudices. As Miles (1991) demonstrated, the single most distressing feature for women with mental disorder is their experience of the process of being referred to a psychiatrist. This 'confirmed that they were mad'. This adds a further twist to the vortex of depression, aggression, guilt and despair and, as the situation tightens, leads to the ultimate rejection of them, of us and, subjectively, of us of them. Sadly one often finds deliberate self-harm appears to be a coping mechanism, albeit one that is self-defeating. In seeking to resolve their distress, they end up shocking those around them and exacerbating the rejection, which, at a cognitive level, is experienced by other people as manipulative, aggressive and an act of ultimate rejection, irrespective of whether or not they die. The behaviour symbolically says that the other person, partner, family member or friend, is insufficiently loved to be a reason for the distressed person to want to go on living. It will be argued that this theme of rejection provides an important insight and possibly an indicator of an area of priority for subsequent intervention and help for the prevention of suicide. In parenthesis, when among the social factors, it is the sense of social rejection, associated with unemployment, for example, that can be most psychically painful.

The book *Learned Helplessness*, by the early cognitive behaviouralist Ernest Seligman, gave an important key for understanding part of the process of depression (note that we write process rather than cause). Brown and Harris (1978) in Britain have provided empirical evidence of how people, especially women, 'learn' to have a poor self-esteem. Further development of the work of Beck (1988) in the field of cognitive therapy has given us a very important insight into the experience of a depressed and potentially self-damaging person, and a key approach to assist our communication with people who are profoundly depressed. They interpret the world in a self-reinforcing negative cognitive way, illustrated in Anne Sexton's poem 'Sickness unto death' (1977). Sexton was a poet of international repute who finally died from suicide (Middlebrook 1992; Hendin 1993). In just a few stanzas she brilliantly illustrated the draining vortex of her depression. She imaged the loss of God, the reverse of the Quaker hope of 'seeking the Godhead in every person'. Her depression immobilized her, transmogrifying her into a statuesque helpless figure, so that death through inertia was a natural corollary of her Nietzschean anomic and self-consuming languor. Not surprisingly, suicide has been seen as a kind of personal cannibalism, eating up one's very being, reminiscent of the self-consuming monster Chernobyl who 'Loves life. Desires it, sucks out its vital juices, and spews out the skeletal debris upon the earth, balmed by tears of acid rain – I am Chernobyl and I Love life' (Anon).

This self-hate and the description of an emotional cul-de-sac are reflected in Sylvia Plath's work:

I am accused. I dream of massacres – hating myself, hating and fearing – arms held out in love.
It is a love of death that sickens everything.

Here is self-rejection and a sense of rejection of others, *par excellence.*

Emerging from this cognitive view of suicidal behaviour are two important assessment and practical themes, which have received empirical support: first, the importance of problem solving; second, reasons for living. Self-evidently during a depressive period people will have difficulty in solving life's problems, either those of long standing or those exacerbated by the depression. This is strongly compounded in people with a suicidal ideation (Linehan *et al.* 1987, 1991, 1993; Fremouw *et al.* 1990, 1993). These are themes to which we shall return.

Social factors contributing to suicide

John Donne's classic statement that 'no man is an island' illustrates a fundamental truth: no matter how individualistic a person is, to a greater or lesser extent he or she is defined by relationships with others. Inevitably people are influenced by their time, society and culture and the formal and informal roles they enact. We shall explore the social factors that influence the individual regarding suicide, before reviewing the macro-sociological factors and critique in Chapter 6.

Gender

We have already touched upon gender in showing that throughout the Western developed world men usually kill themselves at twice or more the rate of their female counterparts. It is easy to consider gender in purely physiological terms, especially within the medical perspective, as there are a number of diseases which differentially discriminate between men and women; for example, coronary heart disease and a number of cancers. Despite familial and genetic predisposition, these conditions are nevertheless increasingly recognized as being strongly influenced by environmental factors (Bodmor and McKie 1994). Gender has an important social meaning, of course.

Kushner (1989) has argued that the different suicide rates for men and women, which apparently do not match the larger number of women diagnosed as depressed, become *concordant* when deliberate self-harm is added. He examined US rates and found that there was virtual equality of the sexes. This may be because of gender differences in method of self-harm, with males resorting to more active and lethal methods (McClure 1987; Wiedenmann and Weyerer 1994). This might mean that differences in actual suicide rates are essentially cultural, a discussion to which we shall return.

One of the seminal thinkers in the field of social psychiatry is Professor George W. Brown, who identified some of the social pressures upon working-class women that lower their self-esteem, often creating lonely and isolated personal situations. He helped us to appreciate that depression and low mood is a significant experience of a large proportion of women (Brown and Harris 1978, Brown 1987; Brown *et al.* 1990). Interestingly, there are some protective elements against suicide found in the gender; being married and having children in particular provides women, more often than their men, with 'a reason for living'. It has been found that within English-speaking countries, paradoxically, women's disadvantaged position in the market place appears to protect them against the demoralizing impact of unemployment (Pritchard 1990). This, however, appears to be changing (Pritchard 1995a, b). As Ferriera de Castro *et al.* (1988) predicted, as socio-economic equality improves, women will have raised expectations, and as equal opportunities increase, women's behaviour will change and the suicide patterns of the genders will converge.

There is evidence that patterns of behaviour traditionally associated with men are slowly beginning to appear in women (Pritchard 1971; Rutter and Gillier 1984; Allen 1990; Hewitt 1993). For example, adolescent and young women engage more frequently in under-age drinking, and fighting, theft, drug misuse and truancy are no longer the exclusive preserve of the young male (Rutter and Gillier 1984; Pritchard *et al.* 1993). The image of the 'new man', who is more sensitive and expressive, may be coinciding with more self-assertive women who have greater opportunities, albeit yet to be fully achieved. Comfortable stereotypes about gender, especially in relation to under-thirties, are increasingly meaningless, if they ever were accurate.

Marital status, support versus isolation

A number of studies have shown that, while marriage appears to add a statistical protection against suicide for both genders, divorce, with its raised anxiety and trauma, is more strongly associated with suicide (Stack 1992). Isolation follows divorce, and despite changes in society's attitudes to divorce, people can feel stigmatized and socially rejected. Not uncommonly, a person has a depressive mood, irrespective of whether it is psychiatric or socially related. If people are alone, there will be fewer supports and less likelihood of anyone being able to intervene should they act upon their misery (Fischer *et al.* 1993).

Age

The key feature in the suicide dimension is age, as suicide rates increase proportionately with virtually every decade. Table 1 illustrates the point well. The average suicide rate in England and Wales in 1974 was 95 per million for men and 64 per million for women. Broadly the rate increased with each successive decade. We will explore other interesting findings contained in Table 1 later, but

Table 1 Suicide by age and gender, United Kingdom, 1974–1992: rates per million

					Age			
	All ages	*15–24*	*25–34*	*35–44*	*45–54*	*55–64*	*65–74*	*75+*
England and Wales								
Males								
1974	95	58	106	114	154	159	189	196
1992	121	115	159	189	170	136	129	156
Index 1992	127	198	150	166	110	86	68	80
Females								
1974	64	29	51	72	111	113	128	95
1992	34	21	37	38	51	45	57	56
Index 1992	53	72	73	53	46	40	45	59
Northern Ireland								
Males								
1974	51	23	29	85	161	131	43	96
1992	114	157	191	110	153	150	152	140
Index 1992	224	683	659	129	95	115	353	146
Females								
1974	29	8	41	48	81	52	16	53
1992	21	16	33	30	34	27	30	18
Index 1992	72	200	80	63	42	52	188	34
Scotland								
Males								
1974	103	78	144	137	164	149	214	168
1992	160	191	293	276	146	257	167	126
Index 1992	155	245	203	201	89	172	78	75
Females								
1974	65	33	51	92	119	113	122	88
1992	36	13	64	48	70	80	62	20
Index 1992	55	39	125	52	59	71	51	23

Index 1974 = 100.

at this point we simply wish to illustrate that usually suicide increases with age. This will be demonstrated in data concerning the whole of Western Europe (shown later). It should be noted in passing, however, that although the Anglo-Welsh rates for the youngest male and female age group are lower than the average, a major change has occurred over the past twenty years, which has seen these rates increase more than those for any other age group (Pritchard 1992a, 1995a).

Adolescent age band

Usually textbooks speak of two age peaks, in that suicide among children under fourteen, both proportionately and in actuality, is extremely rare. For example, in 1992, the latest year for which figures are available for the United Kingdom (WHO 1994), there were only two children who conclusively died from suicide, a rate of only one per million. Clearly one such death is an enormous tragedy, not only for the child but also for the family, but this children's rate has hardly altered over the past twenty years. However, it is not the same for DSH, which will be more fully discussed in the next chapter.

Where suicide begins to soar *relatively* is following the age of sixteen. This age of course coincides, first, paradoxically, with greater social competence and knowledge, so that perhaps the young person knows better how to kill himself or herself, but, more importantly, may be linked with the early onset of schizophrenia and psychiatric depression (Kerfoot and Butler 1988). Practice experience would suggest that young people who are depressed or under tremendous stress, but do not actually kill themselves, are crying for help but this is no reason to take their distress lightly.

The elderly

The other significant factor for age appears to be linked to the economic and social status of elderly people, who are likely to experience personal and social neglect, isolation and rejection, making them especially vulnerable.

For a number of years textbooks have simply noted that with each advancing decade there appears to be an increase in suicide for both genders and in most countries. Usually the highest proportional suicide rate is in the over seventy-fives, though in a minority of countries this peak occurs between sixty-five and seventy-four, with a substantial drop in the over seventy-five group (see Table 1). It has been argued (Pritchard 1992b) that the suicide toll among elderly people was treated by many textbooks as almost 'a natural event', and seldom commented upon. More aware professionals today would recognize the incipient ageism in such a *sang froid*. For example, Italy traditionally has always had a lower male suicide and female suicide rate than the Anglo-Welsh, but actually has a higher rate among over seventy-fives than the UK. This is reflected in another low suicide rate country, Spain (Pritchard *et al.* 1995b). Clearly there are major questions about the significance of such findings. For example, we find in Canada (Agbayewa 1993) that there are differences between certain regions, so that while other suicides are slightly higher in urban areas, the low population rural areas actually have substantially higher proportional suicide rates in people over the age of seventy-five.

Lester (1993) suggested that suicide among the elderly is predominately because of a resurgence of life-long problems, re-exposed as it were when individual resources are diminished by age. There is, however, a growing recognition of linked psycho-social and policy factors, rather than just the assumed physical decline, with associated but understandable mood changes (Henderson 1989), which points to a much more complex elderly–suicide axis than was first thought (Pritchard 1992b; Pritchard *et al.* 1995b).

Two studies merit greater exploration. The first, by Franc *et al.* (1993), was an ingenious review of suicidal behaviour in people over the age of sixty-five in sixty-nine old people's homes in Southern France over a five-year period. They examined one of the regions with a suicide rate lower than the national average, but intra-regional analysis showed that those in old people's homes were more likely to die from suicide than those living ordinarily in the community, at a ratio of 2.9 to 1. Bearing in mind the very strong traditional support of the family, this raised questions about the gap between people's expectations and their reality. We can only speculate, but wonder about the impact of experiencing both personal and social 'rejection', which are so often associated with elderly people being admitted to old people's homes. It would be true to say that France and Italy, for example, have more clearly established extended families than Britain, yet when we examine the elderly suicide rate in relation to the national average suicide rate (Table 2) there are some remarkable differences. Austria, France, Greece, Italy, Japan, Portugal and Spain all have a worse elderly to national average ratio than England and Wales, and only Ireland among the 'traditional' cultures has a proportionally lower ratio for both elderly men and women than England and Wales. How do we interpret this?

The answer may lie in a seminal study by Vogel and Wolfersdorf (1989) from West Germany. They looked at mental illness in an elderly cohort, which included 310 suicides of psychiatric inpatients, in a multi-centre study that included six psychiatric hospitals in the south of the former West Germany. They found that age was an independent risk factor, but was not to be confounded with psychiatric morbidity, and they asserted that psychiatric morbidity was not sufficient to explain the suicide fact. They found that in addition to the chronic psycho-pathology, there was a constant theme of the break-down of cardinal interpersonal relationships, which appears to play a larger part in suicides in the older group of patients. This included deaths of relatives, and in particular the objective or subjective experience of loneliness and being isolated. It was these latter two non-medical factors which played a significant part in two of every three suicides among older patients.

This underscores the elderly's strong sense of being rejected, which is often attendant on isolation and loneliness. Such an interpretation has some support from Japan, which traditionally has a high respect for the suicide. Rockett and Smith (1993), examining suicide among elderly females, found evidence of efforts to hide their suicide by use of the method of drowning. This points to some of the deleterious change in industrial societies, which leave elderly citizens 'like

Table 2 Suicide by age and gender in major Western countries: rates per million and index of change

	Age							
	All ages	*15–24*	*25–34*	*35–44*	*45–54*	*55–64*	*65–74*	*75+*
Australia								
Males								
1974	160	159	167	226	296	254	325	359
1992	191	256	268	232	234	218	245	271
Index 1992	119	161	160	103	79	86	75	75
Females								
1974	74	45	84	126	142	151	127	90
1992	49	50	64	61	58	68	68	80
Index 1992	66	111	76	48	41	45	54	89
Austria								
Males								
1974	340	201	328	453	593	564	663	873
1992	338	244	300	346	442	490	641	1095
Index 1992	99	121	91	76	75	87	97	125
Females								
1974	145	72	93	161	190	275	264	357
1992	117	61	76	135	180	174	148	274
Index 1992	81	85	82	84	95	63	56	77
Canada								
Males								
1974	187	241	232	271	294	255	305	236
1991	214	277	295	269	262	242	241	290
Index 1991	114	115	127	99	89	95	79	123
Females								
1974	71	49	95	121	147	128	100	42
1991	52	40	72	77	70	67	69	39
Index 1991	73	82	76	64	48	52	69	93
Denmark								
Males								
1974	337	171	299	428	598	638	646	709
1992	291	126	246	340	479	394	430	814
Index 1992	86	74	82	79	80	62	67	115
Females								
1974	185	58	103	196	370	383	371	339
1992	151	34	85	146	260	284	276	287
Index 1992	82	59	83	74	70	74	74	85
England and Wales								
Males								
1974	95	58	106	114	154	159	189	196
1992	121	115	159	189	170	136	129	156
Index 1992	127	198	150	166	110	86	68	80

Table 2 Continued

				Age				
	All ages	15–24	25–34	35–44	45–54	55–64	65–74	75+
Females								
1974	64	29	51	72	111	113	128	95
1992	34	21	37	38	51	45	57	56
Index 1992	53	72	73	53	46	40	45	59
France								
Males								
1974	227	115	176	260	362	434	554	780
1991	296	150	312	391	386	383	476	993
Index 1991	130	130	177	150	107	88	86	127
Females								
1974	88	48	69	85	125	168	175	213
1991	112	41	85	134	161	185	186	256
Index 1991	127	85	123	158	129	110	106	120
Germany								
Males								
1974	279	204	288	342	419	476	490	737
1991	250	144	220	267	345	345	380	879
Index 1991	90	71	76	78	82	72	78	119
Females								
1974	147	74	115	142	232	267	258	284
1991	105	36	63	87	135	141	183	295
Index 1991	71	49	55	61	58	53	71	104
Greece								
Males								
1974	46	34	49	54	57	49	136	136
1991	59	40	50	58	70	83	121	178
Index 1991	128	118	102	107	123	169	89	131
Females								
1974	24	17	28	21	19	38	72	50
1991	16	7	14	18	25	25	20	40
Index 1991	67	41	50	86	132	66	28	80
Ireland								
Males								
1974	59	53	110	98	96	116	69	76
1991	160	191	293	276	146	257	167	126
Index 1991	271	360	266	282	152	222	242	166
Females								
1974	17	12	23	46	19	41	18	14
1991	36	13	64	48	70	80	62	20
Index 1991	212	108	278	104	368	195	344	143

Table 2   Continued

				Age				
	All ages	15–24	25–34	35–44	45–54	55–64	65–74	75+
Italy								
Males								
1974	73	31	59	68	95	147	224	302
1990	114	59	99	103	115	156	233	503
Index 1990	156	190	168	151	121	106	104	167
Females								
1974	35	22	30	33	46	66	80	71
1990	41	20	30	38	47	70	75	95
Index 1990	117	91	100	115	102	106	94	134
Japan								
Males								
1974	200	195	232	237	231	317	471	832
1992	223	102	188	240	346	380	330	599
Index 1992	112	52	81	101	150	120	70	72
Females								
1974	150	133	151	131	151	230	409	790
1992	117	47	81	86	137	171	224	418
Index 1992	78	35	54	66	91	74	55	53
Netherlands								
Males								
1974	110	78	86	134	180	222	272	361
1991	139	98	152	182	172	190	190	422
Index 1991	126	126	177	136	96	86	70	117
Females								
1974	74	26	75	108	112	159	171	143
1991	76	36	86	101	86	136	129	114
Index 1991	103	138	115	94	77	86	75	80
Portugal								
Males								
1974	132	38	71	138	246	265	455	722
1992	133	57	131	108	142	210	290	634
Index 1992	101	150	185	78	58	79	64	88
Females								
1974	44	31	36	53	67	72	99	108
1992	46	21	46	42	57	87	70	119
Index 1992	105	68	128	79	85	121	71	110
Spain								
Males								
1974	58	19	38	50	91	139	206	279
1990	112	71	106	95	120	168	234	515
Index 1990	193	374	279	190	132	121	114	185

Table 2   Continued

				Age				
	All ages	15–24	25–34	35–44	45–54	55–64	65–74	75+
Females								
1974	22	10	12	23	30	53	62	69
1990	41	17	30	32	43	68	91	129
Index 1990	186	170	250	139	143	128	147	187
Sweden								
Males								
1974	287	172	313	370	476	400	491	474
1990	241	147	259	272	311	328	393	551
Index 1990	84	85	83	74	65	82	80	116
Females								
1974	115	75	103	154	183	232	170	83
1990	104	53	110	129	149	171	142	149
Index 1990	90	71	107	84	81	74	84	180
Switzerland								
Males								
1974	291	242	276	317	441	527	548	844
1992	313	231	356	318	391	438	472	834
Index 1992	108	95	129	100	89	83	86	99
Females								
1974	125	71	118	173	175	214	257	177
1992	108	63	70	130	140	165	183	218
Index 1992	86	89	59	75	80	77	71	123
USA								
Males								
1974	181	171	233	229	266	302	329	438
1990	204	220	248	239	232	257	322	579
Index 1990	113	129	106	104	87	85	98	132
Females								
1974	65	46	84	111	130	103	80	62
1990	48	39	56	68	69	73	67	60
Index 1990	74	85	67	61	53	71	84	97

shadows, left wandering in the day' (Aeschylus, *Agamemnon*). In Table 2 some major countries' suicide rates are presented by age bands and gender. A brief explanation is necessary before we consider international comparisons.

There is little merit in comparing countries directly with each other in such a complex diagnostic area as suicide, unlike something as diagnostically clear-cut as lung cancer. Hence, when making cross-country comparisons, we must first compare a country against itself over time, as in Table 2. Thus an index for the first year's suicide rate, in 1974, is the baseline, an index of 100, to be contrasted against the latest year available. In the case of England and Wales the male suicide rate went from 95 per million in 1974 to 121 in 1992, an index of 127 or a 27 per cent increase. An examination of Table 2 shows that a crude comparison of the Anglo-Welsh suicide rates with those of, say, Sweden would give a very misleading picture. It would show that the Swedish male rate was almost double the Anglo-Welsh rate, at 241, in 1990. However, since 1974 Swedish male suicide has continued to fall steadily, from a height of 287 to 241, an index of 84, or a *fall* in male suicide of 16 per cent. We would see a very different picture if we looked only at raw rates. The same is true of Denmark, whose current rate of 291 is a 14 per cent decline from the 1974 rate of 337. Germany also has a current level double that of England and Wales, but it is one of the few countries whose male suicide rate has continued to fall over the past twenty years. At the opposite extreme, the male Italian rate is lower than the Anglo-Welsh (114 to 121), but has risen by 56 per cent.

In parenthesis, readers may wonder why it is that Sweden appears to have an unhappy reputation for suicide in our popular press. The opportunity to correct this fallacy is welcomed.

Employment, unemployment and social class

In Britain a person is 'officially' categorized into a social class, defined by the Registrar General's classification of occupations. Though there are a number of different, more refined, measurements of 'social class', including the occupation of one's parents, education and place of residence, the job one occupies defines one's position in society.

It is argued that in Britain social class mediates all other social factors, such as age, gender, religion and ethnicity, so that, for example, middle-class women have greater resources over time and higher social and personal status, and experience a differential referral and treatment process, for both physical and mental health, than the average working-class (unskilled) male. Nevertheless, it is acknowledged that middle-class women are not as privileged as middle-class men, but they are considerably better off in terms of social status and self-esteem than their working-class sisters (Brown *et al.* 1990).

Unemployment is linked to marital disharmony, divorce, truancy, delinquency, drug and alcohol misuse, crime, child abuse and neglect, and, at the extreme, deliberate self-harm and suicide (Platt 1984; Platt and Kreitman 1985; Pritchard 1990, 1991, 1992a, 1995a; Platt *et al.* 1992; Pritchard *et al.* 1993). Unemployment, of course, does not cause any of these activities, but the psycho-social impact of unemployment, especially in the long term, exposes the individual and family to enormous pressure and undermines their morale (Warr and Jackson 1988; Lawson 1994) and destabilizes the vulnerable. Often it is the first link in a chain of events that leads to personal and family disruption, social discohesion and, at the extreme, suicide. Freud said 'work binds people to reality'. Warr (1987), in a seminal text on work and mental health, showed that the vast majority of people, irrespective of their position in the social hierarchy, gain considerable satisfaction from their work, which does indeed socially define them. With the exception of a very small minority of unemployed people who feel liberated from an oppressive work situation, the vast majority of the jobless are diminished by the experience, with a diminution of their psycho-social identity. Often, especially for the chronically unemployed, the only way to deal with the experience is to develop a 'defensive apathy', in effect a withdrawal from society. By this we mean that the person withdraws from relationships and activities that he or she enjoyed while in employment. The immediate impact of being made jobless is somewhat like that of a minor bereavement and, after bereavement, unemployment is one of the most stressful events that can happen to a person (Rahe and Holmes 1980). Within this defensive apathy there is a significant lowering of self-esteem and mood. Not only is unemployment associated with poorer physical health (Whitehead 1990), long-term unemployment induces a feeling of hopelessness, reminiscent of Beck's criteria associated with suicidal behaviour (Beck *et al.* 1993a).

We know that unemployment is also associated with chronic housing difficulties and homelessness (Department of Employment 1992; Pritchard *et al.* 1992; Stockley and Stockley 1993). People can find themselves isolated in the extreme of homelessness, and there is a disproportionate level of suicidal behaviour among the homeless (Yates *et al.* 1991; Marshall and Reed 1992; Scott 1993). This might be partly explained by the fact that a significant minority of the homeless have already had mental illness and other severe social problems (Appleby and Desai 1985) as well as alcohol and drug problems, so it may not be homelessness *per se* that is important, but an accumulative consequence of social and psychological disadvantage. Nevertheless, there can be little doubt that unemployment damages people's health, and the continued statistical association between being jobless and increased suicides across the continents cannot be ignored.

Physical illness

The presence of physical illness, particularly of a long-term chronic type, has been associated with suicide. Ill health disproportionately affects elderly people, and this partly accounts for the presence of physical illness, in conjunction with other factors such as isolation, as a factor traditionally associated with suicide in elderly people (Vogel and Wolfersdorf 1989).

However, chronic illness or diseases that have a chronic prognosis can also affect younger people. For example, in diabetes mellitus (sugar diabetes), at the early diagnosistic stage, there is an association with an increased suicide threat in young men (Kyvik *et al.* 1994). The genetic neurological disease, Huntington's chorea, also has a higher than general morbidity for depression and suicide (Di Maio *et al.* 1993).

It would appear that the mechanism concerned with illness is chronicity, and a sense of hopelessness, often associated with discomfort or pain, with a corresponding reduction in 'reasons for living' (Linehan *et al.* 1991), which perhaps explains the above examples of diabetes mellitus and Huntington's chorea. 'Chronicity' probably explains why the elderly, especially the isolated, and long-term sick people are particularly vulnerable, as it makes a reality of Beck *et al.*'s

(1993a) hopelessness and helplessness. With improved pain control, however, and modern support services, these should no longer be a major determinant, though clearly long-term illness is demoralizing.

Traditionally it was thought that there was a small but significant rise in suicide among people with terminal illness, in particular cancer (Stiefel *et al.* 1989), but as was argued earlier, it is much too easy to link this fact with notions of rational suicide. This may or may not be the case in individual situations, but there is a danger that we ignore the distress of someone who, under improved circumstances, might wish to meet his or her impending demise without wanting to end life. An important longitudinal study by Stensman and Lundquist-Stensman (1988) noted a higher level of suicide in people with physical disease and disability than in the general population, but a much lower rate than for any of the other suicide-associated factors.

In a very important analysis of suicide rates over a decade in a large urban area, King and Barraclough (1990) noted the very high number of psychiatric elements among the deaths, higher than any other factor. We had intended to compare the rates found among the psychiatric cohort with suicide in patients of a hospice in the same area. The palliative care unit specialized in care of terminally ill people, mainly with cancer. In the event the study was simply not feasible, because in the ten years under review, only two people in the hospice were known to have shortened their lives.

It is recognized that patients admitted to hospice may have a range of restrictions, which may make self-damaging behaviour extremely difficult, though it should be recognized that a significant number of people in the palliative care unit are often ambulant. But two life-shortening incidents in ten years reflects the findings of Owen *et al.* (1992, 1994) and Mermelstein and Lesko (1992), who demonstrated that the popular truism that 'I'd kill myself if I got cancer' is a belief held by healthy people. It is acknowledged that it is hardly usual to offer as evidence a study that never took place, but the point at issue is that the quality of care, which involved family members as well as the sufferers, appeared to avoid the pain and isolation noted by Vogel and Wolfersdorf (1989). This should give us pause before we too glibly assume that for elderly and/or long-term physically ill people, even when 'terminal', to commit suicide is either natural or 'normal'.

HIV infection, AIDS and suicide

At the other end of the physical illness–age continuum is the problem of HIV infection and the resultant acquired immune deficiency syndrome (AIDS). The impact of HIV and AIDS in the Western world since the 1980s has been profound. There was early evidence that on hearing the diagnosis, newly infected persons were at real risk of suicide (Marzuk *et al.* 1988; Copeland 1993), especially young people (Brown *et al.* 1992). Fortunately most countries now insist that counselling support services for testees are available, which has appeared to have helped people over the first shock. However, though the infection appears to be spreading more slowly than was first feared, it continues inexorably to rise, and will become a major public health problem (UK Department of Health 1993; US Department of Health 1993). Consequently the risk of suicide may well be an increasing concomitant. There are early indications of a particularly nasty mixture of social and physiological factors coming together. This is the long-term unemployment of youth, leading to homelessness, leading to drug misuse, and male and female prostitution, and eventual HIV infection and AIDS (Cohen *et al.* 1991; Kruks 1991; Schneider *et al.* 1991). Sadly, this is another good example of the interaction of social and physiological factors with suicide risk and eventual death. The one slight positive is that the highest risk of suicide appears to be at the time of the initial diagnosis. Afterwards, it would seem that sufferers are similar to others with terminal illness: the closer they are to the sharp end of the prognosis, the more resilient they become.

It may well be that HIV infection will require the maximum caution for *at least a generation*, because the virus will take forty or more years to work through the body public. The increased risk of suicidal behaviour in new sufferers will therefore, continue to exist for that time.

Religion

Durkheim (1888), in his classic work, saw religion as an important variable and suggested that Catholics committed suicide less frequently than Protestants. It must be remembered that in Catholicism, as in Islam, there are direct and overt theological sanctions against suicide, and the Christian tradition is reflected in Dante, who consigns such people to one of the lower levels of Hell. In Britain it became almost axiomatic that Catholics did not kill themselves and a comparison was often made between countries of the British Isles, showing that Ireland had a far lower suicide rate than Britain. This assumption is now found to be false, if it was ever true. The international suicide rates between 1973 and 1992 given in Table 2, originally used to demonstrate changes in gender and age patterns and the association with unemployment, on closer inspection reveal that the notion that belonging to the Catholic culture is a protection against suicide is patently untrue. Suicide rates in England and Wales, despite rises, have been for many years among the *lowest* in the developed world; only Spain and Italy are lower. But the idea that this confirms the Durkheim hypothesis, given the Spanish and Italian Catholic tradition, is untrue: the *highest* rate of suicide is in Catholic Hungary, while Catholic Austria competes with Finland for second place. 'Catholic' France, Poland and (partly) Germany have between two and three times the rate of Protestant Britain. Stack's (1992) work shows that what matters is not so much the religious culture of a country, though this may clearly influence recording methods and rates, but whether the person actively attends church or not. On reflection it can be seen that church membership will go some way to reduce social isolation, even for the unemployed, assuming that the church membership is not dependent upon being middle class. Church attendance therefore has practical significance, as well as giving spiritual support to the person. It has to be recognized, however, that within depression or schizophrenia, people's religious beliefs can work against them unless they receive appropriate psycho-spiritual counselling (Goold 1991).

Ethnicity and suicide

This appears to be an appropriate point at which to re-emphasize that the vast majority of work already cited has been drawn from research or practice examples from the developed Western world, predominantly Caucasian Western Europe and North America. Yet there are important variations in patterns of suicide among non-Caucasian people.

There are also significant considerations when there is an ethnic difference between the sufferer and the therapist, which can add to the difficulties in communication. It is reiterated that we believe that it is the professional's, not the client's, responsibility to communicate adequately, and in an appropriate fashion. Where there are language barriers, the worker needs to seek the help of an appropriate interpreter. Space precludes a full discussion of this issue, but it is sufficient to say that, generally, clients from an Islamic background, who have major religious sanctions against suicide, appear to have even stronger stigmatized attitudes about mental illness than do non-Islamic people. For example, Levav and Aisenberg (1989) showed that while Israel's national suicide rates were at the lower end of the international scale, Jewish people had a much higher suicide rate than people with an Arab background. Thus, in practice, when a non-Islamic professional is working with an Islamic person, it *may* be that if the interpreter is also Islamic, he or she might be reluctant to 'offend' the client, or his or her family, by asking unpalatable questions such as 'Have you ever thought of hurting yourself – have you thought of ending it all?'

These ethnic and cultural influences appear to last over some time. For example, Sorenson and Golding (1988) found that compared with the average suicide rate in North America, Mexican-Americans had a significantly lower rate in the first generation. This rose over the second and third generations, but current suicide rates remained lower than the average North American level. Conversely, in people from Polish or Japanese backgrounds, whose countries usually have a higher rate than that of North America, first generation suicide rates were higher, but subsequent generations moved closer to the North American mean, though rates were still higher than the overall American average. The most intriguing epidemiological finding to emerge from ethnic considerations of violent death is that while African-Americans are more frequently victims and assailants in homicide, in respect of suicide, despite the history of disadvantage and discrimination, black men and women have *lower* rates than whites of both genders. We also know that there are differences in non-Western countries; for example, between Chinese, Indian and Malaysian people in Singapore, and between Afro-Caribbeans and East Indians in the West Indies (Mahy 1993).

Ethnicity and mental health is of course an area of some controversy because there is evidence, in both North America and Western Europe, that clients from ethnic minorities, particularly Afro-Caribbeans and African-Americans, experience additionally stigmatized and prejudiced referral and treatment procedures

(Littlewood and Lipsedge 1982; Rack 1982; Bean 1986; Fernando 1988; Cope 1989; Fenton and Sadiq 1991; Frederick 1991).

With regard to research from Islamic countries, an interesting study by Eskin (1993), among Turkish high school students, explored attitudes about suicide. Turkey and Jordan are the only Islamic countries that report any appreciable suicide rates, which are still among the lowest in the world. The Turkish young men were much more rejecting in their attitudes, seeing suicidal behaviour as both a form of mental illness (therefore stigmatized) and a behaviour which will be punished in the next world. The young women, however, while still seeing suicide as symptomatic of mental illness, were more accepting and argued that family and friends should be more willing to discuss these issues, though appreciating that their elders might find this difficult.

Soni Raleigh *et al.* (1990) explored suicide among Asian people of the Hindu faith living in Britain, and found two important major differences from suicide patterns in the indigenous population. First, women, especially younger women, die by suicide *more* often than their male peers; second, death by burning is not uncommon among young women. The use of fire is very rare among Caucasians and is usually only seen in the presence of extreme psychosis of a schizophrenic type, whereas there is a tradition in mainland India of suicide by fire, especially among women. The *Bhagavad Gita* gives us a poetic insight showing that the depression–aggression axis is not unknown in the culture; earlier stanzas speak of loss of harmony and then 'desire and the lust of possession' which: 'leads to passion, to anger. From passion comes confusion – from this loss comes the *ruin of reason and the ruin of reason leads man to destruction* (*Bhagavad Gita* 2, v. 62–3, italics added). What better description is there of the vortex that leads to self-harm?

In a generally excellent review of race, ethnicity and mental illness, Pilgrim and Rogers (1993) bring together most of the British-based literature, which not only highlights variations in Afro-Caribbean and Asian culture in Britain, but also illustrates some of the inherent communication problems, which are easy to compound unless one is culturally sensitive. The professional must be willing to appreciate his or her own potential lack of understanding, and how easy it is to misunderstand. However, as mental illness does occur in every ethnic group (WHO 1993), the professional must also be aware of the trap of interpreting the client's experience and behaviour purely as an end product of social factors. At the same time remember that the impact of mental illness upon the sufferer is interpreted and understood through the *person's* own value system and life experience, which is ubiquitous for all people irrespective of ethnicity, gender, age and social class. Thus the meaning of the experience will be strongly influenced by the prevailing socio-cultural aspects of the sufferer, and where ethnicity is different from that of the therapist particular sensitivity is required.

The case of 'Mr Kazim' is a salutary reminder that the professional must always keep an open mind, and respond to the client-specific situation, not the dominant theory. Mr Kazim was a thirty-year-old Asian man who, along with his family, had been expelled from Uganda. His white social worker could not have been more culturally sensitive and concerned, because there was evidence in Mr

Kazim's life that he had been at times a victim of mindless racial prejudice and active discrimination. He had been described by a frankly unsympathetic psychiatrist as a 'depressive personality disorder, tending to hysteria', who had difficulty in 'taking advice, did not comply with treatment instructions' and was considered a 'difficult patient'. Mr Kazim had had a very successful education in Uganda, but had lost everything. On entry into Britain he had 'started at the bottom' but had done well, first getting a job in a bank, and then for four years successfully developing and running his own business. Over the next three years there was a gradual but intermittent deterioration in his general mental health. Finally he lost his business, job and house, and had to return to his parents' home, which exacerbated his sense of failure. The social worker missed two obvious but partly concealed facts: first, Mr Kazim's younger brother had committed suicide shortly after coming to England; second, his mother had a longstanding psychiatric depression, which was intermittently successfully treated. The social worker, who was the key formal carer in Mr Kazim's life, had *over-focused* on the racist issues, and missed the core depressive illness, which led to a serious suicide bid. When Mr Kazim was encouraged to be re-referred to a modern psychiatrist, who combined cognitive behavioural therapy and anti-depressants, he made a swift and positive recovery, taking power over his life again.

This is not to deny or diminish the daily experience of ethnic prejudice and discrimination against many fellow citizens. What is important in meeting the individual's needs is to distinguish what factors are operating. Perkins and Moodley (1993) in inner London explored consecutive psychiatric inpatients' perceptions of their problems. Noticeably the majority of patients *denied* they had a mental health problem, but in respect of compulsory or non-compulsory admission, the key finding was that it was the ethnic status of the Afro-Caribbeans rather than their diagnostic category that was associated with formal admission. Thomas *et al.* (1993), in a study from Central Manchester, explored psychiatric morbidity, ethnicity and admissions. They found, over a four-year period, that Afro-Caribbean patients were admitted more often than Asians and Europeans, and had markedly poorer socio-economic antecedents. Similarly to the Perkins and Moodley results, compulsory admission was more strongly associated with socio-economic factors, including ethnicity, than diagnosis. This socio-economic theme further demonstrates the double jeopardy of people who belong to the least powerful and more disadvantaged groups, i.e. social classes 4 and 5 and/or the unemployed. This is confirmed by the longitudinal study of McGovern *et al.* (1994) in the Midlands. They followed up a cohort of black and white patients with schizophrenia for between five and ten years. Again there appeared to be little doubt about diagnosis or any statistical association in relation to either ethnic group in respect of diagnosis. The differences that did emerge showed that Afro-Caribbeans had poorer outcomes, despite having similar types of treatment and after-care to the whites, and, crucially, that the poorer outcome was associated with factors *prior* to first admission: Afro-Caribbean patients more often lived alone, were unemployed and had previous convictions and custodial sentences. This is a classic example of disadvantaged social circumstances, compounding the negative impact of mental disorder.

It has long been argued that racial prejudice is incompatible with social work in a democratic society (Pritchard and Taylor 1978), and we take it as self-evident that social work seeks to make a contribution to the pursuit of social justice, which at a minimum is founded upon the Universal Declaration of Human Rights (Cox and Pritchard 1995). But irrespective of the societal context, we must always focus primarily upon the person in the situation, be ready to consider alternative explanations for the person's experience, lest paradoxically, in our desire for equal opportunities, we fail to see the person's central crisis.

Nevertheless, the importance of culture in understanding another person and his or her experience of mental disorder cannot be overstated. In Chapter 6 new evidence is explored that gives further weight to the combined influence of culture and gender upon suicidal behaviour.

CHAPTER 5

DELIBERATE SELF-HARM
AND SUICIDAL BEHAVIOUR
IN YOUNG ADULTS AND
ADOLESCENTS

In our effort to unravel the complexities of suicidal behaviour, we have risked fragmenting the problem, and creating artificial schematic paradigms. Nowhere is this more pronounced than when we try to make sense of suicidal behaviour in young adults and adolescents. With this caution in mind, we turn to the area where we are most likely to err. On the one hand, the most appalling situations are survived by young people; on the other, out of the blue, apparently in response to a minor stressor, the young adult or adolescent become involved in the most extreme, dangerous and sometimes fatal behaviour.

Young adults

It was mentioned earlier that suicide is virtually non-existent under the age of sixteen, but the second largest *relative* increase is in the fifteen to twenty-four group (after the over seventy-five group).

In a detailed and brilliant study of patients admitted to a regional poisoning treatment centre between 1968 and 1985, Hawton *et al.* (1993) demonstrate the accumulative impact of psychiatric- and stress-related factors, which are associated with DSH predominately among young adults. A multivariate analysis showed that, compared with patients who did not kill themselves, those dying from suicide or probable suicide scored higher on a series of odds ratios. These were as follows: previous psychiatric inpatient treatment, 4.9:1; substance abuse, 3.3:1; unemployment, 2.8:1; belonging to social classes 4 or 5, 2.7:1; being involved in a previous attempted suicide, 2.3:1; a diagnosis of personality disorder, 2.1:1. Thus people involved in DSH who eventually died were almost five times as likely to have had a previous mental hospital admission, were likely to have had longstanding difficulties as reflected in their previous DSH and were relatively poor. It must be stressed that no one single factor necessarily led to suicide, but all these features are interactive in a very client-specific way.

Deliberate self-harm

Perhaps the most difficult practice problem is coming to terms with the fact that while suicide is associated with deliberate self-harm, DSH is not always, thankfully, associated with eventual suicide. Yet the frequency of DSH is considerable, and it will be found in the caseload of virtually every community-based professional. It creates enormous demands and distress – both for themselves and for those around them – with a high level of attendance at the emergency centres of general hospitals (Peterson and Bonger 1990). Thus DSH requires study in its own right, quite apart from its link with suicide.

Deliberate self-harm is sometimes explained as 'a cry for help', which, while it is sometimes true, can lead to a belittling of the meaning of the behaviour, especially if it has occurred frequently in the same person. This is seen in the continued fact that although hospital staff who receive drug overdose patients are more sympathetic than they were twenty years ago, such staff can feel irritated and unsympathetic to people whose response to their problems appears to be so ineffectual. This is partly no doubt due to the fact that various forms of DSH account for the highest acute medical admissions for women, and the second highest for young men (DHSS 1984; Peterson and Bonger 1990; Department of Health 1992). As we will see when we discuss suicidal behaviour in adolescents, the self-damaging behaviour can range from children putting their head underneath the pillow to try to suffocate themselves, to impulsively shooting themselves in a fit of despair; the second example comes from the USA of course (Holinger 1987; Brent *et al.* 1991; Heim and Lester 1991). Cullberg *et al.* (1988), in an eight to ten year follow-up of people who had attempted suicide, found that 6 per cent eventually died from suicide. Hawton and Fagg (1988) found that death from suicide was at more than twenty times the expected rate within eight years, and the former DSH people had double the expected death rate from natural causes.

Averaging out DSH behaviour, between 15 and 20 per cent will repeat the behaviour within a year, especially if they are younger people, and 2 per cent of all previous DSHs will die within twelve months. Hawton and Fagg (1988) found that the highest risk for eventual suicide was during the first three years, and especially the first six months, following a DSH incident, and they, and others, demonstrate quite clearly that DSH is associated with a far higher level of mortality, not just from suicide, but also from other forms of deaths, including accidents and undetermined causes (Barraclough and Hughes 1987; Hawton and Fagg 1988). Actual suicides are mainly a male activity. However, Asguard (1990), in a consecutive study of 104 Swedish female suicides, found that two-thirds had been involved with previous DSH, which complicates the problem of distinguishing risk levels. Perhaps at this stage it is worth stating what may be obvious: those who *repeat* DSH are very often more disturbed and have a greater degree of psychiatric and substance abuse problems (Crumley 1990; Peterson and Bonger 1990; Cohen *et al.* 1991; Hawton *et al.* 1993). Finally, between 10 and 20 per cent of all DSH people will die by their own hand within two to three years. Thus DSH is clearly an important indicator of psycho-social distress and is clearly associated with eventual suicide. It should never be discounted or taken too lightly, as what some might describe as 'merely' a cry for help.

This is a salutary reminder that, like mental illness, deliberate self-harm carries a far higher morbidity and mortality risk than would be expected. Thus it is certain that there is no such thing as a safe attempted suicide. The person always and most at risk is the client. It would seem that the more often people indulge in such extreme behaviour, the more others are desensitized to the enormous risks they may be running, especially in the case of younger people.

'Lynne Lane' came from a very disturbed background, in which she had seen her mother frequently involve herself in acts of deliberate self-harm and mutilation. By the time she was twenty-two she was 'an expert' in a whole range of self-damaging behaviour. In her adolescence she was often the mainstay for her mother and younger siblings, but she seemed destined to repeat her mother's pattern as she staggered from one short-term relationship to another, which invariably collapsed when the other person could not meet her demands for perfect and total acceptance of frequent testing out behaviour: 'He wouldn't mind if he really loved me.' Sometimes Lynne's DSH appeared almost consciously manipulative of those around, including harassed social workers. After a short but chaotic period of relationship crises, she overdosed after a drinking bout. The dosage was not fatal, but the resultant vomiting was. Sadly she never believed that she was in danger: 'You know I don't mean it.' When one examines high-profile deaths, such as those of the poets Sylvia Plath and Anne Sexton, it becomes easier to understand the allure and excitement that may be unconsciously associated with Russian roulette. As Sexton said, 'suicide is addicting'.

Deliberate self-harm resulted in over 100,000 admissions in 1984 (DHSS 1984). It is also far more frequent in the case loads of British social services and probation departments than is the high-profile child neglect (Hudson *et al.* 1993; Pritchard *et al.* 1993). Thus, despite media images, the average social worker will meet more self-damaging clients then cases of child neglect or abuse! Not surprisingly, therefore, there is considerable national and international interest in this phenomenon, reflected in the establishment of a WHO and European Union multi-centre study led by Platt *et al.* (1992).

Preliminary results have shown a wide variation in the eight European centres, although generally women have the higher rate. Mean rates, across all the centres, are 2,220 for females and 1,670 for males per million population. There is a clear confirmation that the greatest incidence occurs among under thirty-five-year-olds, with the lowest rates being for those over the age of fifty-four.

Platt *et al.*'s work (1992) merits closer investigation and what follows is a new analysis of their data, which juxtaposes national suicide rates with the various city rates, as if those cities were 'representative' of the country. One feature that should be pointed out immediately is that of the fifteen cities involved in the work, a number were in one country, and they showed that different areas of the same country had markedly different levels of DSH, which has been noted in respect of suicide in other studies (e.g. Obafunwa and Busuttil 1994a, b, in the Lothian region of Scotland). Thus, for example, Bordeaux had almost half the DSH rate of the other French city of Pontoise, which we use as a comparative marker against the national suicide rate of 1989. Unfortunately there was no British centre in the Platt *et al.* survey, but in our multi-cultural society, and given the UK's membership of the European Union, the comparison is hoped to be useful. Over the past twenty years, there has been a fairly close similarity between Anglo-Welsh rates and those of the Netherlands, which might be a point of possible comparison, as a Dutch city was included in the survey. Table 3 compares male actual suicide and DSH rates per million population in the countries represented; Table 4 gives the female equivalent.

The first point to note is that male suicide was always higher than female, ratios ranging from 1.8:1 in Denmark to 4.0:1 in Finland, whereas the reverse is the case for DSH. The lowest average male DSH rate was the Dutch (570); the Finnish rate was 3,230. Female DSH levels were almost as wide-ranging, from 850 in the Spanish city, to 5,160 in Pontoise, France. It will be remembered that when we make international comparisons, because of variations in recording methods in such a complex diagnostic area as suicide, we must first compare a country against itself and then compare between the states. In the analysis that follows, however, the focus is upon the DSH:suicide ratio, rather than differences between nations.

The ratio of male deaths to DSH ranged from 1:3.2 in Germany to 1:8.1 in France, and Table 3 clearly shows that young men, aged from fifteen to twenty-four, had the biggest gap between actual death and self-damaging behaviour (1:7 in Finland to 1:19 in France. Table 4 shows the same trend for females, but much more marked. The lowest ratio of deaths to female DSH was 1:12 in Germany, but 1:44 in France. In the fifteen to twenty-four age band the ratio ranged from 1:25 in the Netherlands to a staggering 1:141 among French young women.

The other key practical finding is that, in all countries, the over fifty-five-year-olds easily had the lowest death to DSH ratio. The elderly rates compared with the average ratios for all age groups were as low as 0.03 in Finland and only 0.34 in Sweden, showing the high follow through of death following DSH in older people.

Can we extrapolate from these suicide to DSH ratios to Britain? The averages are worth noting. In respect of males, the two younger age bands have ratios of almost 1:11 and 1:8. The female ratios are about 1:68 and 1:38. Thus the *statistical* risk of a female DSH carrying through is quite low, but one would not bet one's mortgage on the result.

There have been efforts to try to differentiate between deliberate self-harm that is an actual, but failed, attempt to kill oneself, and DSH in which people are making a 'suicidal gesture', driven by the need to gain attention and help, with no real suicidal intent (Kreitman 1978; Leenaars 1989; Kosky *et al.* 1990). This issue is at the centre of the notion of suicidal intent, which Beck has used to

Table 3   Comparison of parasuicide in selected cities with national male suicide rates per million, 1989

			Age			
	All ages	*15–24*	*25–34*	*35–44*	*45–54*	*55+*
Odense (Denmark)						
Parasuicide	2050	1950	3540	3090	1710	670
Suicide	344	146	266	436	514	678
Ratio parasuicide/suicide	5.96	13.36	13.31	7.09	3.33	0.99
Helsinki (Finland)						
Parasuicide	3230	3550	4750	4020	2110	1400
Suicide	464	504	518	616	609	679
Ratio parasuicide/suicide	6.96	7.04	9.17	6.53	3.46	2.06
Pontoise (France)						
Parasuicide	2460	3010	3590	2350	1170	170
Suicide	305	158	322	374	392	663
Ratio parasuicide/suicide	8.07	19.05	11.15	6.28	2.98	0.26
Wurzburg (Germany)						
Parasuicide	750	1450	1100	540	640	260
Suicide	235	147	227	216	308	488
Ratio parasuicide/suicide	3.19	9.86	4.85	2.50	2.08	0.53
Padua (Italy)						
Parasuicide	610	690	1010	450	430	460
Suicide	112	51	99	92	135	286
Ratio parasuicide/suicide	5.45	13.53	10.20	4.89	3.19	1.61
Leiden (Netherlands)						
Parasuicide	570	720	750	620	530	190
Suicide	130	89	154	156	173	233
Ratio parasuicide/suicide	4.38	8.09	4.87	3.97	3.06	0.82
Guipuzcoa (Spain)						
Parasuicide	670	1160	650	660	360	400
Suicide	116	84	106	102	149	297
Ratio parasuicide/suicide	5.78	13.81	6.13	6.47	2.42	1.35
Stockholm (Sweden)						
Parasuicide	1700	1560	2070	2170	1900	1010
Suicide	268	198	337	310	354	413
Ratio parasuicide/suicide	6.34	7.88	6.14	7.00	5.37	2.45
Bern (Switzerland)						
Parasuicide	1200	1340	2220	1280	840	470
Suicide	328	281	417	300	384	595
Ratio parasuicide/suicide	3.66	4.77	5.32	4.27	2.19	0.79
Ratio average	5.53	10.82	7.90	5.44	3.12	1.21

Table 4 Comparison of parasuicide in selected cities with national female suicide rates per million, 1989

		Age				
	All ages	*15–24*	*25–34*	*35–44*	*45–54*	*55+*
Odense (Denmark)						
Parasuicide	2400	2830	2710	3440	3460	1080
Suicide	196	42	102	256	385	324
Ratio parasuicide/suicide	12.24	67.38	26.57	13.44	8.99	3.33
Helsinki (Finland)						
Parasuicide	2340	3300	3490	3110	2350	780
Suicide	115	65	107	164	211	150
Ratio parasuicide/suicide	20.35	50.77	32.62	18.96	11.14	5.20
Pontoise (France)						
Parasuicide	5160	6490	5960	5420	4170	1670
Suicide	117	46	92	130	174	218
Ratio parasuicide/suicide	44.10	141.09	64.78	41.69	23.97	7.66
Wurzburg (Germany)						
Parasuicide	1220	2370	1920	2090	630	290
Suicide	100	42	69	79	130	182
Ratio parasuicide/suicide	12.20	56.43	27.83	26.46	4.85	1.59
Padua (Italy)						
Parasuicide	910	1260	1450	780	870	480
Suicide	41	16	32	35	51	82
Ratio parasuicide/suicide	22.20	78.75	45.31	22.29	17.06	5.85
Leiden (Netherlands)						
Parasuicide	1050	1120	1110	1630	1420	390
Suicide	75	44	72	75	138	123
Ratio parasuicide/suicide	14.00	25.45	15.42	21.73	10.29	3.17
Guipuzcoa (Spain)						
Parasuicide	850	1120	1800	770	600	190
Suicide	39	19	26	23	46	95
Ratio parasuicide/suicide	21.79	58.95	69.23	33.48	13.04	2.00
Stockholm (Sweden)						
Parasuicide	2970	3530	4490	3430	2890	1470
Suicide	106	83	126	114	125	155
Ratio parasuicide/suicide	28.02	42.53	35.63	30.09	23.12	9.48
Bern (Switzerland)						
Parasuicide	1650	2650	2650	1780	1280	660
Suicide	132	83	117	161	179	207
Ratio parasuicide/suicide	12.50	31.93	22.65	11.06	7.15	3.19
Ratio average	20.82	61.48	37.78	24.35	13.29	4.61

indicate a level of risk of suicide amongst a range of patients. However, Beck has come to the conclusion that it is hopelessness which mediates between the depressive state and the suicidal state, though the assessment scales used by Beck are more appropriate to research projects and are seldom to hand in a practice situation. Maris *et al.* (1992) conclude that between 10 and 15 per cent of all individuals involved in what he describes as 'non-fatal suicide attempts' go on to die from unequivocal suicide. Maris has probably produced the most definitive essay, based on current research, about the relationship between non-fatal suicide and completed suicide. Drawing upon his earlier 1981 work and other North American research, he produced some intriguing figures. Interestingly, it seemed that 70 per cent died from their first effort, and a third of this number had already been involved in DSH. One word of caution is needed. Maris's data came from major American cities, and firearms are the major contributor to all violent deaths in the USA (Holinger 1987). However, Maris did find a high level of mental health problems, and age seemed to make a crucial difference, though there were fewer physical problems and apparently more interpersonal problems among the DSH group than among the suicides. This would not be too far from the findings of Hawton *et al.* (1993) in Oxfordshire: significantly more people who carried out DSH were from social class 5, were unemployed, had had previous psychiatric treatment and had a history of substance misuse, highlighting the clear overlap with the dominant features associated with suicide.

What can we make of this complex range of research findings? Cautiously, let us attempt to draw together the distinctive themes in DSH.

First, there is no doubt that people involved with DSH are younger and more often women. Second, their mental health status is more likely to be in the 'personality disorder' area, rather than in a clear psychiatric depression. Substance abuse and impulsivity, and, possibly, premenstrual tension, are factors in younger women. Psychologically there seems to be very much a precipitant problem, caused by distress at relationship problems, and tensions with authorities, such as school, the law and, of course, parents. There are possibly imitatory elements in younger people, with the dynamic being 'flying from' a situation or crisis, rather than seeking a definite 'destination' of death.

We are almost tempted to describe DSH as a form of reaction to a psycho-social situation, whereas with suicide the problem is experienced more as stemming from within oneself. Table 5 is a schematic guideline that attempts to differentiate suicide from deliberate self-harm or parasuicide. In both types of behaviour, the impact on others – family, friends, neighbours and professional staff – can be very significant, with a considerable degree of distress. Wherever there is *depression* there is often *aggression* as a co-morbid emotion.

Adolescents and suicidal behaviour

Elizabeth Barraclough said 'I have lost mother, father, brother and sister, husband and friends, but nothing is more bitter than losing a child.' This must be the secret nightmare for the vast majority of parents, who have a sense of natural

Table 5 Schematically differentiating suicide from deliberate self-harm

Suicide	Deliberate self-harm
Wishes to die	No decisions
More males (3:1)	More females (2:1)
All social classes (including professionals)	More classes 4 and 5
In spring	No seasonal variation
Divorce	Divorce
Unemployed	Unemployed and sickness
Living alone	Living alone and crowded
Psychiatric illness (over 80 per cent, dominant variable)	Affective symptoms (sadness)
Physical illness	
Stress	Stress
Previous DSH	Previous DSH
Alcohol, drugs	Alcohol, drugs
Age-changing, but elderly at most risk	All ages, but under–35 at most risk
Emotionality and violence different between genders	Potential against, so reactive problematic

Note that this is a guideline only: there is no such thing as a 'safe cry for help'.

justice and balance in their expectation that they should die before their children. Consequently, the presence of suicidal behaviour in adolescents creates the strongest imaginable reaction in all around them. At the same time, as Brent (1989) demonstrated, certain adolescents are more susceptible to imitative suicidal behaviour than others. It must be appreciated that adolescence is a time when a number of psychiatric disorders begin to manifest themselves, though adolescent suicide is very rare throughout the developed world, even allowing for the reluctance of coroners to record such a verdict (Chambers and Harvey 1989).

Hazel and Lewin (1993) described a 'post-ventilation' initiative in two schools following adolescent suicides, which enabled their school counsellor to differentiate between adolescents who had a high suicidal ideation and those who did not. However, while this was of immediate benefit, they could find no difference in terms of outcome with a matched group a year later.

Fremouw *et al.* (1990) measured a small sample of hospitalized suicidal adolescents who were indistinguishable in terms of current life stresses from a controlled group of non-psychiatric young people, though the analysis had been undertaken almost a month after their admission. This is a worrying feature, as older people trying to respond to adolescents can become exhausted by the typical 'labile' state of the adolescent, who moves from 'agony to ecstasy', reflected in Wordsworth's *Prelude*: 'I speak of a race of real children, not too learned or too wise, but banded up and down by love and hate.'

The key characteristic of adolescents is that relatively they respond to the immediate present with great intensity of delight or despair. There is a danger of uncritically accepting this *Sturm und Drang* as normal, of not recognizing the extra quality of despair in some young people and of missing the underlying psychiatric depression.

Rende *et al.* (1993) explored genetic and environmental influences on depressive symptomatology, and found a moderate genetic influence on the range of individual differences in depression, though clearly familiar influences contributed to the experience. This may partly account for the findings of De Chateau (1990), whose thirty-year follow-up of 2,364 former patients of child guidance clinics in Stockholm found that they had a significantly higher mortality rate than the general population. Within these deaths, a staggering 82 per cent were related to suicide, accidents and/or substance abuse. It was clear that an interaction between depressive mental disorder and criminality was more prevalent among these adolescent patients, and that aggressive feelings and acts against themselves and others were over-represented in the child guidance population.

Pfeiffer *et al.* (1991) carried out a six- to eight-year comparative study of 100 pre-adolescent and adolescent inpatients in New York. They had been involved in deliberate self-harm, and were compared with an adolescent population who had not attempted suicide. Encouragingly, no subsequent deaths were found within the period. However, the former DSH adolescents were seven times as likely to have a mood disorder as the non-DSH control group. This seems to imply potential life-long vulnerability, and while the greatest care should be taken not to reinforce these young people's 'patient role' with the wrong kind of reinforcing attention, their problems should be taken very seriously. Consequently the professionals involved should incorporate into their intervention plan not only immediate considerations of risk, but also medium- and long-term preventative measures.

While it is clear that actual suicide under eighteen, and especially under sixteen, is rare compared to road accidents for example, the frequency of DSH can alarm all. We must again caution against false reassurance, because adolescents do die. Despite the disproportionate rate of DSH among young people of both genders, it must never be seen as 'normal', because we find significantly higher rates of eventual suicide among adults, and a higher degree of psychiatric morbidity, among people involved in DSH as adolescents (Beck *et al.* 1985; Allebeck 1988; Cullberg *et al.* 1988; Kosky *et al.* 1990; Marttunen *et al.* 1991; Pfeiffer *et al.* 1991). Consequently, the minimum the services should do is to recognize that even an apparently 'mild' DSH is a clear manifestation of the current distress of the adolescent and a potential indicator of future problems as an adult. Hence it merits a proactive preventative response, despite the fact that the relatively transient nature of the situation makes longer-term prediction extremely limited.

Kerfoot (1984) looked at older children and adolescents, and he, like others (Brent *et al.* 1993), believed that you can differentiate between adolescents who attempt suicide and others, in that they appear to *experience more turmoil* in their families, which are not stabilized during their adolescent development.

Brent *et al.*'s (1993) recent study from the USA provides a useful point, as they found sharply defined stressful life events associated with adolescent *suicide*, and not just DSH. Among sixty-seven actual deaths (which exceeds the annual rate of the UK), they compared the stressors in the adolescents' lives with those of a matched group of controls. In respect of demographic characteristics, there was a slight, but significant, difference regarding living with both parents, as fewer than half of the suicide completers lived with both parents, as opposed to two-thirds of the control group. The strong features which appeared to differentiate the two groups were: stressful life events in terms of interpersonal conflict with parents or boy or girlfriends, a disruption of a romantic attachment, and conduct that led to legal or disciplinary problems, especially in the presence of substance misuse.

Very significantly, and reflecting the culture, 70 per cent of the victims had died from firearms, and the remainder from drug overdose, which is the more frequent method of self-harm among European younger people, particularly women. The presence of such lethality, and its immediacy, matched with the volatility of adolescent life, speaks volumes of the danger. Very significantly, almost a third of Brent *et al.*'s group had experienced interpersonal conflicts surrounding their boy or girlfriend, and more frequently than any other actual or threatened loss, two-fifths of them thought they had lost their would-be partner. Finally, a quarter of these young people had disciplinary problems related to school and work, and almost a third were facing some legal problem related to conduct disorder.

This last point might give a salutary warning of the need for caution to ill-informed politicians seeking immediate responses to the social 'plagues' of adolescents. They should consider the relatively high rate of young adult suicide in British closed institutions (Dooley 1990; Gunn *et al.* 1991), which is replicated throughout most of the Western world (Green *et al.* 1993; Johnson *et al.* 1993).

Adolescents, eating disorders, depression and suicidal risk

We do not wish to over-emphasize the association of eating disorders, depression and risk of suicide in adolescence, but from a preventative and therefore a forward-thinking perspective, it seems that a number of practitioners are noting that young men, as well as young women, appear over-preoccupied with body image. King *et al.* (1993) explored self-image in a group of adolescents with depression, and found that body image was an important factor. Lawrence (1984), in a sensitive exploration of the 'anorexic experience', pointed to this problem being on the increase in the affluent West, while Chiles (1986) found a number of clinical examples where adolescents' DSH seemed to centre on their distress about body image. As Plath put it, even before the era that created the androgynous media image of young adulthood: 'she would rather be dead than fat, dead and perfect, like Nefertiti'. It is easy for older adults to forget the intense media pressures of style and fashion, which are ubiquitous within the West. At present the slender, if not downright skinny, person, especially woman, is the object of emulation wherever Western television reaches. In crude terms, women face procrustean pressures as the fashion world dictates size 10 as the idealized 'norm', whereas size 14 is the norm, which in purely statistical terms is likely to create a degree of dissatisfaction in a fair proportion of women.

Therapists can perhaps be disadvantaged by their gender and age, as it is easy not to appreciate the extent and frequency of relatively mild dissatisfaction with body image in younger adults. Within the present context of their lives, this can be the crucial factor in maintaining their psycho-social equilibrium. Body image may not be a major factor in adolescent DSH, but it might be the last straw among a number of other stressors. Only when we no longer suffer the pangs of adolescent unrequited love can we laugh at *our* blue-suede shoes, Tony Curtis or Elvis Presley hair style.

What can we conclude from this overview? Abbar *et al.* (1993) sum it up neatly. Suicidal behaviour is best understood as being multi-determined and *a result of interaction between state and trait, and related effects.* The factors include not only the psychiatric and bio-physiological, but also psycho-social stress, which can include medical illness. O'Carroll (1993), however, rightly warns us of over-emphasizing one particular feature, be it psychiatric- or stress-related, and says that we need a more explicit understanding of the nature of multiple causation. This would allow us to obviate some misguided arguments that seek a kind of totalitarian orthodoxy. It seems to us that different negative triggers will be more distressing for some than others, and again we have to stress the value, in preventative efforts, of responding to the specific person in his or her situation. This sums our position up perfectly, as we try to understand the patterns of rejection in people's lives associated with the risk of suicide.

Child neglect, abuse and sexual abuse, and their links with suicidal behaviour

There has been some suggestion of sexual abuse being associated with adolescent suicidal behaviour (Stone 1993; Wagner and Linehan 1994), and at the same time a high degree of psychiatric pathology among survivors of child sexual abuse, which at the extreme includes DSH (Van Egmond and Jonker 1988; Pritchard 1991). There are, however, real difficulties in teasing out cause and effect, not least from definitions of abuse, which can be so broad as to be meaningless. There is also the problem of 'the helping hand strik[ing] again'. Newberger (1983) found tragic consequences following an inappropriate handling of 'disclosures' of apparent sexual abuse (shades of the Cleveland and Orkney enquiries). We must be extremely cautious lest we compound the family's and young person's distress by acting on unfounded suspicions.

Conversely, there appears to be no doubt that child neglect, abuse and sexual abuse have a relationship to subsequent mental health pathology (Egeland *et al.* 1987; Finkel 1987; Oliver 1988; Bland *et al.* 1993), though the problem is a major topic in its own right. Medium- and long-term negative effects, including subsequent suicidal behaviour, have been found among people who have been neglected and abused as children (Allebeck and Bolund 1991; Bayatpour *et al.* 1992; Hibberd and Zollinger 1992; Kinzl and Biebl 1992).

In brief it appears that the mechanism involves low self-esteem, and an adult person who has experienced little love and affection as a child, or indeed rejection and hostility, is more likely to be vulnerable to a depressive mood and suicidal behaviour. Child sexual abuse is especially problematic, first because it is more extensive an activity than was previously thought. This was exemplified by Freud's response to the frequency he found among his earlier patients (Masson 1990). At core, the destructive element is how abuse pervades early *relationships.* For us the most balanced study, and there is a need for balance, is from Freda Fromouth (1988), based upon a large sample of female undergraduates. She found that about 10 per cent had been involved in inappropriate sexual relations under the age of sixteen, but only 10 per cent of these had felt long-term damage to their sexual functioning, or relationships with peers or men. The damage and distress centred on the breaking of trust, so that experiences with a stranger, even though they could be frightening and distressing at the time, were far less damaging than the persistent, insidious and deceitful destruction and exploitation of the girl by a man whose role should have been protective, not corrosively exploitative. One among a number of problems is that a person feels diminished, undervalued and worthless (Fromouth 1988; Patton 1991), which may go some way to explain why Van Egmond and Jonker (1988), in an outpatients' centre for women involved in deliberate self-harm, found that 40 per cent of the sample had experienced some form of sexual abuse as a child. At this extreme end of the continuum, we examined a cohort of families who were on the 'at risk of abuse' register. We found that 50 per cent of the women had themselves been neglected or abused, and a fifth of the families' men were involved in current sexual abuse of their children. Half the women had some form of recurrent depression and, significantly, a third of these women had been involved in deliberate self-harm (Pritchard 1991). With regard to suicidal behaviour, therefore, a person who has been neglected or abused as a child, sexually or physically, appears to be more likely to be vulnerable to depression and suicidal behaviour, which is yet another variable the therapist needs to consider when making assessments and predictions about suicide risk.

How big is the problem? It is feared that while modern society has been relatively slow to appreciate its extent, there are equal dangers in exaggerating the problem, which is in danger of explaining 'everything', from enuresis to cancer (Patton 1991). The concept then becomes meaningless and the 'theory' dominates, to the detriment of the vulnerable person. If we take Fromouth's figures as a baseline, allow for social class bias and early damage disrupting potential female students coming into college and say that not 1 per cent but 2 of *all* women have been seriously damaged by their experience, would this seem a reasonable estimate? This is not in any way to belittle the trauma. Extrapolating from Fromouth's study and taking the current total population of British women, we might find between 414,000 and 550,000 who had been abused as children and had some distress that *continued* into adulthood; formidable figures indeed. But we must not extrapolate further and assume that all psycho-social distress is the product of child sexual abuse.

There is of course one area of 'sexual abuse' that puts young people at special risk, which comes out of the relationship between poverty, homelessness, physical *and* mental illness, and substance misuse: via a market exploitation of young people's sexuality, they are at special risk of HIV infection and AIDS. It is not very fashionable to highlight the overwhelming evidence that, despite the *early* impact of AIDS in the West, the impetus that started the epidemic was the link between poverty and sexual exploitation. Unemployed, homeless, ex-offending young people are at higher risk of finding themselves involved in HIV risk behaviour.

'Michael' was eighteen years old and had no previous psycho-social problems whatsoever. He did suffer, however, from part-time structural unemployment, jobs at his skill level only being available in the summer months. This was typical for the area and his working-class family accepted that with no difficulty. Suddenly his father was made redundant and having Michael and father at home was catastrophic for family relationships. Michael had to leave and sought the anonymity of a south coast resort. The contrast with his small rural town could not be more drastic. After becoming homeless, he was exposed to hard drugs for the first time. To fund himself, he made an 'alternative market response' to his economic plight, found his bisexuality an asset, and entered part-time male prostitution. His DSH response to a positive HIV test was perhaps to be expected, not least because he did not really know about AIDS and the 'scene'. His story is repeated again and again among the 'runaway youths' in the inner cities of the USA *and* increasingly Britain (Stiffman 1989; Joseph and Roman-Nay 1990; Bell *et al.* 1991; Brudney and Dobkin 1991; Yates *et al.* 1991; Kufeldt 1992; Graetz 1993; Pritchard *et al.* 1993; Pritchard and Clooney 1994). Almost by definition such young people will be alienated from families and society, few having experiences which lead them to believe they can trust the adult and established world. This might account for Runeson's (1992) findings of youth suicides who were virtually unknown to psychiatric or welfare services, casualties found among 'yesterday's neglected children' who are today's disregarded young adults.

The media and suicide

Finally, linked to suicidal behaviour and young people is the issue of the media and suicide. There has been a longstanding belief that the public presentation of suicide might influence the vulnerable and particularly adolescents (Stack 1992). There is a tradition that if a suicide occurs on the London Underground, it is not usually publicized, and certainly there is evidence to show that insensitive reporting by the media of a suicide can have deleterious affects upon the survivors (Shepherd and Barraclough 1978).

Biblarz *et al.* (1991) tried to explore how the media might influence attitudes towards suicide. As might be expected, the conclusions were equivocal, depending upon the current and prevailing circumstances of the person involved. However, after the dramatic suicide of Jan Pallach in Czechoslovakia there was an increase in death by burning in the rest of Western Europe, which is a very atypical means of death. That the media influences our society, and therefore individuals within it, cannot be doubted, but the mechanisms are not understood, least of all the *specifics*, if there are any.

Neither Stack (1992) nor Kessler *et al.* (1989) were able to demonstrate a statistical link over time with either popular films or reporting, other than of 'political' figures. There is a greater concordance between short-term exposure to violence and arousal (Biblarz *et al.* 1991). In conclusion, it would appear that how the individual responds to portrayed violence depends upon age and state of mind, and in terms of general population, the response is likely to be very short-lived and minimal. It may be that the most important feature is how the *local* community responds to the public presentation of suicide, which can compound stigma, isolation and rejection.

CHAPTER 6

THE SOCIOLOGY OF MENTAL HEALTH AND SUICIDE

The contribution of sociology: Durkheim

Richard Titmus once said 'reality begins with history', and the search for the sociology of mental health and suicide must commence with Durkheim. The publication of Durkheim's *Le Suicide* in 1888 saw the first major international landmark in the development of modern sociology, and rightly he is considered the 'father of sociology'.

Durkheim's great project was concerned with the social causes that contribute to suicide, yet his opening sentence reflects his innate 'integrationalist' approach. This is often forgotten by some social scientists who, blinkered, miss the other elements, acknowledged by Durkheim, in the conundrum that makes up suicide.

Durkheim said that there are two sorts of 'extra-social' causes which might, *a priori*, influence the suicide rate. They are 'organic psychic dispositions' and the 'nature of the physical environment'. Durkheim agreed with Escarole that 'suicide may be seen as resulting from many different causes'. Durkheim acknowledged the 'organic-psychic' constitution of individuals, but focused primarily upon social causes that influenced national rates.

Modern scholars, such as Berrios and Monaghan (1990), while accepting Durkheim's seminal contribution to the study of suicide, gently chide him for being somewhat selective in choosing as protagonists those who would see suicide and mental illness as predominantly having a physiological ideology, thus schematically generating antagonists, which inadvertently created an unnecessary schism. Berrios and Monaghan point out that in Britain, Germany and France, there were already psychiatrists who recognized the importance of social and environmental factors in the suicidal phenomenon. In Britain, almost a hundred years before, the Yorkshire Quaker William Tuke sought to further the 'moral treatment' of the mentally ill, based essentially on a humanitarian enlightened approach, which was pre-medievalist and reminiscent of the classic tradition of

Marcus Aurelius. Tuke quoted Juvenal's analogy about children and the mentally ill: 'When you meet such, treat them with the care and consideration you would if they were distinguished foreigners visiting your country, who do not understand its customs.'

Nevertheless Durkheim's contribution was seminal and there are still interesting findings to be discovered in Durkheim's international comparison of nineteenth-century suicide rates. Bearing in mind the varying population in Great Britain in the 1860s, so that numbers must be seen as estimates, his figures for England, between 1863 and 1867, suggest a male suicide rate of between 94 and 102 per million, and a female rate of between 34 and 37 per million. It is fascinating to consider that these rates are close to rates found in a non-recessionary England and Wales in the early 1970s. He argued that 'the suicide rate is even more stable than that of the general mortality', which is a very important concept. In effect, if one accepts this degree of stable mortality, any substantial changes suggest influences upon the morbidity, pointing to new influences in the environment.

Female suicide was much higher in post First World War times, reaching almost double the Durkheimian and current levels. Extrapolating from Kreitman (1978), this appears to have been owing to the simple social fact that a distressed and despairing woman had easy access to the relatively new lethal method of self-slaughter, domestic coal gas, and quickly became a victim of the highly toxic and speedy effect of coal gas poisoning.

Durkheim was also the first to link the presence of alcohol with a predisposition to suicide. In addition, he noted the association of divorce and suicide, even in nineteenth-century Europe, and of homelessness. He also appreciated that general social attitudes to suicide might well have an influence, seen in the variations of social beliefs, systems and sanctions against suicide. However, the question must be asked as to whether these attitudes are 'reactive' to the social 'reality' of the society. While highlighting for the first time these social factors Durkheim also acknowledged that between 25 and 30 per cent of men and 40 and 54 per cent of women had some form of mental illness.

As already intimated in respect of suicide and religion, Durkheim was in our view wrong in his generalization that suicide occurs less frequently in Catholic cultures. This is based upon the simple fact that Catholic Hungary has had for many years the highest suicide rate in the world, even in the nineteenth century (WHO 1994). It was somewhat disingenuous of Durkheim to ignore the fact, based upon his own calculations, that suicide rates for Catholic Austrian men were almost three times those for the 'Protestant' English, and one and a half times the rate for English females!

Durkheim's greatest understanding was his concept of an anomic suicide in which individuals, in the face of the experience of a rejecting, excluding society, were in their desperation more likely to die. He crucially demonstrated the association between increased suicide and economic recession.

In the case of economic disasters, indeed something like a declassification occurs which suddenly casts certain individuals into a lower state than their previous ones. Then they must reduce their requirements, restrain their needs, learn greater self control – but society cannot suggest them instantaneously to this new life and teach them to practise increased self repression to which they must become accustomed. So they are not adjusted to the condition forced upon them and its very prospect is intolerable.

'Declassification' is the very essence of the notion of 'underclass' as people are excluded, rejected from full, adult, independent citizenship.

Modern research on the interrelationship of 'economic disasters', e.g. unemployment, and suicide and suicidal behaviour continues to validate Durkheim's great insight (Brenner 1983; Platt 1984; Dooley *et al.* 1989; Pritchard 1992a; Fischer *et al.* 1993), and Warr and Jackson's (1988) finding of what we describe as the 'defensive apathy' of the long-term unemployed, is an almost exact concordance of what Durkheim predicted.

Invaluably, Durkheim, even while identifying major social factors, never lost sight of other interactive factors that might lead some people to suicide, though perhaps he *under*-stated them. His genius is seen in the fact that despite the passing of a hundred years since the first publication of *Le Suicide*, his main premise, though perhaps not its detail, remains intact. One wonders how many social scientists' contributions will still have relevance and validity in a hundred years from now.

Perhaps the second most important theme identified in Durkheim, and still relevant today, is the idea that there are some deaths which are constant but influenced by negative changing circumstances. Suicide is not the only category that fits this notion; for example, child mortality is very reflective of the social circumstances of the society. Durkheim's great contribution was to show that there is a degree of stable mortality associated with mental illness and/or suicide rates, which are indicative of the cohesion of a society, be it during war or major recession.

That suicide is reduced in war time is the obverse proof of Durkheim's anomic suicide, as society appears to reach out to all individuals, being anxious to be integrative. This, of course, is the very opposite of the experience of unemployed people, who in today's Registrar General's phrase are 'unclassifiable'. This is equivalent to Durkheim's term *déclassé*, and reflects the modern concept of 'underclass' (Jenck and Peterson 1991). Yet interestingly, even during war time, unemployment was found to be a continuing important variable (Vigderhaus and Fishman 1979). To be excluded from the market place, at a time of social exhortation to join in collective action, must truly be declassifying and stigmatizing, and it must be remembered that even in the first two years of the Second World War, there was still considerable unemployment in Britain, which might partly account for the relatively slow decline of suicide in the first two years of the war.

In search of typologies

The study of suicide does attract controversy and this text may be no exception. While it does not seek to be controversial it may be that this chapter will attract the most disagreement, as one may be accused of being a 'structuralist', a 'determinist' or, in the terms of Sibeon (1992), an 'anti-reductionist'. It may be worthwhile, therefore, to declare the author's own historical antecedents, which are virtually coterminous with the developments stemming from the mid-1950s in sociology, psychology and clinical psychiatry.

I was taught an organic base to psychiatry that was very restricted, not least by the contradiction in the definition of a psychiatric problem: if no neurological or organic base could be found for the behaviour, then it was assumed to be 'mental/psychiatric'. This innate inconsistency was highlighted by Thomas Szasz (1960) in his classic paper and then book, *The Myth of Mental Illness*. This author, like many young professionals of the day, found considerable limitations in a purely medical explanation for individuals' crisis and distress, while the newly accessible Freudian psychology and Goffman-type sociology were truly psychedelic and liberating. They appeared to give a greater understanding of the factors that accounted for variations within individuals' behaviour, and to provide a better explanation of some of those accumulative stresses which led to people becoming labelled psychiatrically ill and, at the extreme, suicidal. Consequently, in addition to the organic typology, two other typologies emerged that sometimes became complementary and at other times antagonistic. First was the psychological explanation of mental illness and suicidal behaviour, very strongly influenced by Freud, whose approach was archetypal individualistic. It is perhaps difficult to understand the impact that Freudian and later neo-Freudian ideas had upon society and people's beliefs about mental illness. Indeed there is a paradox of Freudian *psychology* shaping societal attitudes and transforming itself into a major social influence, which still continues to define its psycho-social problems in terms of *social* casualties. However, despite Freud's assertion that his methodology was scientifically based, and that one day it would be overtaken by an organic explanation, the emphasis upon the individualistic has meant for some critics that Freudian psychology has little empirical basis.

The second approach was the very antithesis of Freudian psychology. It came from psychologists from the behaviourist school, exemplified by Eysenck, whose attacks on psychoanalytic treatments became increasingly vitriolic from 1952 on. In parenthesis, when Eysenck's classic critique of psychoanalytic treatments was first published in German his disavowal of psychoanalytical effectiveness was cautious and modest. But the further away from his original work he moved, the fewer were his qualifications, so that his unfettered anti-Freudian criticisms were eventually almost pure polemic.

Here there is a current paradox, as this author has considerable reservations about the *effectiveness* of psychoanalytic treatments, but recognizes that Eysenck's critique was seriously flawed. Two psychoanalysts drew attention to this but published in German (Duhressen and Jorswieck 1962) and were not translated into English until 1974. It transpired that in Eysenck's original analysis of psychoanalytic treatments there were some remarkable arithmetical inconsistencies, which were clearly not noticed by many who later quoted Eysenck. This led us to believe that the original work was never perused by the 'behavioural' critics of the Freudians. Nevertheless, to be fair, they probably *reflected* Eysenck's reaction.

Eysenck's critique reverberated throughout the mental health field well into the 1960s and 1970s, so that it was not easy to find ego-dynamic and behaviourist therapists who could be polite to each other. The first relevance of this old controversy is that it taught the author to be very cautious about 'big ideas' which sought to explain everything, and that the essence of any informed practice must be based upon *reliable* research (sometimes researchers are fallible in their enthusiasms). Second, as will become clear, there developed some very strange professional and ideological alliances, or mis-alliances, between psychologists, sociologists and political analysts in their consideration of mental health issues.

The sociological basis of anti-psychiatry: strengths and weaknesses

The seminal figures in post-war sociology (Talcott Parsons and Reisman) gave us an insight into how people are described by their functions. People fulfil their social roles within, and belonging to, the group, but if this breaks down they become 'outsiders' and are labelled deviant, which fuels the inherent conflict between the freedom of the individual and the controlling and behaviour-shaping society and state. The success of Western post-war economies came to a peak in the 1960s, and coincided with a new questioning of the traditional norms. Sociology was at the forefront of this new iconoclastic age.

It might be argued that sociology at this time was influenced by what might be called the 'Pausanias factor'. Alexander the Great's friend, Pausanias, had consulted the Oracle at Delphi about how he might become famous. He was told – Plutarch reports some cynics as saying with Alexander's connivance – that to achieve instant fame one should kill the most famous person of one's times, in this case Philip of Macedonia, Alexander's father. That this has an element of truth is echoed in the fame of John Wilkes Booth, the assassin of Lincoln, and Lee Harvey Oswald, the supposed murderer of John F. Kennedy. The sociological 'Pausanian' attack was against the most famous and esteemed professional group, medicine, with its burgeoning scientific technology.

The greatest anti-medical protagonist, who is still relevant today, was the Jesuit Ivan Illich. His classic *Medical Nemesis* (1971) brought together the work of Becker, Mechanic, Parsons and others. His central critique of medicine related to its intellectual imperialism, in which everything was 'medicalized'. Medicine seemed to sanction both 'normal' and 'abnormal' behaviour, setting socially acceptable and desirable against unacceptable and avoidable behaviour.

Two very creative sociologists, Mechanic (1968) and Scheff (1984), were particularly interested in how medicine had socially defined the 'mentally ill'. This was closely allied to Irving Goffman's work, which explored stigma and how society could, in his term, 'spoil an identity' by the use of the demoralizing and excluding label 'mentally ill'. The epitome of maturity and independence was someone who was self-sufficient, who met the expected roles and routine requirements of society and, crucially, was an active participant in the socio-economic field. Thus a person's identity, status and resulting psychological self-esteem came from how he or she was defined by social circumstances. Apart from the label 'mental illness' there were other examples of 'spoiled identities' caused by 'labelling': 'deviant', 'offender', 'claimant', 'social security scrounger', 'cripple', the 'little woman', other sexist denigrations and a range of racist epithets. The current critics of the 'politically correct' may have a point that language has almost become totalitarian (Davies 1994), but it should be remembered just how demeaning and damaging such thoughtless adjectives can be.

Medical consultants, especially psychiatrists with their frequent problem of imprecise diagnostics, were special targets, and it is true that a whole range of medical consultants did behave in a somewhat Olympian manner. Indeed, the occasional intellectual dinosaur can still be found browsing and roaring in some psychiatric units. However, medical sociologists so successfully took them to task in the 1960s that they became 'straw men' to be 'burnt up' by the new iconoclasts.

This was a lot of fun, not least because medicine at this time had become intoxicated by its own massive success, and its arrogance was rightly criticized when it inadvertently made claims that far exceeded its scientific base.

One of the reasons, apart from merit, why the medical profession is held in high esteem, is the inevitable involvement of *every* member of society: at some time, everyone requires the services of the doctor. Thus, in almost Freudian terms, we all collude in wishing to placate the great 'priests' upon whom we shall be dependent at times of illness and vulnerability. We avoid offending the 'gods' by challenging their omnipotence. There is a paradox here. When doctors were scientifically and objectively *less* competent, they attracted even *greater* reverence. But major changes over recent decades in medical schools' curricula and changing social mores have meant that doctors have never been more responsive, and have been measurably influenced by the positive impact that the sociological critique has had upon their claims to omnipotence. This said, however, even in the 1990s one can still find supreme examples of medics whose arrogance is only matched by their ignorance when they unknowingly step outside their area of expertise.

Thomas Szasz, a professor of psychiatry no less, reminded us that the language of psychiatry in the 1960s and early 1970s was a language of metaphor and analogy that tried to describe people's behaviour in the absence of organic lesions or toxins. People in a psychotic or distressed state were described 'as if they were mentally ill'; Szasz reminded us that we dropped the 'as if' component of the analogy, and began to reify, that is to make concrete, those metaphoric explanations. A good example was mentioned in respect of 'refrigerator parents', i.e. parents who were reacting to their children's autism. Szasz was a 'libertarian', and attracted considerable enthusiasm from the broad left and progressive liberals among humanistic professionals. However, the brilliant analysis and exposition of Peter Sedgwick (1982) demonstrated that Szasz *was* a libertarian, but from the far right. We suspect that many of those who were enthusiastic about Szasz in the 1970s and 1980s had not read him in full, as his position was 'Kantian' in the extreme. He believed that people who behaved deviantly should be punished, because to do otherwise would infringe their human dignity; and as mental illness was *not* an *illness*, it was wrong to excuse socially a whole range of behaviours. The essence of Szasz is reflected in the following complaint:

> The altruistic imperatives of religion are part of the cause of the present mess. Both Jewish and Christian teaching abound in rules that reward sickness, malingering and poverty, and include brief disabilities of all sorts, whilst at the same time invoking penalties for self-reliance, competence and effectiveness and pride in health and well-being.
>
> (Quoted in Sedgwick 1982)

The great tragedy of Peter Sedgwick's early death is that the potential synthesis of a neo-Marxist sociology with an integrated humanistic psycho-social philosophy never came to fruition. When the 'New Right' speaks in libertarian terms, they are not based upon notions of 'liberty' in the great trilogy with 'equality' and 'fraternity', but upon the Hayeckian 'liberty' of the market-place. The New Right, ideologically at the centre of government since 1979, argues ahistorically for 'liberty' that ignores inherited socio-economic disadvantage, and concentrates upon 'the right to one's own', which is predominantly concerned with avoiding any infringement of fundamental property rights. Thus the 'libertarian' right, embodied by Hayek and Szasz, demands the 'liberty' to continue to enjoy inherited inequality untrammelled by notions of a real search for equality of opportunity. In the United Nations Declaration of Human Rights there is no equivocation about the need for 'active rights':

> Whereas the peoples of the United Nations have reaffirmed their faith in fundamental human rights, in the dignity and worth of the human person and in the *equal* rights of men and women and are *determined to provoke social progress* and better standards of life in larger freedom. [italics added]

Szasz was joined in the great 1960s pantheon by Ronald D. Laing whose contribution was based upon the idea that the 'mentally ill' were labelled victims of families, and that the 'schizophrenic' experience was the effect of a supremely 'sane' person trying to come to terms with an 'insane' world in the search for his or her real 'inner self' (see Friedenberg 1973, for an outline of Laing's contribution). This was attractive to the intellectual adolescents of the day but had little validity when examined more closely. Yes, the world could be stupid, cruel, barbaric, and even evil, deliberately ignoring or denying knowledge – seen in the Korean, Vietnam and Angolan wars, apartheid, the military-industrial complex, world pollution, Bosnia, Rwanda and the oppression of ethnic minorities – but this is *not* mental illness. There may be inadequate words to define such abominations, but to label them as mental illness was and is a misuse of language, and an inadvertent manifestation of the prejudice against the mentally disordered.

The third in the trio was Goffman, whose *Asylums* (1961) taught us to understand the impact of 'closed' institutions, such as mental hospitals, which shaped and restricted people's behaviour.

These three appeared to be great apostles for progressive humanism in the pursuit of social justice and freedom for the mentally ill. However, Sedgwick's brilliant demolition of some of the uncritical attributes of the 'big three' still merits the closest scrutiny. Szasz, in particular, he saw as a conservative libertarian, whose acceptance of the given, within a capitalist society, simply meant that 'liberty' was the freedom to continue to be poor, disadvantaged and exploited.

Goffman was praised for his liberalism, of the democratic variety, but Sedgwick showed how even Goffman, with his very humane understanding of the impact of stigma, as seen in his *Stigma* (1968), was committed to the *amelioration*, not the change, of an innately morally unjust capitalist society.

Sedgwick's criticism of Laing was very much made more in sorrow than anger, for Laing had originally challenged the establishment, and sought to free the sufferer from social and psychological condemnation, but had simply changed the *focus of blame* from the sufferer to the family. Laing failed to recognize that in a structural sense both sufferer and family were victims, and the neo-Freudian concept of scapegoating not only had little empirical support, but failed to address the *causes* of mental disorder, by over-focusing upon the reactive mechanisms. Laing failed to understand that despite life-long need and dependency, it is the primary family that is still the major support for mentally ill people in the vast majority of cases (Gibbons 1987; Stockley and Stockley 1993; Pritchard and Clooney 1994).

Sedgwick, who, unusually among sociologists, had had first-hand experience of mental illness, understood that Laing had failed to explain the origins of mental illness, and by concentrating upon the process and reaction, had simply moved the target of disapprobation. Thus it was no longer the sufferer's fault but the family's.

As a young psychiatric social worker, I was excited by the contextual insight of sociology and by the awareness of the centrality of communication that Laing had highlighted. However, I became cautious very early on, when individual cases were helped by neither the macro approach nor Laingian concepts, which in the majority of family situations simply did not appear to be valid. It was difficult to say this too loudly lest the 'political correctness' of the day be infringed.

Nevertheless, the psychiatry of the early 1970s took very seriously the critique of the 'anti-psychiatrists', and of Laing in particular. Two eminent researchers, Stephen Hirsch and Julian Leff (1971), empirically sought to explore some of these ideas, and looked at communication patterns of families in which there was a person with schizophrenia. In a controlled study, family communication patterns were compared in families with a schizophrenic member and no schizophrenic member. They found no validity whatsoever in terms of *causal* factors of schizophrenia. In respect of hostile and critical forms of communication, there were no differences found between families *with* or *without* a person with schizophrenia! However, the hostile and critical type of communication *added* (naturally) to family stress. It appears that what Laing had picked up was the family's 'natural history': if a family was mutually sustaining before the illness, it was more able to respond more positively to its ill member, whereas families who had stress and strife before the onset of schizophrenia continued to be hostile to each other. In the latter family settings, not surprisingly, the ill member was even more rejected, criticized and ostracized.

The importance of accessible communication was reaffirmed. As will be discussed later, Hirsch and Leff's work was developed further, and offers one of the most progressive and exciting developments in one approach to treating schizophrenia and mental illness (Falloon 1985; Leff and Vaughan 1985). So, perhaps after all the inadvertent misery associated with Laing's work, some good has evolved.

The damage of Laing, however, is that the blame *continues* to be 'popularly' associated with parents of disturbed or mentally ill adolescents and young adults. This persists in society via films and media, and while Laing actually *refuted* this notion, he did so within academic journals and not in the public arena, which would have encouraged wider debate and perhaps some public re-evaluation. Consequently the 'devil myth' of a schizophregenic parent continues in popular fiction, feeding the ambivalent love–hate response of adolescents, who seek to establish a 'new independence' by shattering and then, typically, re-forming the images of control.

Sociology and the professions

George Bernard Shaw's dictum, 'professions are conspiracies against the laity', contains sufficient truth to have become a cliché, but it contains an innate error. The sociological critique of the professions, after its assault upon medicine, turned to psychology, psychoanalysis, social work and later those in the mental health and child care fields. This really reflected the common elements of the progression, with the push–pull of an objective client-specific science-based art versus a concentration of exclusive and excluding power. An illuminative critique was Peter Noakes's (1967). He saw social work as an extension of the priesthood and he coined the phrase 'secular priest', which many social workers might well accept. However, the 'established priesthood', brilliantly analysed in Edward Thomson's *Whigs and Hunters*, were exploitative and cohesive and some feared that such a nineteenth-century 'priesthood', and therefore social workers, were potentially or actually a part of the 'management' of discontent (Milliband 1969). Social norms and therefore social control were reinforced.

Raymond Plant, who acknowledged the discipline's priestly origins as reflected in the Jesuit Biefsteck's casework, was sympathetic to disciplined commitment to the pursuit of social justice, but noted that many of the attributes of the good therapist or social worker boiled down to 'friendship'. Plant asked the devastating question: 'Can you have *professional* friendship?' The answer is yes and no. Friendship assumes altruism, spontaneity and the personal – friendship is a two-way process. Yet social work implies a willingness to subordinate the personal for another's and, it is hoped, society's benefit. What few textbooks acknowledge is the reality in daily practice: upon knowing another person from his or her perspective, you begin to understand and 'like' the client, which is the basis of any relationship. The interaction *is* two-way, albeit consciously controlled by the social worker: the client *gives* to the professional, and the supportive relationship is often the effective change agent. Frankly, we seldom admit this two-way liking, which is so rewarding.

'Mr Neil', a man with a longstanding criminal record and intermittent depression, was seeking to take control of his life. A crisis arose, and Mr Neil eschewed his previous pattern of criminal response, saying to his probation officer, 'You don't know what I'm having to give up for you', i.e. seeking alternative social networks to avoid crime. Recent empirical research confirms the central *value to the client* of this sustaining and behaviour-shaping relationship (Bailey and Ward 1994; Pritchard and Clooney 1994; Ford *et al.* 1995; Williams *et al.* 1996).

Pilgrim and Rogers (1993), in their excellent *A Sociology of Mental Health and Illness*, give considerable attention to the mental health professions, and build upon the early sociologists, spending considerable time on the issue of compulsion, which, in the mental health field as in child care and protection, is the key issue, with the inherent dilemma of 'care and/or control'. Sibeon (1992) comes right up to date when he explores welfare politics in social work. There is a very interesting balance between him and Pilgrim and Rogers, who identify important sociological contributions in the mental health field and examine how the role of the professions has developed. This is strongly influenced by how society views the sufferer, and how in turn professionals are influenced by societal expectations of 'normality' with regard to gender, ethnicity and age, which can be reflected in professional intervention and 'treatment'. In practice this means how we respond to individuals and families, and guard against potential preconceptions. We would reiterate that all have a tendency to share the cultural perspectives of their time, and one of the most important contributions of sociology was to emphasize how *relative* our health beliefs are, and how they are shaped by current ideologies. Thus modern social workers and therapists need to be aware of how, as actors, they are partly constrained and directed by these subtle and less subtle social processes, which are sometimes expressed in statutory requirements. Thus a prerequisite for all professionals should be to understand something of these sociological and, eventually, interactive psychological processes. The father of modern empiricism, Francis Bacon (1561–1626) said: 'If a man were to begin with certainties he shall end in doubt, but if he be content to begin with doubt, he shall end with certainties.'

It is the experience of many professionals that often, when they are uncertain, paradoxically they feel constrained to present certainty, decisiveness and decision, sometimes colluded with by anxious relatives or sufferer. Shaw's *Doctor's Dilemma* from 1906 highlighted, albeit with poetic licence, the 'guessary' of professionals dealing with the unknown. Irrespective of inner qualms, social workers as well as doctors are often forced to present an opinion based on sketchy knowledge, with all due *gravitas*, to reassure all, not least themselves. Another complaint comes from Pilgrim and Rogers, who argue that 'modern professions are not simply the dominant or most important providers – they effectively monopolize a service market'. One can feel libertarians' hackles rise, but if this is true, is it necessarily a bad thing?

Surely there is a need for some form of regulatory mechanism and protection for the consumer. Yet part and parcel of statutory provision is the confidence that the public has that the 'practice' is knowledge-based, and that the professional will attempt to be objective, client-specific and non-exploitative. At the same time, if a professional is incompetent, or exploits the privileged position, all the statutory professions have systems of discipline to expel the erring member. That the balance of colleagueship may disadvantage the would-be consumer is not gainsaid, but it is suggested that the criteria for professionalism outlined above are not inherently bad or injurious to the consumer, but rather that there is insufficient rigour among professionals themselves to evaluate what they are doing.

The danger can be seen from the work of Bean (1986). In his earlier study, he demonstrated that when the consultant psychiatrist is called to an emergency involving a previously known patient, section papers are signed within an average of three minutes. This is self-evidently an inadequate time. Yet surely the consultant should respond as speedily as possible to reduce the crisis and drama surrounding the event, which apparently precipitated the emergency. However, professionals should take sufficient time to realize that despite their previous knowledge of the person, this situation might very well be *different* and merit an alternative assessment or, more importantly, action, especially to seek the least constraint. We go further, to say that professionals are most likely to make their biggest mistakes when they know the client well. It is so easy to assume that the situation is broadly the same, and to miss crucial new elements that can literally be fatal.

Can we imagine a world without professionals? Before 1859, when the medical profession got its General Council, anything went. It has to be acknowledged that examples of middle and late nineteenth-century medical treatment hardly give rise to confidence. For example, during the final illness of Queen Victoria's father, a former Duke of Kent, the constant bleeding and purging of the poor man probably killed him. It took them two months to finish him off, for following a slight recovery from the first 'treatment attack', they attacked him again, until he succumbed. How did this type of treatment become redundant? It was essentially because of clinical empirical research. It is a paradox that modern high-tech medicine can do remarkably clever things, sometimes truly life-saving, but usually in the arena of acute infections, toxins or traumas. When professions confront the more diffuse problems, such as mental disorder, they are less dramatically successful, and sometimes fall into the macho curse of all professional disciplines, of feeling that they 'have to do something'.

Such a response, while it is led by professionals, is actually *shared* by the culture, and therefore it is up to the professional to be aware of these pressures and not to capitulate to them. But it is hard to say 'I don't know what to do next'. Think how you would feel if this was said about you or your partner! Consider how many academics admit that they have not read the latest work: 'Well I've seen a review and [*ipso facto*], I think . . .'.

It does seem from reading some sociological critics of the professions that openness should be total and the professional should always share the truth. This is very alluring, as it seems to take the burden from the professional and to empower individuals by giving them full recognition of their unique individuality.

Such a response, while undoubtedly right and proper for all the best sociological and Utopian reasons, in practice could be cruel, damaging and occasionally technically wrong. For example, at the advent of AIDS, because of the potentially suicidal response (Mazruk *et al.* 1988), one might have to phase the giving of the information. Modern technology can test a persons's blood and decide within hours whether he or she is carrying HIV, but such knowledge can be experienced as a sentence of death. Consequently, we now seek to prepare the person carefully before the test to protect against self-damaging despair. This is an extreme example, but there are many to be found in daily practice throughout the human service professions.

Consider Huntington's chorea, a neurological disorder that has a very severe prognosis and is known to be genetic. Some families want to know, and make it clear that they want to know; some say that they want to know, but only if the result is going to be a good one; other people utilize enormous psychic energy to escape such knowledge. In practice this means that the professional can only seek to act in a client-specific way and try to respond to their needs.

Seldom in sociological literature is any acknowledgement given to the honourable intent and vocational aspirations of the professional. Is it really believed that men and women enter the field of social work so that they can exercise power over children and families, compel people to enter mental hospital or force an elderly person into an old people's home, in effect committing someone to prison? There may well be people who get a kick out of exercising 'power' as there may be some men and women whose motivation for surgery is sadomasochist, for medicine is delusions of grandeur, or, for oncology because they enjoy seeing people die. It is suggested that if such people exist they are a very, very, very tiny minority.

Nevertheless, the great value of sociology to the professions is to remind us that we can be inadvertently harsh, unthinking, insensitive, colluding or controlling if we do not keep central to all our activities the crucial question of 'who is the primary beneficiary'. Any professional in, for example, the mental health field will find himself or herself frequently confronting the dilemma of a clash of interests of equally vulnerable people. Take the case of the Alzheimer's sufferer who is riven by the worst scenario, of intermittent self-awareness and understanding, mixed up with confusion, anxiety, panic and aggression. His or her elderly arthritic partner, or middle-aged daughter (and often the carers will be female), having endured eighteen turbulent, disturbed and disturbing months, desperately needs some respite care, but the *sufferer* does not want to go into hospital. Unless mutual relief is given, crucial family supports may be irretrievably broken. A similar situation often surrounds those who suffer from recurrent and disabling schizophrenia, when the actors in the situation find it difficult, if not impossible, at that time to take a medium- and long-term view.

Puritan theoretical sociologists may sit in their offices and think great thoughts, identifying what could and should be objective rational processes, but regrettably life is messy and often confusing. Do those who would act on behalf of the client have the moral and emotional right to answer Philip Bean's questions about whether the sufferer has insight? Are they all equipped with appropriate information? To what extent are there elements of collusion in this situation? This raises questions about truly 'informed consent' by patients and relatives, which is invariably based upon advice from professionals. All these are very laudable aims and one must constantly strive to operationalize them, because undoubtedly professionals, if they are not part of the solution, can well be part of the problem. One can well understand Rogers and Pilgrim's sense of outrage at the fact that, apart from the 8 per cent of psychiatric patients who were overtly compulsorily detained, four-fifths of the technically informal patients in their sample felt some degree of pressure and coercion about agreeing to go into hospital.

It is not doubted for a moment that this is probably an accurate reflection of these patients' experience, but two points arise: were there any alternatives and, if not, who was to 'blame'? It must be admitted that some people remain in hospital inappropriately because there are no reasonable alternatives; that some people's situations deteriorate into crisis because there is no adequate care in the community, which could have defused the situation and ensured that the crisis did not become an emergency. Despite the arguments that Britain is not a perfect democracy − indeed nor are any of the North American or Western European states − in essence these countries *are* democracies, and through its elected representatives each society in effect determines the extent, nature, organization and quality of care it gives its citizens. Certainly over the past five or more years, the British Association of Social Work, the Association of Directors of Social Service Departments, the Association of Chief Probation Officers, the Royal College of Psychiatrists and the British Medical Association have been persuasive and active on behalf of those whom they would serve, seeking to draw, within the democratic system, the public's attention to accumulative deficits. Matching the efforts of those from the voluntary field such as the National Schizophrenia Fellowship and Mind. There are also examples of professionals who are former members of service executives but who, rather than receiving placatory research funds, asked 'questions' and drew attention to the inconsistencies between political rhetoric and service delivery. They were removed for their pains and replaced by more 'realistic' and compliant 'professionals'.

Duster (1994) and Lawson (1994) have shown that in both North America and the United Kingdom the growth of poverty has coincided with reductions in service. For example, the British National Health Service has lost a third of its hospital beds in a little more than a decade. If professions are the power-crazed incompetents that they are presented as in some sociological texts, then self-evidently their empires have been reduced and they have 'failed', as they have little vested interest in the diminution of service provision. The responsibility for deficits lies with the *demos* and *then* the politicians, but this should never excuse professionals who act less than competently or respond in a less than client-specific way. The reality is that their commitment is undermined, and not that they demonstrate 'burn-out', but much more insidiously and less dramatically, the potentially more corrupting 'erosion' of professional commitment (Pritchard 1987). The professional, whether doctor, social worker, nurse, teacher or even manager, finds an erosion of compassion, sensitivity and energy, so that he or she develops a survival mechanism against the constant clamour of distress and hurt surrounding him or her.

Martin (1984), in a brilliant intellectual analysis, examined the enquiry reports on some of the hospital scandals of the 1970s. He came up with a chilling phrase, 'corruption of care', and traced the theme in institutions and staff, as well as their inmates, who were isolated, stigmatized, under-resourced, under-scrutinized or under-evaluated, and accumulatively under-valued. It was not successive Ministers of Health who were held responsible, nor the chairs of the regional, area or district health authority, nor the consultants, nor even the matrons; in the dock, exposed to the calumny, were the front-line staff, the equivalents of 'Big Nurse' in Kesey's *One Flew Over the Cuckoo's Nest*. She is a classic example of a professional whose original vocational commitment had been eroded by organizational, political and public neglect, so that her care has been corrupted. The stereotypical horror of the hospital ward described by Kesey may in part still exist. But how did Big Nurse become what she became – a bullying, undermining petty tyrant? The answer is often that she was an equal victim of an uncaring society whose response to people with 'a spoiled identity' (Goffman) was to give them services that were 'good enough for them'; out of sight, out of mind. Consequently, when scandals break, surprisingly infrequently, it is the next least powerful who are castigated: the front-line professional staff.

The British public, in response to a number of long-stay hospital scandals, were treated to an object lesson in political buck passing. In 1968 the then Health Secretary, Richard Crossman, with great indignation, told a television audience that he was making available an immediate release of two million pounds for patient care, which was less than £4 per week per patient for a year. In the words of Iain Macleod, 'Politicians have more in common with each other than the people they represent.'

More recently, following the warmly welcomed initiative of the Department of Health (1992), whose aspiration is to reduce suicide by a third, the Health Secretary, Virginia Bottomley, in response to a media question as to why suicide remained high, expressed some 'disappointment' that the 'services' had not yet begun to make inroads into suicide levels. The new 'health targets' for mental health are couched in terms of reducing suicide levels. Suicide has therefore become a paradoxical indicator of the effectiveness of the community and psychiatric services (Pritchard 1995b). Yet there is an implicit acceptance of the Durkheimian sociological understanding that suicide, in relation to gender and unemployment, has both social and psychiatric features. It is predicted that suicide will rise over the next few years, and not decline. If suicide does not fall, it will be the professionals who will be blamed, not the Secretary of State or the *demos*.

Sociology and the political

Freud, the quintessential individualist, attracted other critics of the establishment, and in particular those with a wider political and social perspective. This is seen in the work of Erich Fromm, who began to merge ego-dynamic insight with a Marxian critique of society. In parenthesis, two of the heirs to this unlikely alliance were Habermas and Laing, who saw the fulfilment of Marx's dream of a post-revolution society, cleansed of the 'birth marks' of that society's capital-ist origins. The new emancipation would be led by the former down-trodden, whose particular hell in the trough of despondency and alienation might give fresher and more creative insight, teaching us how to preserve our humanity under prolonged pressure. This coincided with interest in social control and, as in the work of Foucault, in particular his classic *Madness and Civilization* (1965), the mentally ill were given special status in what with hindsight might be seen as almost a parody of their stigmatized social status.

In the 1960s there was a flowering of Marxian critique of a wide range of social problems. Its targets were not only the established right, but also centre and left-of-centre parties – the progressive liberals on the continent and the Labour Party in Britain – that were 'agencies of the welfare state', such as social work and NHS medicine. This critique was epitomized by Ralph Milliband (1969), and in Britain the rising New Left allied itself with Laingian critiques of psy-chiatry and professionalism in general. It was a very fruitful time for the far left, whose apogee was the so-called 'student rising' in 1968 and the creation of a mass protest movement in Britain, the CND. This was a time of political correct-ness indeed, even though the term had not then been invented. However, there was instability in what were really quite disparate collections; for example, CND activists spanned a range from apolitical Christians to Marxists and libertarian anarchists (Taylor and Pritchard 1982). Closer inspection highlighted the logical inconsistencies (e.g. Sedgwick 1982). Pearson *et al.* (1988), in their devastating critique of the link with anti-psychiatry, showed that the Marxism was quite tenuous and the libertarianism confused, as exemplified by the idealization of Szasz, whose idea of passive 'freedom' was *absolute*, and who trusted only the 'cash nexus' to 'control' the over-mighty professional. Not surprisingly, with such allies the far left amalgam could not hold. It has been argued that as the 'protest makers' taught government how to stifle dissent more effectively, they may well have been almost counter-productive (Pritchard 1986). At the same time, European sociology took up a broadly left or far left position, and judicious use of the media created a set of 'straw men' stereotypes. This union proved, paradoxically, to be politically advantageous to those on the *right* (Franklin and Patton 1990), as shortfalls in the welfare services were brilliantly projected upon both sets of 'victims', the recipients and the professionals. Thus the far left's criticisms were more effectively used by the far right.

A major example from the mental health field is the left libertarian policy attacks upon the then current mental health legislation, the 1959 Mental Health Act. Here such protagonists as Gostin, an American civil rights lawyer, drawing upon examples of politically motivated Russian psychiatry, presented Western psychiatry essentially as a conspiracy against the laity, and as primarily instrumental in social control of 'deviants' who, in Laingian terms, were 'finding their true selves'. The paradox of this 'civil liberties' approach to mental health is that, rather than a focus on improving effective intervention and empowering the citizen sufferer, it resulted in a Mental Health Act 1983 which, despite its rheto-ric, actually *strengthened* the powers of the professional, so that certain treatments can now be compulsorily given. It may not be appreciated, but under the 1959 Act psychiatrists were always unsure as to their legal powers in treating people admitted under compulsory sections of the Act, whereas today there is far less ambiguity.

Two crucial and serious critiques of psychiatric treatment and its infringement upon civil liberties were found in a seminal paper by Rosenhan (1973), the classic 'On being sane in insane places', and in revelations of the infrequent but real misuse of 'electric convulsive therapy' (ECT) as an instrument of control and, at the extreme, punishment. There were sad documentations from such right-wingers as Solzhenitsyn in the totalitarian USSR, in some of the less salubrious states of the USA, and even in the UK. There were examples of the use of ECT that were appalling: treatment given without full anaesthetic, which was meant to intimidate and control. Such unprofessional practice can have no apologist, but it was never anything like the norm; these were very rare exceptions. Almost by definition, such atrocities could only occur in those institutions in which, in Martin's phrase, 'erosion of care' had occurred, which essentially happens only when there is a societal message that 'we do not care'. Yet, as will be seen later, appropriately and properly used ECT can be life-saving; it is time to demythologize this hangover from the 1960s.

Rosenhan's work merits more careful scrutiny. He had people admitted into American mental hospitals who presented the interviewing psychiatrist with vague but psychotic-like symptoms. Once admitted, they then behaved in an ordinary fashion, but they found that this behaviour was interpreted as evidence of pathology. For example, Rosenhan's investigators would take notes of what was occurring on the ward, which the 'patient'-observing nurses interpreted as evidence of suspicious and possibly paranoid behaviour. The reading of a service textbook or literature on philosophy was evidence of 'grandiose ideas'. The long-lasting value of this research is to remind us that professionals must never assume 'they know' in a predetermined way (as, for example, with emergency psychiatric admissions) but respond to the client situation afresh, and should avoid engaging in a prejudged dialogue with the person. This reflects the understanding from education of the power of the 'self-fulfilling prophecy', which can occur in any sphere of human activity. Here is the rub. Some interpreted Rosenhan's study as negating the value of an assessment and diagnosis, and, in Szaszian terms, as questioning whether mental disorder could be said objectively to exist.

What Rosenhan's work did was to highlight the ubiquity of the use of energy-saving categorization, so that we respond to roles and circumstances, not individuals. This is not the monopoly of either psychology or social work, but is paralleled even in the relatively 'exact' field of general surgery. For example, there is a variation of the Münchhausen syndrome, where people have themselves admitted with vague but acute symptoms, often with abdominal pains. The person may undergo a whole range of surgical operations and go to the extreme of mimicking syndromes, to the extent that it appears to be an almost conscious effort to deceive. This is despite the objective fact that, even with modern anaesthetics and analgesics, the operation is a physical attack on the body, and the patient is left recovering from serious wounds. Yet the professional in 'health care' can always *initially* be deceived as it is easy for a person seeking to fool a physician, social worker, psychologist or therapist to do so. It must be remembered that, unlike the police, the 'human service' professional is seeking to enter into an alliance with the client, and has to start with belief in that person. Without such acceptance, the development of trust cannot be established. Consequently, in this sense, we are the easiest people in the world to mislead initially.

Conversely, there is some evidence from psychology that by an unconscious use of approval, in different signals, we can begin to shape our clients' response to fit our theoretical perspective. This appears to occur not only in classic ego-dynamic, but also in behavioural terms. More recently it is seen in concerns about the later effects of child sexual abuse (e.g. Bagley 1984; Egeland *et al.* 1987; Yeo and Yeo 1993).

The alliance between the political and neo-Freudian mental health was best epitomized in a book by Banton. In a brilliant introduction, Peter Leonard (1985) wrote: 'Central to a socialist conception of change, is the process of practice.' He then drew upon Mao, who said: 'If you want to know a certain thing, you must personally participate in the struggle to change the reality of that thing.' Leonard went on: 'The separation of theory from practice is a feature of the bourgeois social order, which socialists consistently struggle against.' This matches Marx and Engels's view that 'in revolutionary activity, the changing of one's self coincides with the changing of circumstances'. Leonard stated that it is a pity that this complexity is not better understood, as there are far-reaching implications for the politics of the far left.

This is a very insightful statement, as the problem of lack of awareness of how people are 'socially constructed' is especially significant in the field of mental health and mental illness. The dominant models of treatment are based upon an understanding of the individual as essentially prior to the social order, rather than as historically constructed within it. Social factors are seen as influencing the incidence and distribution of some mental illness, but the absence of some theoretical appreciation of the deeply embedded structural determinants of health leads to a practice which remains fundamentally individualistic and asocial. Leonard argued, and we would agree, that no approach to mental health is conceivable unless account is taken of class, gender, ethnicity and, we would add, age, physical health and sexual orientation as other significant determinants. Leonard urged a subversive approach in mental health, and persistently argued that 'mental health care is a significant arena of socialist, feminist, and anti-racist practice'.

It was 1984 when Peter Leonard wrote this, almost at the height of the power of the New Right in Britain and North America, and perhaps this reflects the dilemma for all practitioners: that writers are always perhaps a decade late. This is exemplified by what was called the 'psychiatric deluge', written about in the 1960s, which was said to reflect the ego-dynamic-dominated British social work, but this was already *passé* by the late 1950s. The 'political deluge' of the 1970s, seen in writers such as Pritchard and Taylor (1978), culminated in Day's *Social Work and Social Control* (1981), which reflected an apparently politically pre-occupied social and health care profession. Yet another paradox is that in Day's small empirical study he found that the clients of probation officers accepted the control as well as the care elements as compatible in the service. As far as political subversion went, the reality was that in the public agencies, such as the NHS, social services and education, the 'deluge' had passed and almost the opposite situation existed, with a majority of public sector professionals voting Tory, or certainly not Labour. Even at the height of the political interest, a quarter of social workers voted Conservative, and Marxist social workers were conspicuous only by being vociferous, to hide their essentially minority status (Walton 1976).

Let us ask the question, have the past twenty years improved the state of the mentally ill? While we might say we have a better understanding of the social constraining and shaping factors, it must be very questionable whether more has been achieved. Rolf Olson's early critique of the libertarian campaign for the Mental Health Act 1983 still stands: 'too much about rights, and not enough about resources'. This is confirmed when levels of national expenditure are reviewed.

The obstacles and opportunities of a sociological perspective

It is reiterated that a sociological perspective is a prerequisite for any informed, progressive field of study concerned with the human phenomena. Without a sociological perspective, observers, researchers, practitioners and actors are restricted by a set of social predeterminates, which means that all that will be seen is what will be expected to be seen, as we will be unaware of the influence upon ourselves and others of power hierarchies, be they gender, ethnic, age or sexual orientation. All these are interactive and collectively are inimical to an objective analysis and evaluation. Crucially, perhaps, a sociological approach shows the potential for confirmation of the *status quo*, seen in the phenomenon of the 'self-fulfilling prophecy'. The 'iatrogenesis effect', technically a doctor-caused disease, is a phenomenon that, it is now recognized, can inadvertently affect any professional, because a less than insightful and aware response might damage clients. Thus, for the person, family, community, professional and politician alike, there are a series of interrelated external social factors which are undoubtedly associated with a whole range of positive and negative social attributes, and which along a continuum may be contributively causal. The classic example is seen with unemployment. For a minority, to be out of work is liberating and a beginning of humanity. For the vast majority, however, it is a distressing experience, and for a significant minority it is the lip of their own particular precipice (Warr 1987).

Without the iconoclasm of sociology, we would still be worshipping the idols of yesterday. We would not be able to use the Popperian insight of the relativity of science and of scientific investigation. We could not even maximize our knowledge from history or geography, or the 'individualistic' knowledge base of psychology or the bio-medical sciences.

A sociological approach is a prerequisite for any practitioner who would engage in life-affecting practice, which includes social work, teaching, medicine, the law and even the priesthood. Indeed we would claim that the imperatives given by Jesus of Nazareth – 'Judge not that you be not judged' and 'Why beholdst thou the mote that is in thy brother's eye but considerest not the beam that is in thine own eye; first cast the beam out of thine own eye and then shalt thou see clearly' (Matthew 7 : 2) – are a kind of early sociology of psychological sequelae. Without understanding social antecedents and extant and possible future influences, we can never see clearly. However, all these positives can, if *misused*, become obstacles to the practitioner, not least because: 'The old order changes, yielding place to new, lest one good custom should corrupt the world' (Tennyson).

The biggest critique of sociology actually comes from an important sociological insight, that of reification. This is where the individual is replaced by the concept, or role, so that an idea is converted into a material objectification, and in effect the role carrier becomes a thing. In practice, this means that some sociological insights become corporate or concrete 'facts', so that the critique about compulsion and control, while very valid, is transformed in the minds of the reader, who assumes that *all* psychiatrists, social workers and doctors are motivated *only* by an obligation to the state. Extreme critics, such as Gostin, could sombrely juxtapose British psychiatry, with its history of progress albeit yet incomplete, with the totalitarian abuse of some psychiatrists in Russia, and at the time be taken seriously. Gostin and the like failed to point out that these undoubted abuses were the minority, not the norm. And even such balanced and empirically influenced sociologists as Pilgrim and Rogers (1993), in their desire to combat racism, which we all share, allow themselves to slide over into hyperbole, as they link the British mental health service with the worst of the USSR and Nazism. This is not to gainsay that bad psychiatric practices, and regrettably there are still a fair number, are dehumanizing and degrading. Nor is it wrong to say that some wards, units, old people's homes and the rest are sometimes run for the convenience of staff to the detriment of patients, but they are not the majority, and often the staff are common victims. 'Convenience' is a rational response to an irrational and under-resourced situation, and sometimes it can be the only feasible way to run the inadequately funded service. So the staff do their best, but fall short of what they know to be the most effective.

There is a lovely Yiddish word 'kervetch', which describes the kind of person who watches another work, criticizes him or her for shortcomings, but stands on the side, keeping his or her hands clean and giving no practical assistance. This can be not only demoralizing, but sometimes counter-productive, and almost a form of sociological iatrogenesis. The danger is that, in our focus upon the imperfect, we perpetrate the English attribute of only blaming and never praising. Sociology must ask the question, even with the restricted NHS resource, as to why it is that, of all professions, nursing and medicine still top the list of public approval and admiration. It should be remembered that today's general public have never been better informed or more willing to be critical, but still recognize that their dominant experience of the NHS is positive. Not surprisingly, some doctors would challenge sociologists to a public appreciation competition, and qualifying arguments on the part of sociology about alienation would not get us very far. To be fair, sociology is coming back into the mainstream of making a positive contribution to social work and medicine, seen in the work of the likes of Turner (1992) and Shilling (1993), who recognize that 'the body is more than just a mere social construct'. Experience suggests that most sociologists with an abdominal pain, other than one caused by the excess of the night before, quickly seek the secure reassurance of modern clinical medicine.

Power to the consumer – empowerment

There has been a growing focus upon 'empowering' the client, user and consumer. Yet there is a longstanding truism of 'ask the patient' within medicine. We followed this approach and sought user views about our practice, in a series of consumer surveys, which produced what some would think were very unexpected findings.

The first concerned a sample of 153 single homeless people (Pritchard and Clooney 1994). In brief, we found these quintessential victims of modern capitalism to be surprisingly orthodox in their attribution of what causes homelessness. For them it was not unemployment but predominantly drink and drugs. Clearly they needed more psycho-social information to understand why people take up such lifestyles. But, more importantly, we asked to what extent people from among a range of agencies and practitioners had been either helpful or unhelpful, and for examples. Families and friends were voted the most important; almost by definition there was a fair degree of ambivalence, but clearly they were still the most important source of support. There then followed probation officers, general practitioners, hospital staff and the rest, about whom the vast majority gave positive examples of general helpfulness and only a minority held negative views. There were, however, three groups who received a majority of negative responses – the police, social security office and housing benefits staff – predominately because they had failed to deal with them as 'individuals, just bloody numbers to them'. Yet for all three groups some respondents described positive experiences, respectively 15, 20 and 35 per cent.

A second consumer survey was carried out among current probationers, who more or less confirmed the profile we had discovered earlier among the homeless. Among these former offenders the police were not totally castigated *provided* they offered a person-specific response (Ford *et al.* 1995). It must be stressed that the psycho-social antecedents of both samples were archetypal for disadvantaged people. For example, among the probationers, a third had experience of being in care when they were children, yet they appreciated the efforts made on their behalf.

A third survey concerned current adolescent clients and their parents in the caseload of the education welfare officer. Over 90 per cent valued the experience. What proved to be important to all groups of respondents, irrespective of service, were the common humanizing attributes of interest, trust, confidentiality, respect and reliance, which actually scored higher than practical aid, although this was also seen to be important.

Thus, despite the sociological critique of professionals, it would seem that most human beings not only appreciate but also gain benefit from a client-centred approach, which seeks to maximize potential resources available and crucially engages in a rapport that enhances the individual's self-esteem, individuality and citizenship. Before the surveys, as Bailey and Ward (1994) showed, practitioners were not optimistic about how they would be viewed, apparently because of a combination of the undermining of sociology and a scapegoating 'bad press'.

George Bernard Shaw criticized the social sciences for illuminating yesterday, but leaving the present and the future in inky blackness. This was perhaps classically illustrated by Kathleen Jones who, in her very important and influential work *Social Policy and Mental Health* (1959), demonstrated that the imperfections of the mental health service had evolved from the nineteenth century. She, like the rest, 'blamed' the professionals. In an incredibly ahistorical review she condemned a Lord Chancellor, Eldon, for the shortcomings of the old Lunacy Act 1890, which undoubtedly contributed to filling up the asylums, for at the time there was little appreciation that the mentally ill could and did recover. Thus, with the advantage of 20/20 historical hindsight, Jones could ignore the knowledge of the day and convict on the evidence of today's knowledge. Unfortunately, she had learned little because, while her work supported the 'treatment' and therefore medical orientation of the 1959 legislation, she joined the politically correct, highlighted the imperfections of the service, did not lay the blame where the political responsibility was, and supported the 'civil liberties' later incorporated in the 1983 Mental Health Act, which short of resources becomes an attempt to avoid our civil and social justice responsibilities to less advantaged people. Thus Gostin and his allies dominated, screaming for a legal and civil liberties approach to the mentally ill, partly justified by protecting them from wicked professionals. Jones actually castigated this approach in the nineteenth century, as it resulted in the worst excesses and the evolution of warehousing asylums, because there was *only* an administrative, legal, social response to individual need. To us, the safeguard for the citizen who may be a sufferer is that first within any necessary organizational structural protection should be professionals who are committed to preserving and enhancing their clients' individuality and personal citizenship, via respect and involvement with the clients and their families, in a client-specific dialogue.

The 1983 Mental Health Act speaks about a least restrictive approach. We would extend this to the legislation and organizations that seek to give a service. While a minimal bureaucracy will always be essential, not least to ensure equity, the greatest freedom to empower the citizen arises where the individual professional has the greatest discretion for the service of that individual client. We reject utterly the Szaszian view of control via fiscal practice, that the market place frees the patient by creating a service-consumer ethos. Simple empirical evidence from the USA shows that despite the fact that it spends almost twice as much of its GDP on health care as Britain, health care is so market restricted and driven by a *lack of partnership* between client and practitioner, that it has spawned a parasitical legal bureaucracy, which is a major diversion from the primary objectives of health care. What the Americans lack is a tradition of public service professionals whose primary criteria are *professional*, based upon the best available evidence.

The North Americans have yet to learn that such a *social* ethos in the practitioners is the best protection of clients' rights. Conversely, for the practitioner to have a direct financial interest in clients' treatment must always be suspect, because clients can never be sure that they are getting an objective service if there are possible financial incentives to the therapist. This author has seen many American families come to Britain to visit their acutely ill young people, often following accidents. They are simply amazed at what we take for granted, which is that patients should get the treatment they need, the rest being relatively secondary. A great lie has taken hold in British health and community services: 'We can only have the services we can afford', said Margaret Thatcher, but we have not been having what we can afford since 1987, and we still have the third lowest expenditure on health, as a proportion of GDP, in the developed world. Few sociologists seem to appreciate that the health and community service works simply by riding on the backs of dedicated professionals who go the extra mile – sometimes in the rain, and sometimes dangerously.

The socio-economic and services we can afford

The social science perspective has been very illuminating when we consider the financial facts behind the political rhetoric of public services being 'safe in our hands', to quote a phrase. One of the great presentational coups has been in the way government statistics are issued on 'public expenditure', so that the phrase is almost pejorative. In essence there has been a massive shift in income distribution, so that the poor have become poorer and the affluent more rich (HM Treasury 1994), which has been facilitated by the massive switch in taxation from direct to indirect taxes, proportionally decreasing the contribution of the richer citizen, and increasing that of those on modest or low incomes (Lawson 1994).

While most Western European governments have proportionately reduced their welfare support, in particular to the unemployed, the United States, Canada and Britain have seen the biggest reduction, and as Britain is proportionately already spending less of its GDP on health and social services than in, say, 1979 or 1987 (Pritchard 1992c; HM Treasury 1993), this is likely to have further negative and accumulative impacts upon services for the mentally ill and others who face psycho-social demoralization, such as unemployment, and therefore to increase the pressures upon support services. This is at a time when health and social services have 'done more with proportionately less' (House of Commons 1988, 1990), despite the frequent hyperbole of politicians in North America and Western Europe who selectively present expenditure figures to the general public. The fact is of a constant erosion of resources from the support services, which is hidden from the potentially caring general public by the presentation of astronomical figures which, without a proper comparative baseline, such as GDP, are meaningless.

While any person must on reflection agree with Mrs Thatcher that we can only have the services that we can afford, the great skill of British politicians over the past decade has been in hiding the facts from the public. The All-Party

Parliamentary Committee (1992) said that health and social services are 'proportionately doing more with proportionately less', and in the specific field of mental health the real advances are coming from better evaluated and more effective intervention, crucially in partnership with sufferers and families alike, not because of society devoting more to its disadvantaged citizens.

From the United States has come the chilling term 'underclass', which on the one hand is associated with a range of social and psychological pathology, but on the other essentially indicates that such people are excluded from the market place, usually because they are unemployed, irrespective of the reason (Jenck and Peterson 1991). This concept is beginning to be seen as attractive in Western Europe, as the 'underclass' is seen to be a drain on the resources of the rest of us. There are some who are comfortable with the rediscovery of the concept of callous Victorian inhumanity, the 'deserving and undeserving poor'. In essence this reflects the old song: 'It's the same the whole world over, It's the poor what gets the blame.'/It's the rich what gets the pleasure and Isn't it a blooming shame?

Certainly the mentally ill, especially long-term, find themselves lumped within this euphemistic 'underclass', and there is evidence to show that this concept is being actively used by North American and British governments to reduce a whole range of important welfare supports (Duster 1994; Lawson 1994; MacFate *et al.* 1994). This is one reason why the targets for suicide reduction in Great Britain will not be achieved; the other is the impact of unemployment and the differential way in which it has affected previously affluent regions of the UK (Pritchard 1995a). Unemployment, especially long-term unemployment, is almost a coterminous definition of 'underclass'. Is it fanciful to suppose that the 'underclass' will be seen by some as similar to the *Untermenschen* ('sub-humans') of Nazi Germany?

Is this too extreme? Not when we see the whole range of psycho-social problems associated with unemployment. While the vast majority of unemployed people do not become clients of either social or health services, increases in unemployment do engender the classic Durkheimian anomie, and we see unequivocal evidence of increases in anomic behaviour, such as crime and delinquency, child abuse, neglect, divorce, an increase in mental hospital admissions and the extreme of suicide (Steinberg *et al.* 1982; Madge 1983; Box 1988; Dooley *et al.* 1989; Macleod *et al.* 1993; Pritchard 1991; Pritchard *et al.* 1992, 1993). 'Defensive' apathy is one response that blunts the demoralizing effect, and this reaction is easily misunderstood, interpreted as spineless 'acceptance'. But the sense of being rejected by society cannot be over-stressed, and the unemployed are rejected because they are now in the 'underclass'; they are rejected because they are held responsible for their plight; they are rejected because they make us guilty.

Brenner (1983) first developed the empirical model to test Durkheim's notion of anomic suicide, and found that there were statistical correlations of increased suicide with unemployment. Platt (1984), in a seminal review, explored all the methodological difficulties, but could still conclude that there is an interactive link between change in jobs and suicide rates. Platt's work was criticized because it was based mainly upon clinical studies and they possibly lacked national relevance, as people attending as psychiatric outpatients would not be representative. However, when unemployment and suicide rates were examined internationally, evidence was provided to confirm Platt's Durkheimian thesis (Diekstra 1991; Morton 1993). It was found that in the 1960s there was *no* international correlation between joblessness and suicide rates, but by the late 1970s and 1980s there were strong positive associations between rises in unemployment and suicide in the vast majority of the Western world (Pritchard 1990, 1992a). The suicide–unemployment anomic link cannot be ignored, and, in parenthesis, it may be more than coincidence that some of the *worst* increases in child abuse deaths, youth and elderly suicide in the Western world occurred in the USA (Pritchard 1992b, 1993a, b), which had the largest proportional reduction in a whole range of welfare supports (MacFate *et al.* 1994; Duster 1994; Lawson 1994).

Unemployment leads to poverty, and, as the Tory Samuel Johnson knew, 'poverty is the enemy of liberty'. The socialist George Bernard Shaw said: 'it blights all who comes within its purview'. In more enlightened times, we had grown out of the need to scapegoat the poor and tried to create 'one nation', as reflected by Winston Churchill: 'I do not like mixing up morality and unemployment. It is the fact of unemployment that concerns us, not the morals of the unemployed.' How can people exercise comprehensive citizenship, if by virtue of being unemployed their life opportunities and those of their family are reduced (Kong *et al.* 1993)? For some people, who already come from the least advantaged socio-economic groups, unemployment has become an almost permanent state.

At the extreme, unemployment appears to release a whole range of aggressive emotions, fuelling the fires of French and British racism and the revival of German neo-Nazism, and acting as the bedrock of American ghettos of despair. Unemployment creates a mood of rejection, echoed by a minor character in *Macbeth* (III, i) whose words are a chilling prophecy: 'I am one . . . whom the vile blows and buffets of this world hath so incensed that I am reckless what I do to spite the world.' This recklessness not only damages others, but can be turned against the self, into deliberate self-harm, as the person is rejected by and rejects an uncaring society, which declares him or her redundant from citizenship, a member of the 'underclass'.

Influence of culture upon suicide

What can a sociological approach teach us about suicide and, more importantly, its prevention? Of course grand theoretical ideas and broad brush painting are stimulating, interesting and useful, but, almost like Freudian psychology, something that explains everything explains nothing in the specifics. But when the sociological allies itself with other disciplines and other perspectives and examines its insight impartially then there can be real progress.

An example of such an approach is current work on the influence of culture upon patterns of suicide. We have mentioned how in the West, and in Japan, Hong Kong and Singapore (oriental countries strongly influenced by Western structures, both social and economic), men killed themselves significantly more

Table 6   Suicide by age, gender and place of domicile in China (rates per million)

| | | Age | | | | | | |
	All ages	15–24	25–34	35–44	45–54	55–64	65–74	75+
All China 1988								
Males	150	158	138	154	160	277	499	901
Females	195	304	177	184	186	265	443	710
Female/male								
ratio	1.30	1.92	1.28	1.19	1.16	0.96	0.89	0.79
Rural China 1990								
Males	203	162	188	191	252	463	800	1395
Females	246	351	320	217	245	325	510	743
Female/male								
ratio	1.21	2.17	1.70	1.14	0.97	0.70	0.64	0.53
Urban China 1990								
Males	81	61	76	86	85	131	252	589
Females	91	103	93	77	89	122	201	463
Female/male								
ratio	1.12	1.69	1.22	0.90	1.05	0.93	0.80	0.79
Rural/urban ratio 1990								
Males	2.51	2.66	2.47	2.22	2.96	3.53	3.17	2.37
Females	2.70	3.41	3.44	2.82	2.75	2.66	2.54	1.60

often than women. Suicide also occurred less in the apparently cohesive areas of rural Europe and North America, and more often in the large alienating urban conurbations. Recently we used a social science perspective to look at the suicide mortality statistics for the People's Republic of China. It became clear that the profiles we had earlier identified and expected to be found in China, namely the gender and urban bias, were highly specific to what has become a ubiquitous Westernized culture (Pritchard 1993a, 1995c). We have mentioned how parasuicide rates in twelve European cities were very varied, even within the same country. Table 6 displays figures of immediate sociological import. A brief explanatory note is needed. The first part of Table 6 shows an 'all China' rate for 1988. The later figures are for 1990 and are presented for 'certain rural and urban' areas representative of China (WHO 1994). The differences in rates between male and female, and rural and urban areas, are remarkable, especially when compared with Western patterns.

The 1988 all-China figures reverse the Western suicide patterns, with *more* female suicides than male until the late fifties age group. The dominance of female rates over male is confirmed in urban and especially rural China. Perhaps the biggest surprise was the substantially higher suicide rate in the rural rather than the urban areas throughout *all* age bands for both sexes.

It should be noted that the all-China male suicide rates were not especially high; for example, Australian, Canadian, French, German, Japanese and US male rates were higher. However, all-China female suicide rates are the *highest* in the world, though urban China female rates are actually lower than those in Austria, Belgium, Denmark, Finland, France, Germany, Japan, Sweden and Switzerland.

The significance of this is the overwhelming evidence of a *socio-cultural influence upon suicide rates*, which frankly we did not expect to be so clear-cut. What the influences are is difficult to say. Mainland Chinese colleagues, in confidence, were not surprised as they saw the rates as a reflection of the lower status of women in China, but especially in the rural areas. Zhang Xianliang's (1989) stark description of life in rural China helps Westerners to appreciate something of our affluence, but it would seem likely that compared with facilities in urban China, there will be fewer psychiatric services, which must make some contribution to the huge disagreement between urban and rural rates. Experience of urban Southern China suggests that it is probably more affluent than some of the former Warsaw Pact countries, such as Bulgaria, Hungary and Romania.

Recently evidence has emerged of marked improvements in female status in China, particularly in urban areas (Shenon 1994). This has followed the effect of the traditional emphasis upon having male children, within the context of the 'one-child family' policy. There is now an absolute shortage of females, a gap of 2 per cent in rural China and 3 per cent in urban areas, with a 6 per cent difference between males and females in the fifteen to twenty-four age band in urban China (WHO 1994). As Shenon puts it, women's 'scarcity value could raise women's status'.

There are, of course, many questions we cannot answer. For example, is this apparent gender bias due to the fact that women are undervalued? Within a culture that prizes family almost above anything else, and in a culture that has a highly stigmatizing response to mental illness, the Chinese statistics, if nothing else, give rise to a whole new range of hypotheses that merit testing, and show quite clearly that by using the broad brush of the sociological approach, we can say with confidence that social, cultural and gender factors do influence suicide and suicidal behaviour.

This result had not been expected because the variation in international suicide rates suggested that, while we accept cultural influence, there may also be different constitutional loadings for mental illness, psychiatric depression in particular. This might partly account for the high rate among Hungarians and their ethnic cousins the Finns; or for the lower suicide rate among Hispanic and African Americans than Anglo-Saxons, although in second and third ethnic generations in the USA the rates move towards the mean, probably reflecting the interaction of *both* cultural and constitutional endowment (Holinger 1987; Sorenson and Golding 1988; Vernon and Phillipe 1988). Until we undertook this analysis, though we recognized that cultural factors do influence suicide, we had not thought that the effect was so pronounced. In the Chinese data there are virtually no grounds for a 'genetic weighting' argument that would account for the rural and urban discordance; perhaps Durkheim was more prescient than we had thought.

Gender and Western suicide: paradox in the triumph over sexism

Women have had a 'bad press' and treatment from a male-dominated mental health service over the past 200 years (e.g. Millett 1991; Usher 1991). Although it is not yet fully complete, there has been a revolutionary change in the status of women in the past twenty years, seen in women's improved educational and occupational opportunities (Allen 1990; Hewitt 1993). There are as many women in higher education as men, and they are almost co-equal in numbers in the employed workforce, although differentiation continues, especially with women in more part-time and lower paid jobs (CSO 1994). We would not subscribe to the notion that for progress to be made it is necessary to suffer, but there is evidence pointing to a paradoxical outcome within the social paradigm of suicide of women. Ferriera de Castro *et al.* (1988) noted the growing confidence of women in Portugal and predicted that as women's socio-economic aspirations came to fruition, especially in relation to work, their patterns of suicidal behaviour would become similar to those of men. To some extent this has happened in mainland Europe, as can be seen in the positive correlations between women's unemployment and changes in their suicide rate (Pritchard 1992a). These trends have also been demonstrated in Britain in the suicide rates of under forty-year-old women (Pritchard 1995a). While women value their socio-economic contribution more than their menfolk, this is age differentiated, suggesting that it is younger women who have benefited from the gender revolution and have equal aspirations (Pritchard 1990). But here lies the paradox: as there is a growing convergence between the gender in respect to socio-economic achievement and aspirations, younger women are dying proportionately more often than older women, which follows the direction predicted by Ferriera de Castro *et al.* (1988).

In a majority of Western countries average suicide rates for women have fallen, reflecting relative improvements in psychiatry, community services and the prescribing habits of general practitioners. However, while the rate has virtually halved in the UK, these gains have not been found amongst suicide in under forty year olds; in *every* region of Britain, younger women are dying significantly more often from suicide than other women. What leads to this?

The answer lies in the biographies of two almost contemporaneous women, Sylvia Plath and Jill Tweedie (Wagner-Martin 1991; Tweedie 1993). Both were born in the 1930s, were middle class and, compared to the majority of women of their generation, were well off. Yet both felt frustrated by the imposition of 'inferior' status. Plath came from a loving and devoted home, but Tweedie's home's male chauvinism was personified in Major Tweedie, who was also a victim, and her home life appeared affectionless. Both women felt the desire to succeed, and felt their intellect and aspirations derided, or at best patronized. Both engaged in acts of deliberate self-harm following an apparent domestic 'failure', though this was on only one occasion with Tweedie. Both felt the dual pressures of having to compete in a male-dominated and therefore discriminating world, while at the same time being expected to be the competent housewife, mother, etc. These are typical of the pressures on 'new women', which were not present for the previous generation of 'successful' women. An example is Virginia Woolf, essayist and novelist, who made major contributions not only to inter-war British literature, but also to female emancipation. While Woolf was sub-jected to many pressures, including mental illness that led to her suicide, there is no hint that she had to be omni-competent in all gender roles (Gordon 1992). This appears to be largely a question of social class. The relative egalitarianism from the 1960s onwards has saddled middle-class women with many extra 'burdens' in addition to their role as professional people.

The author has seen a number of examples where professional women find enormous conflicts in their omni-competent roles, which, like Plath and Tweedie, *they have taken on*: dual workloads no man would even consider; if he is a senior professional, then he feels he is doing well by 'helping occasionally' around the home. Some women feel that they have to be equals in the professional world *and* be 'super mums', and then wonder, unrealistically, why they sometimes feel overwhelmed, inadequate and then depressed about their 'failure'. Experientially this is almost a parody of Brown *et al.*'s (1990) description of the low self-esteem of working-class women, who feel themselves to be so lowly valued. The 'new woman' may be in danger of over-reaching herself, as it appears that the 'new man' has yet truly to equal her contribution in the home. Add the 'baby blues' to this concoction, and we begin to see a worrying trend, as women are in danger of becoming victims of their own success.

Here lies the final sociological lesson, that invariably the social phenomenon described is relative, and is part of a process that will occur at a different pace in different groups or categories of people. The interactional impact of further progress towards equal opportunities has yet to be worked out in society. We must ensure that we do not inadvertently make some pay too great a price.

The social dimension of suicide cannot be over-stressed, but it needs to be examined in alliance with those in the front-line, and not become an obstacle. Practitioners of all disciplines will need to include the social perspective in the search for effective prevention of suicide, the issue to which we now turn.

CHAPTER 7

AN INTEGRATED NEEDS-LED INTERVENTION AND TREATMENT MODEL

An integrated bio-psycho-social approach to reducing suicidal behaviour

Based upon what is known about the causal factors that contribute to suicide, we can develop a needs-led intervention and treatment model. Our model contains three key elements, which are interactive and affected by timing factors. In terms of timing, the greater are the stresses, the bigger is the accumulative impact, which can compound any inherent or predisposing vulnerability.

First, the model consists essentially of the bio-physiological. In terms of mental disorder this initially demands that the treatment approach is the appropriate pharmacology. Second are the affective/cognitive factors such as the individual's mood and belief systems, which are directly linked with his or her behaviour. The third element are those social factors that might retard or speed up the crisis points, which can lead to deliberate self-harm and suicide. One difficulty for sufferer, family and professional alike is that, even in a 'chronic' situation, acute or crisis situations can erupt, increasing the risk of damage. Hence there is an immediacy of need to contain the current crisis, so that it does not become an emergency.

Timing is an important factor affecting the psycho-social elements within the treatment approach. All are influenced by past, current or future situations. Thus, in respect of behaviour, we need to determine what has occurred in the past, whether it is different from the present and how it might, or should, change in the future. These considerations would need to be included in the intervention goals. In terms of affect and cognition, individuals might need to understand their previous as well as current affective cognitive situations, so that they can engage in realistic goal settings, and to understand the previous or current social factors that impinge upon them and their family, as at all times we seek to stall the crisis in the immediate future.

It may at this stage be worth recalling the earlier model for differentiating between bio-physiological and social factors as contributions to suicide and deliberate self-harm, because once we have determined the likely theme, it can assist us in *prioritizing* where our initial and, we hope, most effective intervention will lie. Thus if there is any mental disorder present, the person will require either antidepressants or the appropriate psychotropic drugs to control his or her schizophrenia, as soon as possible. We should never forget, however, that the prerequisite for entry into any effective treatment alliance is the establishment of an effective rapport via a constructive supporting relationship. Experience and common sense would agree with Lazarus (1985), who argued that, irrespective of the type of intervention, it is always enhanced by a positive relationship with the sufferer. Such a comment may seem somewhat of a cliché but it is often missed; the world is full of self-preoccupied people; hence we are highly appreciative of the experience of having someone listen to and concentrate upon us, which may be one reason why short-term work often has such good results. Certainly the creation and sustaining of a rapport is a prerequisite, though the art is in *sustaining* the supportive approach over a reasonable time. But can we assess/predict risk? The following explores a number of predictive instruments.

Predictive scales: assessing risk

Often in the face of suicide the practitioner needs to have some reasonable assessment of risk of suicide. However, as most assessment and predictive scales have emerged largely from research, there are limits to their value in the open-ended hurly-burly situation of day-to-day practice. Pallis *et al.* (1984) remind us that the various scales available have been *validated* on particular suicidal sub-groups, and the tighter the parameters the better the fit. For example, they developed scales based upon former deliberate self-harm patients, who then either had repeat DSH or actually died. However, this would be of little value if it was used on a *non-previous* DSH person, even though Pallis *et al.* were able to discriminate the likely suicides following a multivariate discriminate function analysis. They found in people who eventually *committed* suicide the following relevant factors: they were likely to be older, had some form of communication of their intent, belonged to classes 1 and 2, and were male and living alone.

As the authors of the best predictive scales (Beck *et al.* 1974; Lettieri 1974; Motto 1985) have emphasized, they are essentially research tools or *guides* for practitioners. While they are useful in determining the *degree* of safety, we always have to remember that there will be false negatives as well as false positives. Beginning with cautious qualifications, recently Kaplan *et al.* (1994) compared clinical face-to-face interviews with written self-report questionnaires. They found that the written approach, within the structure of the self-report form, made it easier for some people to admit their involvement in suicidal ideation or behaviour.

The scale of Beck *et al.* (1974) is still widely used, and concerns suicide *intent*. It was developed from a population who had been involved in DSH, and explored the persons' circumstances but also has some self-report elements. There are fifteen separate items to be scored, centred on four themes: the degree of isolation; the timing and precautions taken against discovery; the degree of preparation and planning for the event; whether or not there was an overt communication of intent before the act. More recent research would lead one to include a question about the degree of hopelessness present (Beck *et al.* 1993a), and certainly the factors of past, current and perceived future would be very illuminative. If all four themes were present and the person demonstrated a sense of hopelessness, there would be a very high risk level indeed.

Maris *et al.* (1992), in an ingenious exercise, produced five detailed case records to test out various experts' views, using a range of scales, as to outcome in terms of whether or not there was subsequent suicidal behaviour. This author had three accurate positives and one accurate negative, but 'failed' the test by giving a false negative. The cases were drawn from the United States, and the suicide the author 'missed' died from gunshot wounds, which is a salutary reminder of the importance of the accessibility of lethality. Thus it may have been that such a person would not have died in Britain because his or her impulsive distress was not matched by the accessibility of guns. The author's acknowledgement of fallibility was not too difficult, however, as *none* of Maris *et al.*'s experts was 100 per cent accurate; indeed, I was slightly above average. The most accurate scales proved to be the 'Suicide Death Prediction Scale' of Lettieri (1974), followed by the 'Clinical Instrument to Estimate Suicide Risk' of Motto (1985). What is helpful to the practitioner is that these scales are based on practitioners' observation and knowledge of the client, and do not require direct self-report.

Lettieri scales have a shortened version, and are therefore a useful rule-of-thumb guide. They appear to differentiate between men and women over and under the age of forty. Key factors for *older men* are:

1 Have had a divorce or a recent serious loss.
2 Depression with sympathetic (somatic) symptoms.
3 Element of aggression and anger in their affect.
4 Refuse or avoid help.
5 Have been involved with previous DSH.
6 Failure in a major role area of their lives, such as family or employment.

A clear positive in *all* six means that a person is at extremely high risk.

For *younger men*, and it must be remembered that the scale was based upon an American sample, the factors are:

1 Recently divorced, separated or unmarried.
2 Caucasian.
3 In their mood they have clear suicidal thoughts.
4 And very often persistent suicidal ideation.
5 Particularly dangerous is an element of a homicide component in the ideation.

It will be remembered that there is a longstanding awareness of suicide following homicide.

With regard to *mature women* the factors are:

1 They will be single.
2 More likely to belong to classes 1 and 2.
3 Take great care in timing and planning.
4 Have minimal or no family available.

Finally, for *young females* the factors are:

1 The non-availability of close friends in the immediate neighbourhood.
2 A marked sense of independence.
3 An inability to develop or sustain warm interdependent permanent relationships.

It would be quite wrong to seek to simplify these scales any further. Their real
value is that they can help the practitioner, in a specific situation, to make better
client-specific judgements. They can assist in alerting the worker to the degree
of risk which needs to be addressed by appropriate action or by ensuring that
appropriate process and support is available.

Reasons for living

An old social work truism is that we need to identify not only the negatives,
but also, where possible, the strengths, which we should seek to reinforce and
strengthen. As mentioned earlier, it has been noted that women who have
children commit suicide less frequently than child-free women. Linehan (1985)
developed a scale described as 'Reasons for living' which in essence is made up
of positive counter-indicators against deliberate self-harm or suicide. There are
six themes:

1 Survival and coping beliefs, hopes of change.
2 Responsibility to family and child-related concerns.
3 A fear of suicide.
4 A fear of or concern about social disapproval.
5 Linked to the above, moral objections about suicide.
6 A view that suicide is a sign of weakness and that there are canons against self-
slaughter.

Thus, while we must always consider the risk of suicide with a person who is
depressed, we should also consider both the negative and the positive indicators.
    A major concern for many practitioners is the question: do we ask the person
directly about suicide ideas, or does such a question put an idea into his or her
mind that was not there previously? On balance, certainly with adults, once you
have established a minimal relationship that sets the person at reasonable ease,
you can ask: 'How are you in your spirits? How desperate are things for you?
Have you ever thought of ending it all? Have you ever harmed yourself?' With
adolescents it can be a little more problematic. It may be more constructive to

approach these questions much more indirectly, but they have to be tackled and the practitioner need not be afraid of the answers. One important reassuring element is that the person may well have suicidal ideation, but in purely statistical terms if one predicted that a person would not kill himself or herself, this would be the right answer in nine out of ten cases. However, despite workers' frequent reluctance to ask this leading question, often the sufferer is very grateful to have the opportunity to express his or her sense of stress and desperation to someone who is non-judgemental and accepting, and where necessary, can offer guidance and protection.

Treatment of psychiatric-related suicide

The objectives of any intervention and treatment to prevent suicide must be to reduce the risk, by intervening in those areas which are most associated with either suicide or deliberate self-harm.

The corollary of this means that we deal with the known dominant causes, though we would emphasize that this is schematic. At this stage we concentrate upon the bio-physiological and the pharmacological, but we reiterate the prerequisite of positive therapeutic relationships, as what is important is not pharmacology or psycho-social support or counselling, but the appropriate combination of all elements. Nevertheless in view of the high level of psychiatric disorder associated with suicide we must first address the question of treatment of the underlying psychiatric problems.

Drug treatment: the first stage of a tripartite treatment model

Helen Weisman in the early 1980s developed an integrated approach to the treatment of unipolar affective disorder, which was based upon the combination of antidepressants and social work psycho-social support over time (Weisman 1981; Weisman and Klerman 1990). In brief, cases were randomly allocated to social work and antidepressants versus antidepressants alone, and the combined approach had far better results. Blackburn (1981) brought together the work of the cognitive therapists into a combined treatment format. They found that cognitive therapy enhanced pharmacological treatment and was superior in the treatment of depression to drugs alone or cognitive therapy alone, which matched Weisman's findings. Thus we have known for over a decade that the combined approach has better outcomes with depression than a uni-dimensional approach.

Gibbons (1978) found that while there was no difference between a GP-treated cohort of attempted suicides and a social work treated group, the task-centred social workers were able to demonstrate marked improvements in a range of psycho-social functioning. Generally there is agreement that with unipolar disorder antidepressants are necessary, first to reduce the intensity of the symptoms, and second to speed up the recovery. However, it has to be recognized that because of the extensive prescribing of antidepressants, currently estimated by Henry (1993) to be 1.9 per cent of the whole NHS drug bill, they are the most common self-damaging drug used in Western Europe and North America (Mendleson and Rich 1993; Gunnell 1994; Wiedenmann and Weyerer 1994).

In respect of the acute stages of schizophrenia, the evidence is quite clear that psychotropic drugs are necessary to reduce the impact of the distress and contain the symptoms, and more importantly to enable sufferers to be able to communicate better with those around them. Again there is evidence that, in comparison with placebo alone or psychotherapy alone, drugs are superior, but drugs *and* psychotherapy/psycho-social support is even more superior (Hogerty 1986a,b; Weisman and Klerman 1990).

The combined benefits are probably self-evident. The counsellor therapist can address family issues, social supports and wider communication, and optimal follow-up and close supervision and support can aid proper drug compliance and give an early indication of any side-effects, thus helping to find an optimal drug level for the individual. It must be recognized that after the acute stage of depression or, particularly, schizophrenia, some patients can be extremely distressed by side-effects, and easily accessible support workers can help them to deal with them much more effectively by assisting better individualized prescribed levels.

Drugs and their problems and potential

Considering the frequency of antidepressant prescriptions, it is evident that there is a huge market (Henry 1993), and there has been considerable interest in the benefits of various drug groups. Fluoxetine is one of the newer serotonin drugs (Frankenfeld *et al.* 1994), and there was some suggestion that its use led to more deliberate self-harm episodes. A controlled study conducted over a year found that there was little or no difference between the four main types of drugs used: fluoxetine, impramine, mianserin and traserdone (Montgomery 1993).

Van Praag and Lecrubier (1992) emphasized the importance of minimal toxicity. This is supported by a number of writers (Henry 1993) because undoubtedly these are powerful substances and, in that sense, dangerous. Van Praag and Lecrubier point pretty conclusively to the improved effectiveness of antidepressants, but we reassert that drugs should be used within a combined treatment programme, including psycho-social supports.

One other problem which cannot be ignored is that a third of all suicides, not deliberate self-harmers but actual deaths, had seen their general practitioner and/or psychiatrist within three weeks of their death (Obafunwa and Busuttil 1994b). This suggests that they were not adequately supported, especially, as Modestein and Schwarzenbach (1992) point out, because there was often inadequate compliance in taking the medication. Isacsson *et al.* (1992), in a fifteen-year study, examined the use of antidepressants and suicide rates in a Swedish county. Of the suicides, despite three-quarters of the patients having medical attention, fewer than 15 per cent were on antidepressants. This would suggest inadequate diagnosis, too little use of antidepressants or a lack of community supervision.

There are two other controversial aspects to drug treatment, one of which is the long-term use of Lithium to treat depression. In a Finnish study, Isometsa *et al.* (1994) examined all completed suicides in Finland, and were able to identify a small sub-sample who had prolonged use of Lithium. Lithium had been used as a prophylactic to deal with their mood disorder, and one of its benefits is that people with bipolar affective disorder (people who sometimes have a manic disorder as well as a depression) seem to do particularly well on Lithium. When examining the completed suicides, Isometsa *et al.* found that 85 per cent of the victims had not adequately complied with the pharmacological treatments, but only two out of the almost 1,400 suicides had actually used Lithium to kill themselves. It is acknowledged that for some patients a serious side-effect can be kidney disorder (Van Praag and Lecrubier 1992), but it does seem that with careful monitoring this can be substantially reduced or virtually eliminated. Nevertheless, it is problematic. The second controversial aspect is the use of depot drugs in some forms of schizophrenia. In an attempt to overcome the problem of inadequate self-dosage, the drug is usually given intra-muscularly and released over a period. Thus the person may require an injection only every second month. Modicate is the drug most often given in this way for people with schizophrenia, and generally has good results, except the problem of side-effects. It is believed that with adequate education of sufferers and/or their families, and accessibility to a support worker, side-effect problems could be reduced substantially.

The serotonin and suicide ideation hypothesis provides an example of complexity. One of the most promising developments in psycho-pharmacology has been the identification of the association between impulsivity and low serotonin, which is associated with aggressive and suicidal behaviour (Bourgeois 1991). The problem is that the link is not clear-cut, though it promises to be a potential measure of the risk of suicidal behaviour. Cheetham *et al.* (1991), in a very detailed review, highlighted the difficulties and concluded that low serotonin *may* be associated with impulsivity, which in turn may be linked to suicidal ideation. But as a number of studies have been based upon post-mortem results, are the neurotransmitter patterns the result of the violent action; that is, which is cause and which effect? According to Bourgeois (1991), there is persuasive evidence that the impulsivity link is unequivocal, because of findings of lowered cerebrospinal serotonin levels related to other actions, such as murder, arson and alcoholism. This was confirmed recently by Nordstrom *et al.* (1994) in respect of levels following deliberate self-harm and subsequent actual suicide (incidentally, they found that 11 per cent of ninety-two patients died within a year by suicide). However, the association was statistical in that while people with lower cerebrospinal fluid (CSF) serotonin concentrations had double the subsequent suicide rate, not *all* those with lowered levels re-engaged in suicidal behaviour, though some patients with *higher* than median levels of serotonin concentrations did so.

Relevant in terms of prevention and treatment, especially if we can reduce the impulsive element, is the development of the drug Paroxetine, which is a serotonin re-uptake inhibitor (SRI). Bourin and Turpault (1991) claim that this drug is antidepressant and reduces impulsivity, which Montgomery (1993) supports in his British study. Their study found fewer side-effects, especially fewer sedative effects and no 'clinically significant EEG changes'. Anything that is effective *and* reduces side-effects is very welcome, but insufficient is known about what a clinically significant EEG is, and not all have found such unequivocally positive results for SRIs (Frankenfeld *et al.* 1994). Before we try to conclude which anti-depressants may be the best, a brief word is needed about the potential impact of side-effects.

While we acknowledge the necessity of pharmacology in this field, it has to be recognized that many evidently powerful drugs can also have marked side-effects, both in the short term and over a longer period. They can be extremely distressing for clients. For example, regarding psychotropic drugs, some have said they prefer to deal with the voices, rather than to find themselves with psycho-motor disturbances that cause them to grimace uncontrollably, with a disturbed gait, tremors and excessive salivating. Antidepressants can cause severe dryness of mouth and eyes, tinnitus and imbalance, and this can be unpleasant, but perhaps not as bad as anti-schizophrenic pharmacology.

Second, as indicated earlier, despite better prescribing antidepressants and psychotropic drugs have been used as a method of self-killing (e.g. Mendlson and Rich 1993; Wiedenmann and Weyerer 1994), and having large doses of anti-depressants around the house unsupervised is raising the risk stakes, not least for adolescents. Brent *et al.* (1991) showed that access to lethality, in their case parents' guns, was a major factor in eventual suicide, especially in North America, and drugs could play the same role in Britain. Yet when we examine studies of completed suicides (not necessarily caused by drugs) with respect to levels of drugs present in the USA (Mendlson and Rich 1993), Finland (Isometsa *et al.* 1994) and Sweden (Isacsson *et al.* 1994), there is indisputable evidence that the fatalities with depression were *not* receiving adequate dosages of antidepressants; some were not even being treated for psychiatric depression. In parenthesis, we present two important practice points. First, often at post-mortem there was evidence of recent alcohol intake, which for this author is in problematic situations, invari-ably a complicating factor. Second, quite a number of people had died from a combination of hypnotics and sedatives, which, as all three national research teams independently concluded, are a problem and had possibly been missed by therapists of different disciplines. Hence, they urged that where there are sleep complaints, the professional needs to consider an underlying depression.

A very important role for non-medical professionals is to assist in the moni-toring of the medication taken, not only to ensure proper dosage and safety of the drugs but also to oversee whether or not any side-effects are emerging. Some psychiatrists believe that initially, especially with schizophrenia, an adequate dose to contain the patient's symptoms will invariably bring some side-effects. How-ever, on maintenance doses of antidepressants and psychotropic drugs, severe side-effects are unnecessary and indicative of poor non-specific client prescribing, and can be dangerous in themselves, not only in the extreme, fortunately rare, cases of severe physiological reaction, but also in the psycho-social distress of sufferers and their families, which can precipitate discouragement and a reactive form of depression.

Finally, returning to the serotonin hypothesis, Moller and Steinmeyer (1994), in a short-term six-week trial, found *no* differential reduction in suicide idea-tion of those on SRI compared with those on the tricyclic amitriptyline. However,

Montgomery (1993), reviewing the major range of antidepressants, tricyclics and the new SRIs, on balance believed that the sum of the evidence supported the use of SRIs in preference to the tricyclics, because there did not appear to be any evidence that SRIs provoked suicidal ideation or impulsivity. Indeed, they appeared to be a defence against the dangerous aspects of a depressive episode, as they probably reduce aggressive impulsivity against the self or others. Thus they may make a major contribution in bringing down the toll of self-killings, and reassure professionals who often feel helpless in the presence of a person with a history of impulsivity.

Finally, the complexity of drugs treatment for psychiatric depression is seen in the syndrome known as 'seasonal affective disorder'. With this, the sufferer's depression *appears* to be linked to the season of the year, in essence to a lack of sunlight. Some postulated that this might account for the relatively high rate of suicides among the Scandinavian countries, but it would not account for the Austrian or Hungarian rates. What is clear is that a *minority* of people with depression are improved by the use of artificial sunlight (Avery *et al.* 1990). This shows that there is still much to learn about the syndrome of affective disorders and psychiatric depression. Consequently, workers must always look towards the best empirical evidence to guide them in their intervention.

Electro-convulsive therapy and psycho-surgery

The most controversial bio-physiological treatment, electro-convulsive therapy (ECT), does appear, in selected patients and in particular those who do not respond after a month of antidepressants, to be potentially life-saving (Mendleson 1981). The problem with this treatment is that as yet there seems to be no firm understanding of how it works. Thus we have a treatment which has no validated theoretical underpinning. Moreover, because of its misuse in totalitarian regimes, as well as occasionally in the Western world, there is considerable suspicion about the treatment. This is seen in British anti-psychiatry's response to the use of ECT; thus clinicians are now extremely cautious (Haddad and Benbow 1993).

An interesting paper by Tubi *et al.* (1993) looked at the subjective symptoms experienced by people with depression who were treated with actual ECT and simulated ECT. Based upon standardized measures of Hamilton's depression scale, both groups showed a decrease in acute subjective symptoms, but which was greater with actual ECT than with simulated ECT. It appeared that there was a paradoxical effect, in that there may have been an increase in the severity of symptoms after each treatment, but cumulatively the severity of the symptoms was reduced after later treatments. Black *et al.* (1993) tried to analyse the recovery elements in a group of over 400 depressed patients who had received ECT. Those who had made a good recovery were older and had received fewer ECT treatments, but, most importantly, the recovered were less likely to have a secondary depression or require Lithium.

It has to be said from practice experience that clients who have not responded to antidepressants or social support and who have marked suicidal ideation seem to recover more quickly with ECT, which reflects the findings of Mendleson

(1981). Equally, the treatment process has been brought into disrepute by a sometimes thoughtless 'do something' attitude, when little progress is made. It would seem that all should have an open mind and, as always, be client-specific, considering the needs of the person and whether ECT may in certain circumstances be life-saving.

To complete the review of 'controversial treatments', one must look at the notion of psycho-surgery. This is a highly dubious treatment, not least because with our present knowledge the deliberate creation of brain lesions, which is the core of 'leucotomies', is unacceptable. There are case histories of certain clients with seemingly intractable problems, such as totally incapacitating obsessional neurosis, actively seeking partial leucotomies. Nevertheless, despite the relatively minimal trauma done by modern leucotomies, there appears to be insufficient evidence to override the major ethical, as well as scientific, questions associated with psycho-surgery in which the effects of treatment are irreversible. However, as always in life, one should never say never.

Psycho-social treatments for psychiatric-related suicidal situations

As mentioned already, treatment for depression which uses the behavioural cognitive approach allied with drugs has proved to be superior to either drugs or cognitive therapy alone and we will explore this further.

This discussion is based upon the work of Beck (1987), who in turn had built upon the behavioural view that depression is a learned experience. Beck's crucial contribution was to incorporate the notion of a self-perpetuating and circular mode of thinking, which was negative, self-pejorative and self-denigratory. Thus people would not only interpret a positive situation negatively, but if they were in a new diverse situation, they would have a prospective pessimistic view. For example, the pint pot is half empty; it will probably become more empty; he won't enjoy it; because he is not enjoying it, he is a bad person; because he is a bad person, he doesn't deserve either to enjoy it or to fill the pot; and so on. The particular value of the cognitive approach is that it reinforces the rational, acknowledges the centrality of a positive relationship, and can set reasonable and achievable goals for the person.

Beck and his colleagues have developed a range of techniques that are now well established and accessible, not only in the field of psychiatry (Hawton *et al.* 1989; Scott and Stradling 1991), but also for a whole range of psychological and psychiatric problems. It must be emphasized, however, that although the approach is easily accessible for new therapists, it does demand a degree of structured commitment by both client and therapist, which can be time-consuming over the short and medium term. In these days of excessively limited resources, some colleagues in the statutory services may feel that the model is non-feasible, because of the over-emphasis on statutory duties rather than prevention by social services departments (Huxley and Kerfoot 1993). However, such a position is not tenable, especially in view of the British government's intention to reduce suicide rates.

Scott and Stradling (1991) explored the use of group cognitive therapy with depressed people. Following two or three initial individual sessions, it was found to be very positive, with good outcomes and the additional benefit of group reinforcements, group identity and group cohesiveness. Macleod *et al.* (1993) reviewed the use of behaviourally based cognitive treatments for depression and suicidal behaviour. These are again very promising, and relatively easy to assimilate by professionals irrespective of discipline. Perhaps the only weakness of cognitive behaviourial therapy is the need to remember that sometimes there is a need for an advocacy role for clients in an adverse social situation, which traditional clinical psychological, the origins of the approach, has been slow to recognize. It is interesting that Borga *et al.* (1992), looking at long-term functional psychosis in three different areas of Stockholm county, not only identified a range of social problems (two-thirds living alone, two-thirds unemployed) but also demonstrated that schizophrenia was related to poorer social conditions, and such conditions worsened the state of people's schizophrenia. This vicious cycle matches work in Britain (Pritchard *et al.* 1992; Hudson *et al.* 1993; Stewart and Stewart 1993; Pritchard and Clooney 1994), though the Swedish quality of care and accommodation was above that usually found among the British long-term mentally ill (which may be a contributory factor to the continuous fall in Swedish suicide rates).

It is taken as self-evident that the client's welfare rights, including benefits, will be maximized and this will be discussed in greater detail later. The point is not to make invidious comparisons between social and psychological care and intervention, as both are required to deal with the negative compounding interaction of poor social conditions and the deterioration in clients' functioning.

A particularly important approach that seeks to engage the potentially suicidal patient is the work of Linehan, which is a development of the cognitive behavioural therapeutic approach. Her approach is described as 'dialectic behavioural therapy'. It brings together the cognitive understanding of Beck and the discipline of behavioural therapists, and seeks to respond to needs-led treatment in that earlier research identified potential victims as lacking important interpersonal skills, being unable to tolerate distress and having poor problem-solving capacity (Linehan *et al.* 1987, 1993; Macleod *et al.* 1993). Thus her model recognizes a deficit of motivational skills, which sees the vulnerable person being overwhelmed by any new challenge. The 'dialectic' acknowledges the immediate involvement of the client with the therapist, and contains a major concern about the quality of the client's life. There is an agreed hierarchy of treatment goals, which targets potential suicidal threats found in the social stressors, behaviour and attitudes that undermine the quality of life, and not least interpersonal relationships. Treatment is quite intensive and combines individual psychotherapy with group sessions. This is probably one of the most optimistic psycho-social treatment models, especially if it is linked to appropriate drug treatment and any necessary advocacy response. The two most important elements appear to be improving the person's 'problem solving ability' and stimulating 'reasons for living', both factors associated with suicidal behaviour (Strosahl *et al.* 1992; Mzraz and Runco 1994).

This very integrated but focused approach can benefit from the use of reinforcing groups, which, for some clients (after initial reluctance that perhaps typifies those in Britain), brings with it an additional supportive network of mutually sustaining and encouraging people. This is, in other words, a combination of a cognitive behavioural approach and the essentials of social work (Davies 1994).

Recently Linehan and colleagues evaluated the use of dialectic behavioural therapy (DBT) versus usual treatment with that most difficult of groups, people with *borderline personality disorder* with a history of deliberate self-harm. It has to be recognized that DBT was not 100 per cent successful in avoiding repetition of deliberate self-harm, but it was superior in reducing the rate of parasuicide to virtually a third of that with the usual treatment. DBT had only a quarter of the treatment-as-usual hospitalization (11 versus 40 per cent), and over the next eighteen months had fewer suicidal episodes or medical treatment. Interestingly, after the eighteen-month period of DBT, the patients reported less anger and subjectively better social adjustment, which was confirmed at the end of two years by an independent reviewer. No differences were found between either work performances or anxiety states in the two treatment groups (Linehan *et al.* 1993; Sherin and Linehan 1994).

One important practice feature of dialectic behaviour therapy is that it makes a bigger impact in the first six months, which reduces the distress not only for clients, but also for their possible supportive carers. This is of particular promise, remembering the finding of Golacre *et al.* (1993) in Oxfordshire that suicidal behaviour was substantially high *after the discharge* of former psychiatric inpatients. In addition, bearing in mind the relatively poor prognosis of borderline personality disorder, the Linehan approach faced the most clear challenge, and merits wider development.

Treating schizophrenia: families as allies

Perhaps the most tragic hangover from the excesses of the Laingian, Szaszian extravaganza of the 1960s was the scapegoating of parents as being causal to schizophrenia (as if there was not sufficient guilt in parents already). One effect of this unfortunate misunderstanding was a degree of covert professional suspicion of or hostility to parents, as professionals almost demanded divine and saintly responses. It seemed they had models of perfection in their heads, which suggested that they were child-free or lacked the imagination to understand the emotional turmoil as the illness drew into the psychotic vortex the sufferer's loved ones. Consequently, the modern and empirically validated family approach to schizophrenia (Falloon 1985) is doubly welcomed, as it gives true recognition of the second most damaged sufferers, parents, and acknowledgement of the centrality that most human beings place their families in, albeit sometimes ambivalently.

This is described beautifully in Lefley and Johnson's work, *Families as Allies in the Treatment of the Mentally Ill* (1990), which is not just about schizophrenia, but emerged out of the work of Hirsch and Leff (1971) and Leff and Vaughan (1985) on family management of schizophrenia. Interestingly, the approach emerged from the Laingian view that communication patterns in families with schizophrenia were abnormal and therefore causal. Hirsch and Leff sought to examine this and found that although there was certainly a great deal of confusion in the communication systems, they did not differ from matched non-psychotic groups. The crucial difference was that the presence of schizophrenia compounded the *usual* tensions within families, which normally were resolved but were impaired by the presence of schizophrenia.

In a series of studies, what became known as 'high expressed emotionality' (HEE) was found to be inimical to maintaining the sufferer's adjustment. The three main elements in HEE are critical comments, resentment and over-involvement, which undermines self-esteem. Thus we aim, via counselling, to reduce this high expressed emotionality, which helps the sufferer and family to cope better with the symptoms, which in turn improves the psycho-social functioning of both individual and family, as family treatment improves the affective climate of families (Doane 1986; Hogerty 1986a). Such an approach leads to fewer relapses; but if relapses do occur, the sufferer requires less time in a psychiatric hospital (Leff and Vaughan 1985; Hogerty 1986b; Falloon 1992).

This approach has been validated internationally (Micklowitz 1984), and in a seminal review, Kupers (1987) demonstrated that an integrated treatment approach based upon family management of schizophrenia had the best outcomes. An interesting study from Greece utilizes the approach to examine comparatively family communication in families with and without a person with schizophrenia. This found that the illness does disrupt intra-family dialogue, not least by breaking up family-specific norms of ritual, which are stabilizing elements in their relationships (Madianos and Economou 1994). The family approach directly tackles this problem by looking at the interactions and how to assist cognitive change and adaptation.

Bearing in mind what is known about the demoralization and erosion of commitment of recurrent schizophrenia, this approach should be able to make a major impact upon the risk of suicide in people with schizophrenia. Thus it seems reasonable that the optimism shown by the British Secretary of State for Health reflects professional confidence that a reduction of suicide is feasible. However, what is crucial is to reach the potential client. A worrying study by Runeson (1992) found that among young people there tends to be a significantly lower level of professional psychiatric contact with those who ultimately commit suicide. One of the difficulties that young adults have is coping with the stigma of their distress. The great likelihood of impulsive behaviour and the more usual distrust of authority figures mean that in both the organization and the structure of community psychiatric services the needs of possibly alienated young people must particularly be considered, especially when they are juxtaposed with drug or alcohol problems (Young and Fogg 1994). This re-emphasizes the importance of establishing a trusting, socially supportive relationship. The centrality of positive relationships has already been referred to but it is worth remembering that where potentially suicidal people come from, almost by definition, there is a degree of self-hate, certainly self-disregard, almost invariably low self-esteem and sometimes a personal history that compounds the lack of self-worth. They feel hopeless and therefore helpless, and often feel rejected by the experience of being cut off from their peers. In their withdrawal, they compound their sense of unworthiness by believing that they are not liked because they are unlikeable. They are unlikeable because they are not liked and the circular pain and distress becomes overwhelming. Not infrequently in post-death written communications, sufferers express the greatest regard for their family members, assert that they love them, but believe that the distress that they bring to their family members makes them more unworthy. Their rejection of life is seen as a positive sacrifice. Neimeyer and Pfeiffer (1994) noted that clients, especially younger clients, who made contact with suicide prevention centres had a lowered suicide rate over time. What the authors failed to take into account, when they wondered why the centres were not used more, was that in depression, both psychiatric- and stress-related, sufferers do not value themselves, and therefore lack the *basic motivation* to seek help.

A therapist who actively seeks to understand and consider the world from the other person's point of view demonstrates how his or her inherent dignity is valued and humanity affirmed, and can have a profound impact upon the depressed and despairing person.

A positive relationship gives the lie to the all-prevailing sense of despair epitomized in Psalm 22: 'I am a worm and no man.' Thus the counselling needs to reaffirm the person's reasons for living. The establishment of the relationship, allied with knowledge drawn from a range of disciplines, allows us to demonstrate to individuals that their problems can be confronted, challenged and overcome. If for a short time people have to be dependent, then so be it. We can establish and enhance people's ability to resolve their own problems and reverse the vicious cycle of the suicidal vortex, so that they neither feel rejected nor reject, and avoid the ultimate personal renunciation of life and their own humanity.

Violence and forensic factors

It is something of a paradox that the crescendo of civil rights criticism against the Mental Health Act 1959, which was triggered by an illegal and totally unacceptable compulsory detention by an unqualified person, sought to place rights and freedoms ahead of treatments. The 1983 Act is concerned with treatment, protection and prevention, and the Approved Social Worker (Mental Health) has an implicit advocacy role, but at two o'clock in the morning, when emergencies seem inevitably to occur, there is some suggestion of greater collusion between the visiting professionals than that resulting from someone asking: is this crisis really an emergency?

Conversely, if the sufferer or others are at risk of suicide or violence, or the person is in urgent need of treatment and is not in a fit state to determine his or her own welfare, then Marcus Aurelius' injunction about our responsibilities is apposite, and the compulsory clauses in the Mental Health Act are invoked without hesitation, not least because of moral and humane imperatives. However, there may be a danger that we over-respond to any threat and take the position of seeking to avoid a mistake, rather than judging the situation on its merits. Against both the spirit of the Mental Health Act and objective need, we might be inclined to pursue admission, with hidden or indeed open compulsion

(Bean 1986). It is always going to be a matter of judgement, and clearly we should always be seeking to avoid either the first incidence or a repetition of DSH, which is one of the most effective ways of preventing ultimate suicide.

Regrettably, while community services deal with their legal *duties* in response to calls for compulsory admission, the responsibilities in terms of prevention of break-down are less supported (Huxley and Kerfoot 1993). The best way to avoid the crisis is longitudinal regular support, and monitoring to avoid any deterioration. If the person develops another episode, the optimum way of dealing with this is to have available the social worker who knows the person best, but perhaps this is not a professional matter *per se*, but rather a resource and organizational matter, and therefore political.

The problem that is often uppermost in the public or political mind is mental illness compounded by violence. Despite this being a minority feature it is a real threat, because undoubtedly the phenomenon of depression/schizophrenia leading to suicide/murder does occur. This may be in response to paranoid ideas and/ or an element of jealousy which reaches pathological levels and can end in murder followed by suicide (White and Mullen 1989; Prins 1992). Where there appears to be any strong theme of jealousy, in the presence of paranoid-like ideation, this threat has to be taken seriously. But life is not like textbooks and professionals still have great difficulty in accurately predicting dangerousness (Floud 1982). Such knowledge is seldom comfort in the hurly-burly of the open-ended, fraught family situation, and social workers know to their cost that despite the UK having the biggest improvement in child protection in the Western world (Pritchard 1993b, c), their rare errors are pilloried by enquiry after enquiry. (Note that the annual number of deaths from 'social work disasters' are one-tenth that from 'unnecessary deaths' in operating theatres, described in the Royal College of Surgeons Report 1987 (Toynbee 1987).) Of course the counsellor, therapist, social worker or psychiatrist feels anxious, especially in the presence of paranoid ideation, where someone might be actively hiding his or her suicidal intent from us, and the professional who is *not* anxious in such circumstances, or who has not made a mistake, is rare indeed; though fortunately not all errors of judgement in the turmoil of the crisis situation end fatally.

A review by Benezech and Bourgeois (1992) of the link between suicide and homicide in France, the UK and the USA suggested that between 10 and 25 per cent of killers are depressed and *not* manic, which partly accounts for between 5 and 30 per cent of murders ending with suicide. Recently Wilson and Daly (1994) found that wives or husbands were actually more often murder victims when separated than when co-residing, which reflects the jealous element, and should alert the supporting practitioner to the risk, especially if there is a *previous* history of violence.

It is not easy, but one way of trying to reassure oneself is to take a narrow and perhaps distorted view of the statistical evidence, which shows that in terms of odds, to predict that people will not kill themselves would be right nine out of ten times; but the odds are only one in three for deliberate self-harm. But what if one is wrong?

Suicide is of course too late for the client and his or her family and there is longstanding evidence of the distress that a suicide can cause not only to relatives (Wertheimer 1991) but also to ward staff, social workers and psychiatrists (Schmitt *et al.* 1992; Horn 1994). To lose a patient is profoundly distressing, and there are examples of people who have left their jobs feeling they have failed, when any objective observer would confirm that they did all that could be done without the soul-destroying and short-term totalitarian response of total compulsory seclusion. Yet, as medical practitioners and nurses learn to their cost, death can be part of their practice, and the threat, fear or actuality of the event can, if we are not careful, impair our judgement.

Let us confront directly the issue of violence and mental disorder, which exercises the minds of media and politicians alike (and gives rise to the desire to develop 'supervised discharge', in response to media–hyped tragic murders committed by the mentally ill (Brindle 1994)). The *Daily Telegraph* of 17 August 1994 had as its main headline 'Mentally ill kill 38 in eighteen months'. This is true, and based upon Department of Health rates prevalence for all psychosis this represents a UK murder rate of 75 per million committed by psychotic people. Bluntly, that is nearly *nine times* the general murder rate of 8.7 per million, including Northern Ireland.

The first point to make is that, as with all violent deaths, victims are more likely to be family members, or in our case social workers. This is why, proportionately to the numbers of social workers in Britain, in the past ten years *more social workers have died in the performance of their duty than police.* Even so, there were only four tragedies. But a murder rate that is nine times that of the general rate seems enormous, until the second qualifying point is considered.

In 1992, 5,106 people died on the roads of the UK. Per capita this was the lowest ever number in modern times. This death rate represents a rate equivalent to 171 deaths per million driving licences, or 235 deaths per million licensed vehicles. Thus, at best, *the general public is substantially more at risk of being killed on the roads than by a mentally ill assailant,* at a ratio of 1:2.28. Conversely, if we take the notion that 90 per cent of suicides are linked to mental illness, then the mentally ill *are significantly more at risk from themselves,* as their suicide rate (compared with the general population rate of 80 per million) is 13,747 per million; thus they are 171 times more likely to die from suicide.

This does not mean that there is no risk to those around the sufferer, especially if there are paranoid ideas or self-damaging ideas that include others. But with sensible precautions and an alert mind to changes or indicators of an episode of mental disorder and aggression in sufferers, especially those with a history of threat or actual violence, then the professional need have no fear. Violence is not a major issue in the *majority* of work with the mentally ill.

The post-DSH interview

Among the many stressful factors for those who work in the suicidal behaviour situation is the need to interview people who have been involved in a deliberate self-harm incident. Meeting someone who has just recovered, one fears that insensitive handling may make matters worse by recalling to the person the impulsive despair that led to his or her desperate act. Conversely, there is the danger of reinforcing the 'attention-seeking' elements, especially in a younger person, by expressions of too much concern and interest. Nor do we want to be drawn into the self-denigrating 'I can't even kill myself' mode, or be sucked into the humiliation and self-loathing. Yet a balance has to be sought, and the best guide is to respond to the obvious *priority stressors* in the client's specific situation. Perhaps most important is that the crisis situation can be used as a positive opportunity to get close to the client, in order to reduce subsequent DSH incidence. Therefore an active preventative position should be taken and the following 'seven Ps' need to be addressed: precipitant, priority, predisposition, planning, psychiatric factors, the positive help required and promise.

1 Precipitant. Why do they think it happened?
2 Priority. What, in order of priority, were their stress points?
3 Predisposition. What predisposing factors were around?
4 Planning. Was the incident planned or impulsive?
5 Psychiatric factors. What psychiatric treatments, if any, were they getting and do they need now?
6 Positives. What positives are there in terms of potential help available and what they need, ideally prioritized by them?
7 Promise. This is perhaps the most difficult point, but ask about whether they feel at further risk, how frightened they are and whether they will promise not to repeat.

Certainly this is not the time to be judgemental, but every effort has to be made to understand what led them to their current plight and to identify an immediate short-term goal, as well as to think ahead about medium-term objectives. While giving recognition to the 'reality' of their distress, at every point we seek to engender hope and add positives to their situation, building up their reasons for living.

How can one appreciate the utter despair and emptiness of someone who feels ultimately rejected and, accepting the verdict of those around, then rejects life in the ultimate of suicide? Alvarez complained that professionals and researchers, almost by their very social competence, are disqualified to capture and distil the emotional meaning of anomie. It is vital that professionals do have some sense of this passive desperation, so that in imagination we can cross a 'black hole' to reach those who would cast themselves down. So often in learned papers and lectures knowledge is distilled, but without the *deliberate* act of imagination of what the situation means for the other person, we may truly be unable to communicate. Here there is value in turning to poets and playwrights. Anne Sexton, whose turbulent life not only appeared to foreshadow her final suicide, quintessentially brings the despairing themes together in her poetry, which according to one commentator and her biographer, damaged all around her (Hendin 1993, Middlebrook 1992). The loss of the sense of God, can be truly catastrophic when we understand how in even non-religious people, the acute onset of either mental or physical illness re-activates our religious and cultural heritage (Goold

1991). The theme of self-immolation and the obscene reversal of 'mother love' that quintessentially feeds, but now feeds upon one self, is a strong theme, so that all the senses are reversed in a harsh parody. Sound obscures hopeful images, sight floods out comforting bird-song, touch heals not but self-condemningly burns.

Porter (1992), the medical historian, writes: 'The pain of severe depression is quite unimaginable to those who have not suffered it and it kills in many instances because its anguish can no longer be borne.' The prevention of suicides will be hindered until there is a general awareness of the nature of this pain. This understanding should be at the centre of all our efforts to reach out to people who believe that they are unworthy of our efforts; in common humanity we cannot accept their rejection.

Community care: an integrated interdisciplinary approach

The need for protection: respite and refuge

Often governments and researchers see admission into mental hospital as failure, and do not acknowledge the often excellent work done in our hospital psychiatric wards when people require *intensive* care in a *controlled*, protecting and protective environment. Such care can be schematically differentiated between 'respite' care, where people need short-term relief or protection, and 'refuge', where their needs demand long-term care because their situation is intractable and they and/or others could be in danger.

It might be thought that if there is risk, then the obvious answer is immediate and total protection by admission, if necessary compulsory. Short-term compulsory admission can be a very traumatic experience for all concerned, and apart from giving immediate protection, can fracture family networks and make matters worse in the medium and long term. The apparently simple protective device of total control in the interest of the person is not very effective. Experience in the closed wards of the 1950s was that patients 'at risk' were given twenty-four-hour supervision, 365 days a year. Such an unwitting totalitarian response actually added to the violence and self-damaging behaviour, rather than reversed it. Few people would prefer the locked anonymity of those wards to an opportunity to live life in the community and, where possible, in full citizenship.

This has been recognized since Enoch Powell introduced the 'care in the community' policy for mentally ill people in 1962. This is still the primary objective for most governments throughout the Western world, inspired by a mixture of varied impulses, including humanitarianism, efficacy and cost savings. As we shall see, there are grounds for *more* than cautious optimism but the policy is not without its difficulties. Let us explore these problems first.

Long-term refuge or asylum for people who are cumulatively irretrievably damaged, to provide them with a compensatory civilized and protected environment, seems to be a positive step. Carey *et al.* (1993) demonstrated a need for this among new long-stay mentally ill people, but they still preferred hostel-type assistance. Though only a minority of mentally ill people became 'new long-stay', as Thornicroft *et al.* (1992) showed, they were much worse when surrounded by other forms of social deprivation, and consequently they could add to the flow of the homeless (Marshall and Reed 1992; Scott 1993). The case for long-term refuge is not really in doubt; the question is how it should be provided. Martin (1984) showed that there are dangers in cul-de-sac institutions, which following the relative neglect of policy makers and politicians, whose covert attitude is 'it is good enough for them', can erode staff commitment, 'corrupting their quality care'. Anything done tends to be minimal, reflecting the less than subtle stigmatizing not only of mentally ill people, but also those who care for them.

It is clear that, apart from those needing the optimal acute and refuge care described, the vast majority of former mentally ill patients prefer to live as normal and unrestricted lives as possible within the community (Lamb 1993). Harrison *et al.* (1994) followed up a cohort of people, mainly with schizophrenia, thirteen years after discharge. The majority, after initial difficulties, had maintained themselves outside hospital and preferred community living, despite some of its short-comings. This was a similar result to that of Olkin and Pearsall (1993), whose eleven-year study of former patients' perceptions found a preference for living outside big institutions. Mercier *et al.* (1994) incredibly traced the majority of a sample of mentally ill people thirty years later, and though about 20 per cent had at least one readmission in a five-year period, the preferred option was for as independent living as possible. However, while much changes in thirty years, Mercier *et al.*'s work demonstrated that although a substantial proportion of mentally ill people can be *effectively* and humanely maintained within the community, there are a minority who probably need a caring refuge or asylum.

Care in the community

The common problems for people who depend upon 'care in the community' are resources, access and continuity (Lamb 1993). Such people include the mentally ill, the unemployed, the homeless and those with substance abuse problems, all of whom may become involved in suicidal behaviour. Yet there is extremely encouraging evidence that good 'care in the community' works for all those needing it, including the potentially suicidal.

In respect of intervention and treatment, differentiating between psychiatric- and stress-related suicide is essentially schematic. Hence we offer the following as a form of *integrated interdisciplinary care in the community*, which appears to have the best results so far.

Bellack and Mueser (1993) demonstrated that, in addition to appropriate psychotropic drugs, people with schizophrenia can receive effective psycho-social care that sustains them in the community. They found an integration of social skills training, cognitive supports and family treatment to be very effective, confirming the work of Hogerty (1986a,b).

Such an approach has important additional benefits for relatives, the most frequent primary carers. Simpson *et al.*'s (1993) comparison of home-based versus hospital-based care, along with the Baker *et al.* (1993) and Dean *et al.* (1993) studies, showed that community support for severely mentally ill people was feasible, particularly when it focused on the sufferers' social networks. This in turn enhanced the primary carer's morale, reversing something of the vicious cycle, and reflecting the value of supporting the 'natural' social networks of individuals and groups (Gottleib 1983). To supplement this further, Schene *et al.* (1993) were able to show that day patient care was, in a number of areas, as good as inpatient hospital care, in that there were no differences in levels of the patient pathology, including suicidal behaviour. It also had the advantage that it maintained the person's social networks better, and of course was relatively cheaper. Conway *et al.* (1993) also showed that targeting the severely mentally ill was feasible but warned that without adequate interdisciplinary support, which unfortunately was lacking, and despite significant reductions in sufferers' psychiatric pathology, their social progress was severely limited. Lowe *et al.* (1993), from the field of 'learning difficulties', reported early improvements with the All-Welsh (Integrated) Strategy. However, Evans *et al.* (1994) reflected Conway's findings that initial improvements are achievable, but need continuity and support from social services, who, it appears, despite the ability and will, do not have the resources to provide the necessary long-term supportive service (Huxley and Kerfoot 1993). The message is clear: an integrated service can work safely, provided it is adequately resourced.

Employment and occupation

Employment is very important as, in our society, the job we do strongly defines our social identity and makes a major contribution to our personal identity. The psycho-social disadvantages of unemployment do not need to be rehearsed here but unemployment often has a double jeopardy effect, in that it not only mars the individual, but also often undermines those in the social network who might have supported him or her (Kong *et al.* 1993). A vicious spiral is created, a reduction in the availability of social supports adding further to the economic problems and increasing the sense of social and personal rejection. At a practical level, any vulnerability to depression is bound to rise. Thus, apart from economic factors, *occupation* is vital for the emotional well-being of the person, because every effort should be made to engender or sustain a sense of hopefulness, to counteract the dangerous engulfment of hopelessness which can lead to suicidal behaviour. But these problems can be overcome.

Reker and Eikelmann (1993), in a long-term study with 'chronically ill' psychiatric patients, two-thirds of whom had schizophrenia, found that sheltered employment, along with community social support, successfully maintained all but the most chronically ill and damaged patients. This was carried out in West Germany, where there is a higher level of resources, but Block (1993) was able to reach a similar group of people in Surrey by designing an individualized 'employment package', which was successful in finding employment or morale-sustaining training, reversing the sense of rejection, helplessness and hopelessness.

People need occupation as much as employment, and Patmore (1987) gives examples of a range of ingenious projects that helped to restore the self-respect of unemployed formerly mentally ill people. The Remploy model is a well established approach, which, as Reker and Eikelmann showed, has long-term benefits. We need to take a 'total management perspective' of the interrelationship that employment/occupation has with many psycho-social problems, including mental illness. It is now manifest that unemployment has public order, public health and public costs ramifications, and only by taking an integrated view of employment/occupation can we reduce some of the accumulative hidden costs, both economic and personal (Catalano *et al.* 1993; Graetz 1993; McGovern *et al.* 1994; Pritchard and Clooney 1994).

Accessibility

One theme running throughout all the 'care in the community' projects is accessibility. Since we know about the dangers of isolation in relation to suicidal behaviour, this problem requires a solution, usually one of thoughtful organization. We cannot of course compensate our client for the lack of a life-partner or family. If the links, for whatever reason, have broken down, we must provide a system of easy access to either a named support person or, more feasibly, a 'team' or agency to whom the person is known. This was shown by Laurent (1993), who worked with young people with previous mental illness and suicidal histories. His clients commented that 'just knowing you were there' gave a constant sense of support and, with ease of access to the team, was quite literally life-saving. Such a procedure has been tried by Morgan and Owen (1993), who organized a 'green card' system with those who had been involved in deliberate self-harm. Not only did the clients appreciate the sense of being valued, but with easier and quicker access, over time there was a significant reduction in repetition of DSH. This has practical implications, as the reverse can be the case when there is too early a termination of psychiatric contact, which has been found to lead to increased DSH and suicide (Hills *et al.* 1993). However, this means more than simply 'turning up' at psychiatric outpatient or GP clinics. There needs to be a focused purpose, which considers *all* aspects of people's lives, not only medication compliance, but also their morale and socio-economic circumstances, which must include the perennial 'chronic' problem, accommodation.

Accommodation

It is clear from a range of studies, in particular in Britain, that when young people become involved with drug misuse they are at risk from both repetitive parasuicide and suicide, which often contribute to homelessness (Brent *et al.* 1993; Hawton *et al.* 1993). Thus the first response to prevent suicidal behaviour is services that will reach the disadvantaged and dispossessed. The profiles of the homeless consist of the triad of drugs and alcohol, mental illness and delinquency, so we need either short-term hostels with active outreach workers, which is achievable (Stockley and Stockley 1993; Pritchard and Clooney 1994), or purpose-built homes for single people, with support from organizations such as the youth service who can specialize in meeting hard-to-reach youths. McCarthy and Nelson

(1993) have shown that supportive housing can be effective for a whole range of people with 'special needs', but especially the mentally ill, reducing the need for alternative group or hospital care. Providing there is adequate and long-term support, relapses that require readmission are significantly reduced.

Wasylenki *et al.* (1993) examined a model based upon 'assertive outreach' from hostels, which aimed to meet vulnerable young people with drug and mental health problems. It proved to be very effective, reflecting the recommendations of Brudney and Dobkin (1991), who were concerned with the multiple pathology of homelessness, TB and HIV infection, with its association with suicidal behaviour. One valuable adjunct to the Wasylenki *et al.* study was that, if there were remnants of the person's social networks, the assertive outreach often enhanced and preserved such natural benefits. It is easy to assume that the 'homeless' have no families. This is not the case, as in the 'passage' through family conflict, which can involve a degree of transient homelessness (Stockley and Stockley 1993), families are, paradoxically, still the most likely source of succour, which community services need to bolster. Experience suggests that while a full 'reconciliation' may not be feasible, a partial positive response can be developed to the mutual benefit of young person and family. The 'maintenance model' of social work (Davies 1994) in the last resort accepts people for what and where they are, seeks to support *their* strengths and acknowledges that we all have to live within our limitations.

One perennial weakness of care in the community is the degree to which it is believed that people will tolerate the mentally ill around them. The response summed up by the acronym NIMBY (not in my back yard) occurs when 'nice people' accept the need for humane care of the mentally ill, but not next door to them. A study by Wahl (1993) produced at first sight a surprising result. It surveyed neighbours who lived near relatively new group homes for the mentally ill. The majority of the 'neighbours' hardly knew the purpose of the group home (a quarter did not know there was one) and the vast majority were not unduly disturbed or distressed by the residents. This is a classic manifestation of the phenomenon that the most prejudiced have least first-hand experience of the stigmatized person.

Of course, an optimal care in the community service would be easy to establish. But the expected massive financial savings have not materialized, as good and effective care is only marginally cheaper than hospital or residential care (Lamb 1993). In the longer term it appears that there are better prospects (Bond 1984) but cost is a major factor. An extreme example was found by Beecham *et al.* (1993) who examined the cost of domiciliary care for elderly people: despite the better quality of life than in hospitals, it was actually dearer than the hospital, ranging from £900 to £950 per week. This study concerned the elderly, who would require considerable nursing as well as psycho-social support, but it is an indicator of the potential long-term costs that policy makers have to consider. Healey (1993) explored the costs of new anti-schizophrenic drugs, in particular the 'budget busting' clozapine, and argued that not only must professionals confront the ethical issues, but the case must be made for comparison of *effective* costs in terms of patient care over time. Comparison must be made with the cheaper but less effective psychotropic drugs, which may well be more costly to all, especially the sufferer.

Practical steps for intervention

The first point is to recognize that the 'assessment' of the person is the beginning of the 'intervention'. What follow are twelve practical steps for offering a service to any person facing psycho-social distress and mental disorder, which includes the worker's conscious consideration of the potential risk of suicidal behaviour.

Rapport. Everything in the counsellor's demeanour works towards establishing a rapport with the client and is specifically focused upon that person's situation. Simultaneously, the worker must be making an assessment and therefore be information-gathering. The immediate practical difficulty with people who may be under particular stress or depressed is that a less than sensitive approach may initially *add* to the client's pressure, and anxiety on behalf of the worker may result in the client feeling that he or she is under inquisition. However, despite some of the barriers that the client may present, people almost invariably welcome the experience of interest and concern. However, in the presence of depression, clients may lack the energy to respond or may be so overwhelmed by their worthlessness that they feel guilty about our concern. This demands that we must be more positive in demonstrating our concern and understanding. The importance of establishing the relationship cannot be over-emphasized because from this early base we have to build 'the question' (i.e. are they contemplating suicide?) and seek to obtain 'the promise' (that they will not damage themselves).

Current stressors and prioritization. The need to understand the current situation is self-evident, but we need to discover from the client: (a) which is the most pressing problem; (b) what this means to him or her; and (c) what resolution he or she would seek. Realistically, some stressors may not be immediately resolvable, which means we address the next one down in the hierarchy. The primary aim is to reduce the client's and family's immediate stress levels, with the direct intention of engendering a sense of hope and reasons for living. With our special concern about suicidal behaviour, we do not have to reel off the 'signs and symptoms' of depression, but if we allow the *client to tell* his or her story, in his or her own sequence, with patient gentle questions of clarification, the absence or presence of symptoms associated with self-damaging behaviour will become clear.

Lessons from the 'prediction' scales. The following checklist is based upon an amalgam of the most practical prediction scales. A simple presence or absence will quickly allow one to assess risk levels, but it is offered as a guide, and should not be completed until close to the end of the first or other early assessment sessions. Consider the following within the context of the client's age and gender.

1 Is the person depressed?
2 Is there a sense of hopelessness?
3 Are there reasons for living?

4 Has the person avoided or refused help, or is he or she inclined to do so?
5 Has there been previous DSH?
6 Is the person involved in drug or alcohol misuse?
7 Has there been a fairly recent (six months) major role failure: divorce, sep-aration, unemployment, end of emotional attachment, etc.?
8 Is suicidal ideation present?
9 Is the person isolated or does he or she lack close relationships?
10 Is there a history of aggression and violence?

Deliberate self-harm and suicide: the evaluation. Based upon the above, we should be in a position to have some idea about risk and to differentiate between potential deliberate self-harm and suicide. It would be helpful for workers con-sciously to ask themselves the question: is there a risk? A positive answer does not give cause for panic, but allows a review of what is required to reduce the risks to reasonable levels. But it should be remembered that there is no such thing as a risk-free DSH that is 'just a cry for help'.

Lethality. Consider what lethal means are available to the client, and how these might be controlled. This might depend upon family (see the following) or the removal of objects.

Medication: plusses and minuses. Is the person being treated with anti-depressants, psychotropic or hypnotic drugs? You need to consider: (a) whether the person is taking the medication properly; (b) whether he or she is suffering from side-effects; (c) what is the level of supervision of potential lethal drugs? How regu-larly and frequently is the person in touch with his or her psychiatrist or general practitioner?

Family support. In evaluating the risk, we need to know whether there are people around the client who can offer emotional support and a degree of supervision. Their presence may well ensure that risk factors will not arise, but they need to know a risk exists. We also need to discover the family members' perception of the problem, and what it *means* to them. In addition, while the client may share with relatives the level of his or her despair, the worker is then faced with the problem of how the family will respond, because such knowledge, emotionally, can be experienced by the family as rejecting and an indictment of their relationship. In practice we are often a conduit between the sufferer and family, and may have to tolerate a considerable degree of oscillating anger and dependency, as the complex and mixed emotions are worked out. In particular, though perhaps not early in the contact, it may be important to determine whether other family members have had previous problems, which may have included suicidal behaviour. These might well complicate their emotional response to the current client.

Previous behaviour and problem solving. Further understanding is needed of the explanations for current difficulties, which means we need to know about past behaviour, affect and cognition, the social situation, how they managed in the past and what their usual coping strategies were. It can be especially helpful to identify and reinforce positives with clients or family, thus enhancing their sense of hope and purpose.

Employment and finance. Determine the client's current employment status, and whether there are acute financial difficulties, i.e. is there sufficient income to meet primary needs? If he or she is unemployed, begin to consider employment and/or training needs, or potential opportunities for an occupation that offers satisfaction and avoids solitary brooding.

Accommodation. Consider what if any accommodation requirement there is, and whether the accommodation provides secondary support and *de facto* supervision. If possible, avoid the isolated 'bed-sit', which can be highly demoralizing.

Accessibility. There is a need to consider how accessible you or your team are, to meet current or future crises. While it is seldom possible to provide the optimal twenty-four hour cover, ensure that the person knows how to contact help, if required, and reinforce the 'promise' that, should you be unavailable, he or she will if necessary contact the team or emergency cover.

Avoid inadvertent reinforcement of the 'sick' role. The subjective reality of the person's distress can be experienced as manipulation, aggression and hostility by those around them. Moreover, the person appears to have 'secondary gains', such as an inappropriate feeling of importance brought about by the apparent 'control' he or she has over other people. This is especially important with younger people, who may well 'learn' that threatening, or going to the extreme, can gain attention and be immensely powerful. This can be almost 'addictive', so that the distress, social disapproval and physical discomfort or pain, as well as the reality of risk, are forgotten.

The spiritual or religious dimension

The value of a client-specific integrated bio–psycho–social approach appears to be well established. But to be fully comprehensive, and to respond appropriately to all aspects of the client's life, it must not ignore the spiritual and religious dimension in our pluralistic, multi-ethnic society. Goold (1991) examined the significance of religious beliefs among three samples: a non-patient group; samples from acute surgical admissions; and acute psychiatric admissions of people with schizophrenia. He found that the non-patient group had relatively low religious ideation, and church attendance similar to average levels, but was markedly different from *both* patient groups, who expressed high religious ideation; there was little difference between the psychiatric and surgical admissions.

Classically, in times of trouble, religion is a potential source of comfort. Kehoe and Gutheil (1994) expressed concern about the neglect of the religious, the failure to utilize the potential support for people involved in suicidal behaviour. It is not an easy area, and the idea that this is a time to proselytize is abhorrent, but practitioners should be willing to consider whether this is a legitimate area of client support. This author, as a non-theist, recognizes that throughout re-corded time, in every culture, there has been overwhelming evidence of human-kind's search for a spiritual and religious fulfilment. All the great faiths of the world – Buddhism, Christianity, Hinduism, Islam and Judaism – have within their teachings the imperative of compassion and care towards the suffering.

While some believers' claims to exclusivity and authority exclude those of us who differ from them, experience has taught that with patience and humility, people of good will can come together in the service of others. Where spiritual and religious aspects are important to the client, the worker should acknowledge them and if possible respond appropriately, or if necessary refer to someone who can meet this need.

For me one of the great liberating documents of humankind this century is the United Nations Declaration of Human Rights, and it is not without significance that members of the great faiths can subscribe to its tenets. In Isaiah we read, 'Comfort ye, comfort ye my people'. The Prophet Mohammed wrote the Koran in 'the Name of God the Compassionate, the Merciful'. These are echoed in the Beatitudes of Jesus and in the *Bhagavad Gita*. Humanist or believer, who could quarrel with the prayer of Krishna?

> Freedom from fear, purity of heart, constancy in learning and contempla-
> tion, generosity, self-harmony, adoration, study of the scriptures, austerity,
> righteousness; non-violence, truth, freedom from anger, renunciation, serenity,
> aversion to fault-finding, sympathy for all beings, peace from greedy cravings,
> gentleness, modesty, steadiness; energy, forgiveness, fortitude, purity, a good
> will, freedom from pride – these are the treasures of the man who is born
> for heaven.

With such a prescription, and the knowledge that we can positively and effectively intervene, people of good will can unite in the Quaker injunction to 'seek the Godhead in every person' and reduce the unnecessary toll of the ultimate rejection.

CHAPTER 8

FAMILY 'SURVIVORS' OF SUICIDE: HIDDEN CASUALTIES?

The famous quotation from John Donne, 'no man is an island', is almost a cliché because it has become an accepted truism. Of equal relevance, however, is a subsequent line, 'any man's death diminishes me'. If this is true for people generally, how much more diminished will the family feel, following suicide or suicidal behaviour? Suicide is seldom neutral in its effects, and after the immediate family, it has impacts upon the professionals involved and the local community. How do these respond both to the death and to the family? There may well be an unconscious collusion to 'blame the family', because of the sense of guilt felt by all, including professionals, who may be subtly 'laying off the responsibility', as we have a sense of guilt because we 'failed' to prevent the tragedy. Yet both community and professional share a sense of the core hurt of the family, of rejection by the person who has died or apparently attempted to die. It will be argued that the families of people involved in suicidal behaviour, especially those who survive their family member's death, often become hidden casualties.

In the British way with death, we are embarrassed and 'pass by on the other side', especially if it is a 'dubious death'. We ignore the evidence that death not only 'diminishes us' but also damages surviving people's health, especially those experiencing post-suicide bereavement (Pennebaker and O'Heeron 1984; Keitner et al. 1990; Reed 1993).

This dynamic is an outcome of two converging almost covert pressures: one is the professional shuffling off the blame; the other, echoing the rejection theme, is the feeling that the deceased did not value the family sufficiently to want to continue living. It is known that the living have an element of guilt in respect of the deceased, and for those in the community faced with an 'intentional death', the family is an easy target to blame. If the family is not blamed, then the professional is, but it is far simpler to infer the family's failure. This enables the local community to abdicate any sense of responsibility for the perceived dual rejection of someone who was part of their society.

The 'suicide survivor' family, while sharing certain common attributes with other bereaved people, is subjected to extra pressures compared to the ordinary bereaved (McIntosh and Wrobleski 1988; Barrett and Scott 1989; McIntosh 1993). As a 'group category', survivors will be unique in their response to the various pressures, but because of the 'collusion of silence' that surrounds bereavement, especially post-suicide, few families will have someone to 'tell them what is a common reaction to suicide' (Wertheimer 1991). This in turn may further exacerbate their pain and sense of rejection. It is not surprising that we have known for some considerable time how the 'anniversary' of an earlier family death reactivates the bereavement, which at the extreme can add further to the suicidal toll (Bunch and Barraclough 1971). What is certain, across all cultures, is that the family survivors of suicide are unlikely to remain unmoved by suicidal behaviour in the family (Takahashi 1989; Chan and Lau 1993; Rockett and Smith 1993).

If one looks at some of the things experienced by families, there are common elements of grief where death has occurred, with guilt, anger, stigma and a sense of rejection as well, which are made much more intensive and disruptive in the presence of a suicidal death (Dunne *et al.* 1987; Barrett and Scott 1989; Farberow *et al.* 1992; McIntosh 1993). This should not be unexpected because, following a deliberate self-harm incident, the family's own networks, strengths and weaknesses, tensions and conflicts are tested to the uttermost. Thus, depending upon the previous and current quality of relationships between the victim and family, as with the impact of a mental illness on the family, the reaction will be coloured by the immediate past and current event. Unlike in death from an 'illness', however, which one did not choose, it is the apparently deliberate nature of the behaviour that is so difficult to accept or understand. It cannot fail to hurt.

In a text that will become a classic, Alison Wertheimer (1991) explored the extent of this hurt when she examined the experiences of survivors of suicide, eloquently called '*A Special Scar*'. The work followed the suicidal death of an older sister, and Wertheimer begins with her own 'survivor's story', which is virtually an epitome of the other case histories. The sister had much, husband, children and family, who therefore, research would suggest was safe. Typically, the death 'came as a complete shock'. Though Wertheimer later learned that perhaps the suicide should not have been unexpected, but she learned '*survivors only achieve understanding with hindsight*', and 'talking to people other than very close friends was hard. Because most thirty-six-year olds don't die suddenly'. Wertheimer appeared to be in an almost cocoon state, pulled between feeling 'ashamed', 'freakish'. Survivors however, not only their own distress, anxiety, confusion and guilt to contend with, but also other people's response: 'I could see the horror in their faces.'

Another theme mirrors Elizabeth Irvine's old adage about family reactions to mental illness: 'Who done it?' Family members begin to blame themselves for possibly contributing to the difficulties, as 'suicide leaves the survivor with a rag bag of painful and conflicting feelings, and guilt and anger at oneself, and the deceased, seem to be the conflicting themes'. There is also a tendency in retrospective analysis for the survivor to begin to wonder about Elizabeth Irvine's next family question: 'Who next?' That is, is anyone else thought to be at risk?

Suddenly, said Wertheimer, 'the world began to feel very unsafe – there was no one to tell me that this is a common reaction to suicide'.

In the United States of America there has been a considerable growth in mutual self-help groups for the survivors of suicides, who come together to provide much-needed support. Edwin Schneideman, one of the founders of the American Association of Suicidology, argued that for every suicide there are at least six other 'casualties'; that is the likely average number of people who would have a sufficiently close relationship with the deceased to bear the 'special scar'. The usual bereavement process takes between eighteen and thirty months to traverse (Parkes 1986). This would imply that, based upon the average annual UK suicide rate, there will be at least 27,000 people annually who are learning about the negative effects of post-suicide bereavement. Despite the efforts of a few voluntary bereavement support groups, such as The Compassionate Friends, Cruse and the even smaller local Suicide Bereavement Groups, there is virtually no formal acknowledgement that such people have any continuing post-bereavement needs. Yet the extent of distress in terms of physical and mental ill-health will surely add to the double sense of rejection.

Of course those taught in the British way learn to suffer 'silently', and not to make a fuss, which allows the rest of us to take advantage of their inhibited reluctance to draw further attention to themselves and to expose their tragic stigma further. Unfortunately, with a few honourable exceptions (e.g. Barraclough and Shepherd 1976; Parkes 1986; Wertheimer 1991), there is a dearth of British empirical work in this field. This is doubly regrettable because when the excellent work of the palliative care movement is observed, with the involvement of families post-bereavement, it is clear that much can be achieved, and the extent of unmet need in this vulnerable group is thrown into sharper relief. It is suspected that if there was a fiscal analysis of the concomitant costs in terms of health and employment following a suicide bereavement, then there would be a speedier recognition not only that families merit help in their own right, but also that such a service, in terms of a total management perspective, would pay for itself by reducing the effects of post-traumatic stress. This is not special pleading, as there is good evidence that post-suicide survivors experience more distress, and damage to health and employment, than that following a non-suicidal death. This was reviewed by McIntosh (1993), who examined the American research of the past fifteen years. It is appreciated that there are some real methodological difficulties, not least the ethical one of intrusion into appropriate controls; for example, exploring what if any differences there are between suicide, accidental death, unexpected death and 'ordinary medical death'. The different responses will probably be dependent upon the link between the 'deceased' and the mourner, and the interrelationship with the disease, 'timing' and 'expectedness' of the death.

A particularly rigorous study was carried out by Barrett and Scott (1989), who identified eleven 'grief' elements and designed a Lickert scale which contained five items for each element. It is an especially useful scale in that it has potential for practice use, not in a straight question and answer format but as the core of a post-bereavement interview. Barrett and Scott were able to demonstrate identifiable differences in terms of not only levels of disruption, but also the intensity of the grief reactions of survivors, compared with mourners from accidental, unexpected and expected natural deaths.

They were able to illustrate and confirm the 'normal bereavement processes' identified by Parkes (1986), and while there was *no* difference in the general nature of grief reactions between the three groups, there was a much greater intensity for the suicide survivors, reflecting the case histories of Wertheimer (1991). Many families were very much concerned with the prolonged and painful 'search for an explanation', which manifested itself in guilt, shame and stigmatization, compounded by a 'rejective' loss of social support. Rejection was an enduring concern, as well as increases in self-destructive behaviour, and what the researchers described as unique reactions to the particular circumstances. These were very typically more frequent among the suicide survivors than the other bereaved groups. It would seem, therefore, that survivors of suicide are at greater risk from some of the secondary psycho-social impacts of bereavement, and are at greater risk of ill health and, in particular, a dysfunctional reaction at the anniversary of the death (Shepherd and Barraclough 1976). This should give impetus to efforts to reach out to people who experience the double jeopardy of the rejecting death of a person who is important in their lives, and being exposed to the loss of social support, stigmatization, guilt and shame that are associated with this ultimate rejection.

In the search for meaning, interpretation of the events may well be different for the various actors. For the victim the deliberate self-harm or actual suicide, may be intended as an end, following perhaps the longstanding deteriorating distress of prolonged mental illness; or an impulsive response, which may be fuelled by anger and depression and have manipulative elements, as well as despair. Canetto *et al.* (1989), exploring the immediate interpersonal relationships of partnerships in which one died, found a considerable degree of mutual hurt and confusion, which for the survivor was unresolved. He or she could never say sorry or, equally, could not hear an apology from the deceased person.

The various relationships of the survivors to the suicidee are likely to create different reactions, and it is important for the counsellor to understand the meaning of the events within the family, because if we are looking at deliberate self-harm then the family dynamics are the context and content with which the therapist will work, and, as we will see later, if the family are the survivors, it is they who carry that 'special scar'.

If we could share only one single insight into the plight of the survivors, it would be to appreciate that, in many situations, suicide is *not* the end, but a beginning.

In some circumstances, after the initial grief is resolved, there is a feeling of renewal and freedom; for example, after years of devoted support through the turmoil of recurrent schizophrenia. As Parkes (1986) points out, 'some mental illness can be just as malignant as cancer and cause relentless pain not only to the sufferer but to the family as a whole'. But such a clear-cut reason may have elements of solace within it, mirroring the 'normality' of cancer deaths, where there is consolation in having a sufferer 'at peace – it is a blessed relief'.

In other circumstances the suicidal death is the start of an unwinnable emotional war, which, unlike intolerable marital or family conflict, cannot be resolved by a conciliatory divorce, as it can in the bitterness that surrounds longstanding jealousy and marital violence. It must be endured with little chance of absolution from the scourge of guilt.

A search for meaning

George Kelly described the human being as a natural scientist who sought to impose meaning and order on the chaos around them. Consequently, human beings seek to categorize not only for inherent logic but also to maintain some form of control, especially over dangerous issues. Wertheimer (1991) graphically demonstrated how the survivors, in looking back, tried to understand the event, but painfully she appreciated that 'survivors only achieve understanding with hindsight'. Wertheimer explored some of the stresses of shifting balances of power and relationships in the family. The search for meaning and understanding is poignant and sometimes lasts for years, shown in the ambivalence of one respondent, who said: 'I have accepted that I will never know, but it does seem important that I don't know. I should know – I'd like to know why, I don't know why I want to know, it does not change anything.'

This author had the strange experience of talking with investigative journalists who were examining a number of suicides of people who worked in the electronics part of the defence industry. The 'search for meaning' for some survivors became a frantic quest. In discussions, it was possible to demonstrate that at least three-quarters of the deaths appeared to have some clear form of depression, which may have been psychiatric, or severe stress-related; but a number appeared to be inexplicable, and a very small minority did not match any of the models explored. One survivor said, 'We can't understand it – we can't bury him properly.' This was four years after the event, illustrating the desperate desire to understand.

In such a 'vacuum of knowledge' it is easy to see how extreme explanations were offered, ranging from undetected murder to conspiracy. As Tacitus said, 'wonder grows where knowledge fails'. In Collins's book (1990), we see how inference and suggestion were seized upon by relatives seeking to impose some absolving meaning for their tragedy. In the BBC2 programme *Public Eye*, which explored the rise of young men's suicide, families were willing to expose their concern and grief, predominantly in an effort to establish meaning. Some suicides appeared to be a sad resolution of the impact of poverty, such as the experience of homelessness; some suicide notes highlighted how the victims had a sense that their lives were incomplete, and for the survivors there was the continued shadow of an accusation.

Of course some victims try to forestall family distress, but can inadvertently add to it, when they speak about their failure, sickness, distress and desperate loneliness (Maris *et al.* 1992). They try to absolve their parents of any blame, looking back with great sadness to the days *before* the family disruption that contributed to their running away (Leenaars 1989). They apologize for the hurt they cause, though one doubts whether parents could accept their pardon, which might make self-forgiveness even harder to achieve.

Impact of 'timing'

Within the family context there will be an 'ascribed meaning' of the death. Was it broadly associated with mental illness, or stress-related, and how did the timing impact upon the different family members? Was it sudden and out of the blue, which can be quite shattering and incomprehensible to family members, who have little or no opportunity to understand why? In effect they are left with an open-ended, apparently meaningless death, which in some cases can compound their grief resolution, at least prolonging it, and make them especially vulnerable to other features, related to the death of a parent (Shepherd and Barraclough 1976), or to being exposed to an insensitive media (Shepherd and Barraclough 1978). Perhaps worst of all is the apparent indifference or minimal response of society to those bereaved by suicide (Wertheimer 1991).

Conversely, was the death the end of a series of deliberate self-harm incidents, which will have built up a meaning and an understandable defensive reaction within the family? If the death came at the end of a long struggle, if this is a prerequisite and if the victim received appropriate support and help for as long as needed, experienced practitioners can help families to appreciate that the sufferer is at rest. Conversely, it may be that the family members feel they have been left to deal with intolerable problems and now, following the suicide, they experience even more disapprobation. This will be the psycho-social context within which the professional must work in an effort to bring some calm and understanding to the family, and, as will be discussed later, where necessary a vindication for the professional.

Parents

Otto von Bismarck, when asked what his greatest satisfaction in life was, replied that 'God has not taken any of my children before me.' He eschewed boasting about establishing a united Germany, or making the Hohenzollerns German Emperors. His response echoes across time and cultures, being shared by the vast majority of parents who take comfort in the 'natural justice' and expectation that they will pre-decease their children. A death threat to one's children is the chronic nightmare of parents. Young people, in the competence and confidence of youth, may smile benignly at the 'clucking' of apparently over-anxious (and therefore interpreted as controlling) authoritarian parents. Macduff (in *Macbeth*), on hearing of the death of his family, turns upon the vociferously outraged Prince Malcolm, who has urged him to 'give sorrow words', and, knowing that there are no words to express such devastation, witheringly replies, 'he has no children'. There can perhaps be no greater sorrow. The underlying anger and impotence of blighted hopes is reflected in Macduff's 'Did Heaven look on, and would not take their part?' It is this unjust and 'unnatural' order of things that can be so damaging. So when we consider the stressful life events following adolescent suicide, we will, like Brent and colleagues (1993), find that the reverberations in families will be enormous.

In the Brent study, young people who had died appeared to have a profound interpersonal conflict with parents, a major disruption of a romantic attachment or an earlier conduct disorder, which inevitably involved the parents. Fortunately, in Britain, adolescents usually do not have easy access to lethal means, so relatively we are spared the consequences of the sudden, impulsive, destructive reaction of an adolescent in response to an interpersonal crisis. But it is doubtful whether the family can ever be the same again, even in the face of just one act of deliberate self-harm.

'Pauline', who was sixteen, was fostered and then adopted, relatively late. Her adoptive parents were tolerant, understanding, long-suffering and, most of all, loving. Pauline dealt with the storm and stress of adolescence in extreme testing-out behaviour: 'If you really loved me you would . . . etc.' She began to overdose in dramatic and apparently frank attention-seeking ways, and the frantic concern of the parents was exacted as a due, because Pauline's birth mother had rejected her, and they had to prove their love. A brief but passionate affair ended after a party and was followed by an overdose. With almost tragic inevitability, death was caused by the subsequent vomiting. The adoptive parents felt they had failed, projected impossible standards of omnipotent insight and understanding upon themselves, and felt desolate and rejected.

Parents' reaction to deliberate self-harm or suicide in the face of a 'Romeo and Juliet' attachment will be compounded by projected scapegoating of the rejecting partner of their son or daughter. And, of course, with the increasing speed of changes in socio-sexual norms, it can be very difficult for parents to know where to draw lines; and the young people themselves often feel confused and wish for controls. When it 'all goes wrong', the immediacy of youth can lead to drastic self-harm in flight from the distress, which is not an intended journey into oblivion, but can be catastrophic. This can leave parents overcome with guilt that they should have imposed the older controlling norms of their day – they cannot win.

Consider an increasingly common scenario. A young person has left home, and engages in deliberate self-harm or suicide at the end of two or three turbulent years. This may be the first the parents have heard of their runaway son or daughter, who is then found to be involved with drug and alcohol misuse, and who might have been exploited and dragged into prostitution, and then suicide. Such a profile is regrettably not uncommon in runaway youths (Stiffman 1989; Bell *et al.* 1991; Kufeldt 1992; Pritchard and Clooney 1994). As Yates *et al.* (1991) highlighted, runaway youths invariably avoid health and welfare systems until they are in severe crisis, and then it is too late. Paradoxically, even in times of homelessness, the only aid young people can rely upon is that from their families (Stockley and Stockley 1993; Pritchard and Clooney 1994). When death occurs, added to the parents' distress is anger and not infrequently a wish to blame someone, sometimes themselves.

A very wise paediatrician colleague commented that in his experience of the death of a child, two themes emerge: parents who have a faith blame the hospital; those who have no faith blame God! But in addition to wordless sorrow, anger and projection were the prevailing themes.

Parents losing a child by their own hand truly feel a double blow and are in double jeopardy, and this is nowhere more graphically demonstrated than in the suicide or suicidal behaviour of adolescent or young adult gay men (Schneider *et al.* 1989). We have already discussed the impact of HIV infection and AIDS, but it has to be recognized that though there is greater understanding and acceptance of different sexual orientations, prejudice and discrimination still exist. Sadly, it seems that older people, especially if they belong to the 'working classes', are predominantly the guardians of 'tradition' and 'normality', and therefore more likely to be prejudiced. 'Mr Quin' 'couldn't stand gays', could not understand 'how a son of mine is gay' and some years later was devastated by his son's suicide. His grief was extended into post-bereavement depression as he was tortured by his own ambivalence, blaming himself for his rejection of his son, yet condemning a behaviour 'that I know is wrong'. He felt very rejected that when his son 'was in trouble he didn't come to me'. This is not to castigate people of less advantaged socio-economic status, but rather to acknowledge that they are victims of a system that excludes them from education and the encouragement of reflection, which helps people to think about and reconsider values in a more open way. When this double blow strikes, it is profoundly disturbing, not least because there is less of a tradition of self-care or an ability to use guilt-reducing counselling services. This is one reason why people from classes 4 and 5 often have significant post-bereavement somatic illness and raised levels of dysfunctional stress (Parkes 1986). It is noteworthy that, in the estimate of risk of suicide of Motto (1985), he included an unresolved adjustment for the person's sexual orientation, when a person feels that his or her sexual identity is rejected by either family or society. Mr Quin was another hidden casualty of prejudice.

Spouse or partner

Perhaps the next most traumatic relationship after that of being a parent of a suicidee, is to have been his or her spouse or partner. Canetto *et al.* (1989) examined the interpersonal dynamics of one of the partners being admitted to psychiatric hospital following suicidal behaviour. Not surprisingly, compared with a non-suicidal partner the victim was described as psychologically disabled, but there were clear indications that the suicide had meaning within the dynamics of the partnership, though whether this was in reaction to the earlier illness or the suicidal behaviour remained unclear. Keitner *et al.* (1990), in a more focused study, found strong links between previous suicidality, episodic adjustments and changes in family constellation and family functioning. They stressed that the client's family functioning and social adjustment were important elements in suicidal risk. Important was not only the access and availability of potential help, but also the emotional *quality* of the family situation. In parenthesis, this reflects the results found with family management of schizophrenia (Falloon 1985; Leff and Vaughan 1985; Kuipers 1987), but we would stress that family dysfunction is not necessarily causal, but very often reactive. On the other hand, it is recognized that if the family response is not supportive, it is better, in this minority of cases, for there to be a planned separation, so that the sufferer is found alternative, but supportive, accommodation.

In the phrase of Van Dongen (1990), partners ask 'agonizing questions' of each other, and often feel rejected, with anger interspersed in their distress. Bronisch (1992) asked: does attempted suicide have a cathartic effect? What is interesting about this question is that it suggests that, with a very severe major depression, an extremely violent attempt that is not successful might prove to be cathartic, and somehow resolve the depression. No clear conclusion was found, and though the 'cleansing' effect may appear in some situations, it seems dubious.

Heikkinen *et al.* (1992) demonstrated the importance to spouses of understanding the suicide in a substantial Swedish cohort ($n = 1397$). Spouses related major life events within three months of the incident. Approximately a third had employment difficulties and somatic illness, and there was also another third with family discord, with a small proportion where the family discord had led to separation. Perhaps not surprisingly, former spouses saw this as the most critical event of all, which was accompanied by guilt, distress and stigma.

Siblings

What if the suicide victim was your brother or sister, especially if the sibling was older? It is the general experience that, no matter how mature one becomes, one still tends to see the older brother or sister in the former family hierarchy. When a crisis comes, this inhibits intervention, lest one is perceived as presumptuous.

Alison Wertheimer (1991) movingly relates her response to the death of her older sister, as well as the total surprise, 'after all I reasoned, people in nice, normal families do not kill themselves', reflecting the double blow to professionals who feel they have an additional sense of responsibility to their family. All professionals, carry an extra burden of being perceived to have 'perfect' understanding, so she wondered: 'Why hadn't I made sure she got help?' Thus echoing the anger and sense of frustration of Alvarez at the death of Sylvia Plath, and all who have lost someone from suicide. There is little doubt that major family tragedies, not just suicidal behaviour, but also autism, learning difficulties or serious physical illness can take their toll of a healthy sibling, who sometimes feels resentful or indeed envious of the attention that the depressed, unhappy, physically ill or disabled sibling receives (Dunne *et al.* 1987; Stein *et al.* 1989; Stewart *et al.* 1991; McIntosh 1993).

One feature not often mentioned is the genetic factor (Roy 1986; Rende *et al.* 1993). Siblings are apt to worry about constitutional endowment and, in the words of the classic social work educator and practitioner, Elizabeth Irvine, the family's questions about mental illness – 'Why us? Who next?' – may very well be a chronic subliminal anxiety. In a deeply moving passage, the actress Margaret Rutherford wrote in her diaries of her life-long dread that she would succumb to an inheritance that included violence and suicide. Consequently, irrespective of the relationship held with the sufferer or victim, families are not going to be neutral in the face of suicidal behaviour.

Parents as suicide victims: impact upon 'children'

The opposite side of the coin of 'parental nightmare' is the childhood memory, which most of us hold, of our burgeoning understanding of the meaning of death when we tearfully contemplate the demise of our parents. Irrespective of how old one is, the loss of the parent evokes all the old fears and threats of the lost child. Imagine one's parent deliberately leaving one through death. There is evidence of the family being damaged in relation to elderly people, for while there is a degree of acceptance of the death of someone of over seventy-five, it has been shown that following admission into an old people's home, an associated suicide attempt has profound repercussions upon adult children (Franc *et al.* 1993).

The family secret

We have touched briefly upon child abuse and neglect and the interface with psychiatry and suicidal behaviour. While it is necessary to emphasize that the vast majority of people involved in suicidal behaviour are *not* victims of either child abuse or child sexual abuse, some are (Hawton and Roberts 1985; Van Egmond and Jonker 1988; Wagner and Linehan 1994).

Child sexual abuse is controversial in its own right, and we would not wish to compound the distress of the vast majority of family co–sufferers. Based upon an analysis of Fromouth's work (1988) with an exceptionally large cohort of 'non-patient' women, it is postulated that fewer than 2 per cent of all women experienced an inappropriate sexual relationship that *also* impaired their adolescent or adult lives. This still represents a considerable number of people, and extrapolated to the UK, it is equivalent to between 300,000 and 400,000 women. Van Egmond and Jonker's (1988) study showed that 60 per cent of women in their post deliberate self-harm clinic had *no* history of child sexual abuse, but the remaining 40 per cent did. In cases of the suicide of assailants following disclosure (Wild 1988), and in cases of suicidal behaviour following a history of child sexual abuse (Yeo and Yeo 1993), all involved may well be exposed to the most horrendous confusion of pressures, and we must be careful not to add to people's agony. In the words of Newberger (1983), we must avoid 'the helping hand strik[ing] again'.

There are of course other 'family secrets'. For example, 'David's' mother went to enormous lengths to protect her son from the 'ghosts' of his father's suicidal death. When he 'behaved like his father had done' this almost precipitated another tragedy. On the relatively *rare* occasions when there are such 'family secrets', survivors require our special understanding and the most sensitive support and help, lest we add to the damage.

Finally, it should be appreciated that the response of family members, be they spouses or siblings, will contain reverberations of the typical interactions that occur in ordinary families: love, rivalry, affection, jealousy, support, altruism, selfishness, generosity. Professionals must be careful not to 'pathologize' these reactions inadvertently, thereby adding to, not reducing, the post-bereavement stress upon survivors.

Impact upon professionals: protection and prevention

There are a number of areas of potential stress that can impinge upon therapists working in the suicide field. First is what might be described as a shared grief reaction, which is often felt at the loss of a client, even though the counsellor may be confident that every effort was made to protect the client. Professionals often respond to the suicide with a post-traumatic stress reaction (Schmitt *et al.* 1992; Eudier 1993; Reed 1993), not least to having to convey the message to families, and there is longstanding evidence of how a range of disciplines find this the hardest task (Chambers and Harvey 1989; Brownstein 1992).

A second feature involves professionals and families alike: a significant number of suicides saw their psychiatrist, or had been discharged from hospital, in the month preceding their death (Fischer *et al.* 1993; Golacre *et al.* 1993; Obafunwa and Busuttil 1994b). This almost seems a contradiction of Lester's review (1994) showing how effective suicide prevention centres can be. Yet it is too easy to assume that because experts (i.e. psychiatrists) were recently involved with the depressed person, he or she is safe. Not surprisingly, there can be a considerable degree of anger or at best ambivalence. Yet this ignores a whole range of other potential contributory factors, of which the lack of continuity of supervision and support may have been paramount. It is feared that it is even easier to start blaming each other, rather than the chronic neglect of the mentally ill.

All people make mistakes, including professionals, and it may appear presumptuous, but perhaps we should actively begin to empower the survivors of families of suicide by being willing to review what resource *deficits* may have contributed to the death of the sufferer. It is believed that with reasonable resources, and an integrated and interdisciplinary approach to the care of vulnerable people, we could reduce the suicide rate by substantially more than the 25 per cent hoped by the government. In parenthesis, it might be asked, why not eradicate suicide risk altogether? This will never be possible, even with optimal services and a fully understood and safe treatment of mental disorder, for in a free society there will be always a boundary beyond which people must be allowed to determine their own lives, albeit at a certain risk.

When suicide does occur, do we not owe it to yesterday's victims, today's survivors and tomorrow's fatalities to pose Marcus Aurelius' injunction that the task of mental health workers is 'not merely to stop them from harming themselves, but from destroying others'? And if this happens, 'there is some justification for casting the blame for it on those who were somewhat negligent in their duties'. This perfectly posits the dilemmas inherent in community care. There should be no doubt that professionals must take on the responsibility of protecting others – which can be stressful as it may clash with their primary vocation of care for the mentally ill. But they owe it to society, as well as sufferers and potential victims, to protect sufferers and others from the potential consequences of their extreme actions. As demonstrated earlier, however, the mentally ill are less dangerous than the average driver, being far more dangerous to themselves than others. But was someone to blame?

In law, to convict someone of a crime, intent has to be proven. No one wants the levels of suicide we currently suffer, but we know sufficiently what is required, and the gap between the minimal feasible service and the reasonable – note that we do not ask for the optimal – is still considerable. According to Huxley and Kerfoot (1993) in 82 out of 117 local authorities surveyed in England and Wales, there were only 3,463 approved social workers under the Mental Health Act 1983; this is equivalent to one per 11,575 people in the surveyed areas. Bearing in mind that there is one medical doctor to every 1,425 people, it is easy to see why media, public and perhaps other professionals complain that 'there is never a social worker around when you need one'! It may be time to draw to the public's attention something of the real and measurable shortfall in levels of community care. If a 'case' comes to court complaining of the failure of the local authority, rather than 'blaming' the individual professional, we should expose just how thin is the 'thin red line' of our protective and preventative community care services.

Psycho-social impact

Finally, it is important to explore some of the anxieties carried in grey areas, or hidden agendas, when we are trying to determine the primary interest; say, between the sufferer and the family, or, more subtly, between the client and the organization. There are five sources of stress.

First is the direct impact of the death of another person in whom we have invested effort, concern and care. In this sense, although it less than for the family, there is a degree of bereavement for the professional. Second, we may have to carry the family's 'burden', to ease their guilt, when we as fellow human beings would find our guilt easier to bear if we could displace our feelings on to them. Third is an intrinsically professional dilemma. We know we need to maintain a degree of detachment, while at the same time being involved. We often feel unsupported, and this can be very eroding of our commitment and ultimately our competence. Fourth is concern with the question, did we do all we could reasonably have done in the circumstances? Fifth are pressures from society and agencies, who want to 'blame' someone.

Providing the therapist acts to the best of his or her ability, and utilizes the knowledge reasonably available, both in professional terms and in the specific client situation, he or she need fear no indictment if things do go wrong. As Jasper said, 'Illness I can treat, to life I can only make an appeal.'

A case example

I believe that over the years my practice has demonstrated that good psychiatric social work can contribute to positive change, improvement and comfort in the lives of my clients. I hope too that there are a number of people who have been helped to reject the suicide option. But from a small number of events, two in particular still give me cause for regret from which others may learn.

'Roy', aged thirty, was somewhat 'infamous' in the area, for whenever he had a minor crisis, he acted it out in public and dramatically engaged in deliberate self-harm. Among a range of examples was the swallowing of dangerous objects, often at the Saturday afternoon market. His forte on arrival at the local hospital was pride in being able to undergo endoscopy without anaesthetic, and he was happy to claim that he gave valuable practice to medical trainees. His public acts of deliberate self-harm were clear attention-seeking behaviour, and are too numerous to mention. His climbing of high buildings infuriated the local fire brigade; his jumping into a river by the side of a football ground when thousands were streaming by annoyed the police, who objected to getting wet. Eventually, a job was arranged at the local hospital as a theatre porter. Roy's life was transformed. He was the best theatre porter anyone had ever known, he was superb in his attention to patients, staff and colleagues and he clearly enjoyed life to the full. The crisis brewed in the fourth year, when patients began to mention to the visiting anaesthetist that they had already been cheered up by the surgeon who had visited earlier.

Roy, now clothed in theatre garb, had visited 'his patients'. He was confronted with this, admitted it and was sacked on the same day. By the time I had learned of the event, and made a home visit two days later, Roy had been dead for thirty-six hours. I was too late.

'Stuart' was a middle-aged man with a recurrent depression, whose illness had led to him being divorced and living alone. Associated with his current depression was a chronic anxiety. He lived within 200 yards of my home and on occasions 'accidentally' had 'extra sessions'. While the service did not pretend to offer twenty-four hour cover, there was an emergency service in the town, which Stuart or I could call upon. One Saturday morning as I was hurrying by Stuart's home going to a family engagement, he called to me to say that he was not well and to ask if I would visit. I was not on duty and was not pleased. With hindsight and retrospective review, I did not look closely enough, because I did not want to see anything that might have made further demands upon me. Instead I offered him contact with the emergency officer, which he politely declined, gave him reassurance that he would be all right and offered an appointment for the following Monday evening, but demurred at Stuart's hesitant request that perhaps I might see him later that afternoon. Time was pressing, there was no legal statutory obligation upon me, I had a longstanding though intermittent professional relationship with him and, although he seemed agitated, there had only been the mildest suicidal ideas and there had never been an incident of deliberate self-harm. Therefore I failed to ask the question, was anything different about Stuart? The answer might have appeared to be no, but this was the very *first time* he had ever *asked* for an extra session in this semi-formal way. When the glib reassurance 'you will be all right, I'll see you on Monday evening' was given, it was as if a door had closed, and he was courtesy itself. He reassured me that he was being unfair and intrusive upon my free time, that I had been enormously helpful and that he would always be grateful for all the help I had given over the years, and he shook my hand. This was a valediction, and later that afternoon I was troubled. Early in the evening I walked by his house, to see if he was about. He did not appear as hoped, for he had been dead for two hours, in one of the earliest examples of carbon monoxide poisoning.

The two cases have common themes. First they were well known to me, and did not appear to have any real risk. In the case of Roy, there was something different, and there should have been some communication, no matter how brief, and the promise of advocacy and possible reinstatement in another area of the hospital. I was too slow and the excuse of the enormous caseload and other statutory duties brings no comfort. In the case of Stuart there was also a slight, but significant, change in a client whom I thought I knew well. Roy could not take the communal rejection, or Stuart the passive rejection from a source where he expected succour. The biggest professional mistakes are made when we think we know the situation well. We subconsciously stop thinking and evaluating the situation. More than twenty-five years later, I still feel the scars.

CHAPTER 9

EUTHANASIA: AN EPILOGUE TO CHRONIC MENTAL ILLNESS?

'Is it normal for terminally ill patients to desire death?' asked Brown *et al.* (1986). They made no 'excuse' for the judgemental and medicalized term 'normal', but reflected a growing debate about the 'rational' limiting of life and treatment in the face of incurable and apparently irretrievable situations. Euthanasia, often called 'mercy killing', is where physicians or others assist or permit someone else to die. The issue has even been the subject of a popular play, *Whose Life Is It Anyway*, and the vigil at the death of Peter Bond, a victim of the Hillsborough football disaster who existed in a 'vegetative state' (brain dead) for more than twenty months, could not fail to touch all who heard the parents, nurses and doctors who struggled with this terrible dilemma. In Kentucky, with its strongly traditional religious beliefs, we find a wide 'public acceptance' of the idea of euthanasia and 'living wills' (High 1988). And that most civilized and secular country, the Netherlands, has recently decriminalized euthanasia and allowed people to request assisted deaths (Van der Maas *et al.* 1991).

There is considerable evidence that extreme life stressors, exemplified by cancer, have a co-morbidity of depression (Klerman 1989; Spiegel 1991; Mermelstein and Lesko 1992), but it is believed that the answer to Brown *et al.*'s question is actually in the negative. Generally, people who are terminally ill do *not* take their own lives. While they may consider it, there is testimony that the more serious the prognosis, the *less* likely are they to actively contemplate either suicide or euthanasia, although passive euthanasia has some support (Owen *et al.* 1992, 1994). Careful examination of the evidence in Owen *et al.*'s brilliant and very sensitive study of 100 Australian oncology patients points towards a very important trend. First, those most inclined to suicide are more likely to have had a previous psychiatric illness, or have a family member having depression (hints of susceptibility). When such people contemplate their situation, unsupported pain is also a factor in their projected view (Spiegel 1991). Kuhse and Singer (1986) found similar trends when they asked kidney dialysis patients about voluntary euthanasia.

The most stressed, interestingly, were those who had dialysis at home, and these were more likely to consider euthanasia. This is reminiscent of Vogel and Wolfersdorf's (1989) finding of subjective isolation and unsupported pain among a cohort of elderly suicides. It is normal to *consider or think about* killing oneself when musing upon a hypothetical death from cancer when one is under thirty, fit and healthy. But it is a very different situation when life experience tells one that five or ten years are the maximum one might expect if one has a malignant disease in an advanced state.

For us, the link between euthanasia and suicide, with all the ethical dilemmas implied, is much too close for comfort. Anne Sexton spoke wistfully of the death of Sylvia Plath, and became almost obsessionally fascinated with her rival's death. Unhappily in the poem she almost echoes the Victorian sentimentality of Thomas Chatterton's suicide: seen in the Wallis portrait he appears to 'sleep' and died unscathed, unruffled, a parodic echo of 'They shall grow not old, as we that are left grow old'. This idea of dying perfectly, intact, painless, is a throwback to a child's images of death, totally devoid of the reality of change and physical corruption. But many who repeat and repeat, succumbing to the allure of Russian roulette, forget that mutilation is increasingly certain, as the seductive challenge of the lottery grows – will someone come in time? At the danger of being considered impertinent, when one views the comments about Sexton's life by those who knew her, and tried to treat her, she comes across as a person who can so numb us with a rare intelligence and insight that we miss the fatal flaw, which in all probability is later recognized as an illness. Certainly, a poem that Sylvia Plath wrote less than a week before she died through coal gas poisoning reflects a chilling hopelessness:

> The woman is perfected.
> Her dead
> Body wears the smile of accomplishment,
> the illusion of a Greek necessity.
> – Her bare feet seem to be saying:
> We have come so far, it is over.
> – The moon has nothing to be sad about,
> Staring from her hood of bone.
> She is used to this sort of thing.

('Edge' 1963)

Plath had prepared her children and was careful to protect them from the dangers of the coal gas. Was the expected visitor late? Was this suicide, or the euthanasia of someone who could no longer cope with her own unattainable, autocratic demands? Did she know what she was doing, or rather, despite her high intelligence, her forbidding independence, was she as ill as any who are blasted by the self-fragmenting hopelessness found in psychiatric depression?

Suicide, some would say, is different from euthanasia, as it is essentially about the deliberate act of self-killing, while euthanasia, among many definitions, is classically primarily concerned with the 'good death', eased, comfortable and peaceful. Since 1990, the progressive and professionally advanced Dutch have made it possible to practice not only passive euthanasia, i.e. letting die, but also 'assisted suicide', which is defined as deliberate assistance at a suicide attempt at the request of the attempter (Hellema 1992).

It should be clear that it is conscious patients who must initiate the request, and in keeping with their high standards, the Dutch demand that a second medical opinion be available, often a psychiatrist, because it is recognized that some people may be suffering from depression (Spiegel 1991; Mermelstein and Lesko 1992). Yet there is evidence that it is exceedingly difficult to communicate with people considering euthanasia, not least to disentangle the impacts of physical pain, threat of loss, psychic pain and so on (Cole 1993). The Dutch, with their longstanding tradition of integrated health and welfare services, have elected to cross this particular Rubicon, yet we remain uneasy. Why?

The fundamental divide, which sees one form of self or assisted death as acceptable and the other as unacceptable, is the notion of rationality. What Gillon (1988) in a rather chilling phrase calls 'the benefit–burden balance' is the situation when there is a decision as to whether a life is no longer worth living. Euthanasia is traditionally associated with fears of interminable suffering, following old age or in the condition of 'pre-death', which is defined as a terminal condition in which the person, partly depending on age, takes between three and thirteen months to die (Isaacs *et al.* 1991). Ganry *et al.* (1992) explore the modern cultural fear of cancer, and suggest that one reaction is to consider the last resort of personal self-control, euthanasia. Cole (1993), from the field of palliative care, found that there can be hidden agendas for requesting euthanasia. It might be a form of 'altruistic suicide', where victims or sufferers do not want to expose their families to further distress, or feel that they are being burdensome to the service and family. So it may be that their motivation is shaped by wanting to please others rather than by a primary concern with themselves. It could be asked, why not allow people to make a sacrifice for their families? But would we really want this to become a norm, especially when it must be appreciated that in 'terminal' states a life's length will often be fairly short.

Ten or more years ago, one of the stress factors associated with suicide was physical illness, though a fairly recent Swedish study (Stensman and Lundquist-Stensman 1988) that explored physical disease and disability among cases of suicide found no statistically significant link with cancer deaths. However, others have reported a proportional rise in suicide among cancer victims: 1.3 times higher in males and 1.9 times higher in females than in the general population (Allebeck and Bolund 1991). However, not only is there a link with previous psychiatric pathology, but diseases such as cancer have a co-morbidity of between two and four times the rate of depression of the general population (Spiegel 1991). Mermelstein and Lesko (1992) found this depression to be treatable.

It may be argued that seeing depression as an 'illness' in terminally ill people is the worst example of 'medicalizing', in this case 'psychiatricizing', human experience, a theme that Illich (1971) railed against. But in a review of twenty-five studies of the treatment and outcome of depression in people with cancer, Mermelstein and Lesko (1992) reported that there appeared to be psycho-social benefits in twenty-three of the research projects, with some reduction in suicidal or euthanasia ideation and a concomitant raising of Beck 'hopelessness' scores. This suggests that improved care and management of pain and appropriate psychosocial support for the terminally ill may well have removed a key precipitant, and re-empowered the person. Some years ago we planned to undertake a comparative analysis, over a decade, of suicide rates in an acute psychiatric unit and a hospice that specialized in cancer care. Despite the time period, it proved not to be feasible because there were insufficient self-determined deaths amongst cancer patients, probably only two in ten years.

However, the justification for euthanasia must lie in the motivation for death, and while it is probably true that for many years people have been allowed to die, rather than actively kept alive by assertive treatment (Kuhse and Singer 1986), there is a crucial difference between active euthanasia, with active killing, and the notion of assisted suicide. Irrespective of either single case examples or hypothetical humanistic projections, this must give us pause, for if someone shuffles off this mortal coil, who is benefiting (apologies to Hamlet)?

In 1991 Derek Humphry published the last of a series of popularizing 'do-it-yourself' euthanasia texts, a book called *Final Exit*, with the subtitle *The Practicalities of Self Deliverance and Assisted Suicide for the Dying*. Michel *et al.* (1994) examined a year's Swedish suicides who used lethal drugs, and found that 16 per cent had used a 'drug combination recommended by EXIT'. Recently in Britain, a twenty-eight-year-old woman suffering from an eating disorder read the *Final Exit* text and took her life (Dury 1994).

Humphry's book was unusually reviewed by five different experts in one of the most prestigious international journals concerned with suicide, *Suicide and Life Threatening Behaviour* (Motto *et al.* 1992). Motto refused to 'take a position' because 'the basic issues are philosophical in nature and *can only be answered by society*' (italics added). Maris was far less reluctant, indeed he was caustic, juxtaposing the 57,000 members of the Hemlock Society against the 1,200 members of the American Suicidology Association. But he acknowledged that as more than half a million people bought the book in the USA, far more than would ever read a lifetime's psychiatric and social work texts, the issue must be of substantial public interest. Maris raised many questions. He acknowledged the probable altruism of the author, but also remarked upon his treatment of his second wife, and asked whether, if there can be 'rational suicides, could not there be rational homicides too?' This is perhaps a cheap debating point, but it shows the degree of passion aroused! Battin's contribution sought to offer weight on the other side. She appeared to accept the issue of 'rational choice', approaching the issues from the point of view of defence of the individual against coercion and control by professionals. Especially useful was her argument that the issues fall along the former religious divide: the Christian tradition, which 'set His canon against self-slaughter', versus the Hellenic Stoic antecedents, who urged 'that dying be a responsible autonomous act'. She reminded us that between 75 and 80 per cent of people in the developed world are likely to die of some form of deteriorative disease. While this information might be thought to be double-edged, it strongly indicates that the issues will not go away, and she laments, with a swipe at the professionals, that it is a pity that people in such trouble cannot 'guarantee help from a skilled, loyal counsellor in exploring so important a decision'. Richman was singularly struck by the apparent fascination of Humphry with 'practising' with a plastic bag, but his main criticism was of Humphry's disregard of the social context of the argument, which Richman believed would lead to no further provision of dedicated hospices and the like.

It may be argued that if someone is 'determined to die', then we should not impose inhuman obstacles so that he or she is compelled to go to extreme means. It should be said that I have no intention of imposing upon *compos mentis* fellow citizens a view about euthanasia, for any hidden philosophical, ideological, religious or political reason. I hold a humanistic, democratic socialist world-view, and am non-theistic in religious belief, prizing tolerance above all else, except the pursuit of social justice and the dissemination of knowledge. What I seek to do is briefly to explore some of the complexities inherent in the dilemma, and perhaps to expose some dangers which, at first sight, may appear to be 'nannying' and old-fashioned, authoritarian and 'non-progressive'.

It is acknowledged that the Hemlock Society and the Voluntary Euthanasia Society are raising very important questions and one is not attributing malfeasance, but it does seem somewhat unfortunate, to paraphrase the words of Oscar Wilde, for the protagonist of *Final Exit* to have lost two wives. The husband is reported as saying of the second: 'Right from the first year the marriage was blighted by her depressive episodes – she had a history of borderline personality disorder' (Dalrymple 1991).

In parenthesis, I have always believed that the great personality theorists have inadvertently been 'willing to justify themselves' (St Matthew) by emphasizing the aspects of their personality that they view as important. It is a truism that one way to deal with an anxiety or threat is to talk about it in magical terms, so that it will not happen (Parkes 1986).

One must always ask about 'vested interests', which may not directly be about fees, status, altruism or any of the myriad versions of what 'vested interests' are taken to be. We professionals are always on the edge of being either part of the solution or part of the problem.

On the other hand, take the example of Jill Tweedie, journalist and social activist extraordinary, who developed motor neurone disease (MND). In a most poignant discussion, Polly Toynbee (1993), with the collaboration of her friend, raged against the 'dying of the light'. She raised the question of whether Jill Tweedie would take charge of her own life by ending it because of the unequivocal diagnosis, which has a most horrendous, destructive impact upon mind and body. It would be difficult in such circumstances, knowing what the late symptoms of MND can be, to question a person's right to take the decision, and at this time, and *deo volente* still fit and well (for my age), I find it impossible to contemplate equably a worse death, and therefore perhaps might think of euthanasia; who knows?

Christopher Howse (1993) directly answered the Toynbee article from a self-declared Christian position: 'Some say that killing yourself is brave, [but] it is the ultimate treason', largely because neither life nor one's body is one's own. He could understand Jill Tweedie wishing to avoid counselling by some 'death expert', and he 'bristles at the thought that a healthy living person cannot do much for her let alone tell her how to die'. But Howse claims that we cannot accept such a death for other people or society, saying that the crucial point is that we 'are all dying, it is a question of when, let's not make it now'. In the book of Job, which attracts the approbation of the Hebraic, Christian and Islamic faiths, it is written: 'Who is this that darkeneth counsel without wisdom?' (Job 38: 2). Consequently what is required is to tease out the key issues and, within the spirit of humility, seek wisdom, without imposing one's own value system upon others, but seeking the best available evidence, so that we do not counsel 'without wisdom'. When people wish or actively seek euthanasia or suicide, are they truly acting rationally? We do not know.

Is there a difference between euthanasia and suicide? The term euthanasia was used by Thomas Carlyle, when he said 'not a torture death but a quiet euthanasia', and is described in the *Oxford Shorter English Dictionary* (1969) as 'an abridgement of the pangs of disease', a 'quiet and easy death' and the 'means of procuring this'. Thus there is an intent and an action. Suicide is defined in the same place purely in action terms; that is, 'one who dies by his own hand; one who commits self murder; an act of taking one's life'. Crucially suicide is about the action of the person, and legally in the UK and most countries for another to assist the would-be suicide is still a criminal offence. This is why the Netherlands decision is so far-reaching. And there are active steps in some states of the USA to follow the Dutch line (Owen *et al.* 1994). However, for an indictable offence to be proven, in addition to the 'guilty act' (*actus rheas*) there must also be a 'guilty intent' (*mens rheas*). Eighteenth- and nineteenth-century Europeans 'forgave' self-murderers because the *mens rheas* was not proven, as mentally ill people were not in the position truly to appreciate what they were doing. Such a position is probably no longer tenable, but it is valuable to look at where these ideas came from.

In the United States of America, some have taken one of the most often misquoted and out-of-context lines in an easy defence of euthanasia: 'Thou shalt not kill; but needst not strive officiously to keep alive' (Arthur Clough, 'The latest decalogue'). But more of the poem should be considered, to highlight its underlying cynicism:

Thou shalt have one God only; who
Would be at the expense of two?;
[. . .]
Honour thy parents; that is, all
From whom advancement may befall;
[. . .]
Do not adultery commit,
Advantage rarely comes of it;
Thou shalt not steal; an empty feat,
When it's so lucrative to cheat;
[. . .]
Thou shalt not covet; but tradition
Approves all forms of competition.

The above is potentially very undermining of professional commitment. Yet in the world of hospital trusts and value for money, Wilde is again apt, as it increasingly appears that the world is run by people who 'know the price of everything, and the value of nothing'.

We need to determine the rationale for the death, which raises the question: can we always be sure that there is a rational euthanasia, because, as with suicide, it can get very ambiguous? To what extent is a person truly autonomous, as euthanasia must in one sense, like suicide, outrage our basic belief and knowledge of life? But is this academic sophistry, for there are daily examples in many hospital wards where a person observing the individual suffering might well think he or she is better off out of it? Most sapient people can envisage, in their own peculiar circumstances, 'a situation where if they could their 'quietus make', peacefully and painlessly, they would end their lives. But the question is: would they? Even if they are likely to die in a relatively short time, as in the later stages of motor neurone disease, should they be allowed to go 'passively' or be assisted?

One possible solution sometimes put forward is that we would need some form of advocate, rather like the 'Official Solicitor' or the 'Board of Protection', for incapacitated people, minors and some mentally ill people respectively. But whose cause would this 'advocate' be pleading? From the poetry of the Mass we hear: 'Who shall plead my cause, when even the just sit insecurely?' It is this area of uncertainty as to the *objectivity* of such an advocate, whether an individual or committee, that arouses so much concern and arguments about the dangers of the slippery slope.

Let us try to place the discussion firmly in the practical, rather than the philosophical, domain. It seems evidently true that when a person is fully *compos mentis* is the time to gain his or her view about resuscitation and/or assisted euthanasia. However, on reflection, and apart from in certain circumstances, such as a persistent vegetative state, we must ask whether an early pre-emergency decision can be based upon 'informed consent'. What little research there is suggests that the determining factor lies in the reality of a serious diagnosis. Once the 'sentence', i.e. the confirmed terminally ill prognosis, has been passed, then, as in the 'case' of Mrs Baker, who apparently had all the right reasons to 'end it all', the patient might recognize that life is precious.

Within the Dutch system, the second physician is often a consultant psychiatrist, who can determine the rationality of the patient's request in the light of his or her mental state, though this is not mandatory. It has been reported that most psychiatrists felt that their involvement in such cases should be voluntary, and half believed that their role was 'to support the decision-making process of the ward staff' (Huyse and Van Tilburg 1993). Unquestionably the decision to allow euthanasia must place tremendous stresses and strains upon staff, but at another level it is hardly reassuring that there seems to be no one to plead the patient's cause.

Recently Van der Wahl *et al.* (1994) and Muller *et al.* (1994) examined the practice of the majority of Dutch nursing home physicians (NHPs) in response to requests for euthanasia or doctor-assisted suicide of their residents over the previous five years. Some 78 per cent had *no* such requests from their residents ($n = 582$), and of the remaining 22 per cent ($n = 164$) seeking active euthanasia,

53 wanted physician-assisted suicide. The numbers granted were 51 and 23 respectively. It appeared that in total there were only 300 requests per annum and about 25 approved and carried out. The rationale for a positive decision centred upon: (a) the patient experiencing unbearable suffering and hopelessness; (b) the request coming voluntarily; (c) the request being well considered; (d) a second physician being consulted. Slightly more than half of the granted requests were granted because of unbearable suffering, the remainder because of hopeless suffering. At first sight this is reassuring, as 91 per cent of physicians thought the request well considered and 93 per cent believed there was no alternative treatment. However, when closer inspection was made as to certification and prudent recording and administration, the researchers concluded that the Dutch NHPs observed *all* the requirements in only 41 per cent of cases, perhaps most often erring on the side of certifying death from natural causes. This would suggest that, even at this early stage, not only might there be an under-recording of euthanasia and physician-assisted suicides, but because of the frequent use of 'internal' second opinions, it *might* be that the safeguards are already being overwhelmed by the administrative task. Who then will plead my cause?

It is accepted that most physicians, most of the time, want only what is best for their patients, and they *can* be relied upon, particularly when there is no financial vested interest, to do the 'right thing'. Experienced practitioners know that every day caring physicians and nurses help people towards a peaceful end, based upon their total view of the specific situation. But because of the present state of the law, they must always err on the side of caution and offer a 'second chance'. In a paper by Benatar (1992) from South Africa, the issues of medical progress and what he described as the secularization of life were explored. His views are close to those of Ivan Illich, who complained that there has been an over-medicalization of both life and death. Both Benatar and Illich would want to return to some earlier, less 'overly scientific' era, in which the culture viewed dying elderly people as normal, surrounded by families, making their farewells, without the intrusion of professionals and their technology. 'Die with dignity' is a rallying cry that few would quarrel with (Battin in Motto *et al.* 1992). This is laudable perhaps, and it used to happen before the Second World War, and could again with appropriate care and resources. But there is really no going back, as knowledge brings with it an onerous responsibility, and Illich's lament is as useful as wishing that we did not know about nuclear energy, or somehow could dis-invent weapons of mass destruction. In a Utopia it would be possible, but what part of medical, social and psychological knowledge would we wish to dis-invent? Rather like Szasz's diatribe against psychiatry, this is a dangerous reactionary libertarianism, and for all practical purposes is irrelevant.

There is, says Benatar (1992), a growing acceptance of individual human rights, including the right to refuse medical treatment, which is linked to a better informed public and a sharing in medical decisions. There is good empirical support for this (Owen *et al.* 1992, 1994) as it has been generally agreed that patients at the 'sharp end' of oncology should have more and better information, and be able to take decisions about the nature of treatment, and whether it should be discontinued or not. This places the issue of informed consent at the centre of the debate, yet one of Britain's most eminent and humanitarian research psychiatrists, the late Professor Max Hamilton, in his last publication, a letter to the *British Journal of Psychiatry*, argued that 'there is no such thing as informed consent unless there is equal knowledge'. If this is so, it implies that currently patients have to rely upon the integrity of their physicians; or we need to re-educate *both* physician and the citizen to respond to what would be a massive change in the balance of power between them. Such an alteration would not be without its complications. On the one hand, physicians would have to be more open and accept an overt diminution of their authority, as they engaged in a shared decision-making process. On the other hand, patients would have to decide whether or not to confront the reality, rather than having the comfort of being able to hand over responsibility, which many people frankly still prefer to do. 'Doctor knows best' is sometimes true, and in many circumstances this is an *easier* position to take than handling the burden ourselves, with all the extra emotional involvement this might entail. Experience would suggest that there are currently three types of patient response: those who say 'tell me all' and mean it; those who say 'tell me all, Doctor', but only want good news; and those who overtly do not want to know. It may be that even within the first two groups of people, in some circumstances, the patient does not 'hear' what is said, amply demonstrating an understandable, real, non-communicative ambivalence. None the less, as a society, we should certainly strive towards greater empowerment of every kind of client of professionals, though this is not a 'free good' without possible costs to some people.

Decisions about withholding or withdrawing treatment, argues Benatar, who acknowledges the psychological implications surrounding the open acceptance of such a stance, remain distinct from decisions about assisted suicide or active euthanasia, which are 'generally considered unacceptable perversions of medical practice' (though not in Holland; Van der Wahl *et al.* 1994). However, Benatar has to acknowledge that in many countries, such as South Africa, use of the technical ability to sustain life for long periods is not always a fair, rational and, equally importantly, reasonable use of scarce health care resources (this is a modern example of the classic Benthamite argument of the greatest good going to the greatest number). In view of the totally inadequate allocation of resources for effective medical treatments in South Africa, Benatar advocates an opening of the discussion about allowing to die and killing, though he rightly warns of the slippery consequences. It is interesting that someone who comes from a culture where totalitarian rule existed until very recently warns of the slippery slope.

Could such an incline move from the humanitarian active euthanasia of a terminally ill old person (so as to use the resources saved for preventative child health), to limiting treatment according to age or level of recovery, to diverting moneys saved to more preventative medicine, to limiting psychiatric treatment after a certain number of episodes have occurred. Far fetched? Bach and Bach (1993) explored the linked issues of compulsory sterilization and euthanasia, and traced the roots of such thinking back to the Nazi way of dealing with not just political opponents and ethnic undesirables, but also the other '*Untermenschen*' (less than humans): homosexuals, the mentally handicapped and the mentally ill (Meyer

1988). Christoph Hufeland (1762–1836), a medical ethicist, presciently said: 'If the physician presumes to take into consideration in his work, whether a life has value or not, the consequences are boundless and the physician becomes the most dangerous man in the state' (quoted in Hulatt 1992). This is a salutary warning, but is it 'over-the-top' and do our concerns reflect more the ivory towers of academic detachment, rather than the daily reality of people in extremity?

We were earlier critical of sociologists' extreme use of totalitarian examples of psychiatry, juxtaposing compulsory admission in Britain with the misuse of psychiatry in the USSR. Have we committed a similar hyperbole?

Our critique was based upon practice experience of how difficult it was for a person to be admitted, not how easy. Might there not therefore be a parallel here? Euthanasia, either passive or active, is so much the 'last resort' that some worry it is tardy in its application, but what about the pressure put upon doctors to clear their beds? The hospital bed analogy is a good one, because one of the reasons why hospitals are reluctant to accept patients is the cost. Let us pursue this line of thought a little further. The remarkable reduction of people residing in psychiatric hospitals is not just humanitarian, but is associated with a marked fall in the number of available beds, in both psychiatry and general medicine and surgery (CSO 1994). Of course people prefer to be at home wherever possible, but even the most gimlet-eyed market enthusiast must recognize that the effort to reduce the cost of health and social care has also contributed to a reduction in the availability of admission. Despite all the 'civil liberties' rhetoric – when some governments speak of 'citizen choice', look for a net reduction in funding – sufferers, families and practitioners do not experience the all-compelling asylum-filling mental health system, but an often desperate search for either respite care or protected refuge. Yet it must be remembered that Britain spends a smaller proportion of GDP on health than it did in the late 1980s, and relatively has one of the lowest health budgets in the developed world (Pritchard 1992c; Baggott 1994; Lawson 1994). One begins to wonder about the motives of government and society, which are operationalized by professionals who would potentially make euthanasia easier or, eventually, the desirable norm. Is it just a way of saving money?

In a brilliant essay from Munich, Lauter and Meyer (1992) discuss the role of the psychiatrist in the field of euthanasia, and for us the themes would be the same for social workers and nurses. They argue that the decriminalization of active euthanasia in the Netherlands has fundamentally changed the way in which dying patients are dealt with. They believe this approach will eventually extend to other European countries and the USA, echoing Huyse and Van Tilburg (1993). They cite the influence of moral philosophers like Jonathan Glover (1984), who attempted to marry the utilitarian with the humanitarian approach, with interesting echoes in the United Nations Declaration of Human Rights, which, Glover infers, gives human beings rights only as long as they are 'rational and self-conscious', though his examples are particularly related to people with severe learning disability.

A practical example might concern the 100,000 plus patients who are said to have Alzheimer's disease in the USA. If we extrapolated this rate to Britain, it would be in excess of 25,000 people. With the rise in the use of 'living wills' (High 1988), and the length of time that many people are in the 'pre-death situation' (Isaacs *et al.* 1991), it is not surprising that Lauter and Myer ask the question of whether the next step will be towards the elimination of the very elderly. Just think of the saving to be made; it is enough to make hospital trust finance officers drool with anticipation at the redeployment of resources, or a performance-related pay incentive to reduce overall unit costs. Some believe that the decriminalization of euthanasia is almost inevitable, especially after the innovation of the Dutch experiment, which therefore merits a closer scrutiny. Huyse and Van Tilburg (1993) analysed the requests for euthanasia in 1990 from among the 130,000 deaths in Holland; in 5 per cent the doctors took a decision to alter the duration of the patient's life (more than 6,500), but only 2,300 cases involved the doctor performing euthanasia. Hellema (1992) questions whether the Dutch have over-estimated their euthanasia rates, but Muller *et al.* (1994) suggest the opposite. Yet the official 2,300 cases represent 152 deaths per million population, which is higher than the total suicide rate of 107 per million, or 4.8 per cent of the total 1991 Netherlands death rate. If this 4.8 per cent was extrapolated to the UK, from a total of 634,239 deaths in 1992 there would be more than 30,000 assisted euthanasia deaths!

Huyse and Van Tilburg have conjectured whether this innovation might be followed elsewhere, such as in the USA. The USA has a very different culture from that of the highly secular Dutch, yet 'living wills' have attracted over ten million supporters in the States (High 1988). But if the work of Owen *et al.* (1992, 1994) and Brown *et al.* (1986) is a guide, then the healthier the person, even when he or she is currently a patient, the more likely he or she is actively and positively to consider euthanasia or assisted suicide. But such enthusiasm falls away rapidly among those with the worst prognosis, and Brown *et al.* argue that a large number of seriously and especially terminally ill people are measurably depressed; the Dutch NHP studies showed that in the majority of nursing homes requests were the exception rather than the norm (Van der Wahl *et al.* 1994).

If we translate the Dutch experience into the numbers of equivalent deaths in the USA, an 'assisted' euthanasia rate of 4.8 per cent would represent 103,126 deaths. Can we really contemplate such numbers? Consider how much double-checking any patient-safeguarding 'advocate' would need to do. In Holland this was not as rigorous as might be supposed (Muller *et al.* 1994). Perhaps with numbers like these, even the fit and well might be a little less enthusiastic.

Apart from in the first year of life, the citizen costs the NHS more in the last three years of his or her life than in all the other years put together. It is feared that for economic reasons these very elderly people may (it is emphasized *may*) have life saving medical treatment withheld (*de facto* euthanasia) or have assisted suicide made easier. Soon, with changes in orientation, there could almost be a moral pressure, once prolonged invalidity occurs, for the person 'no longer to be a burden' upon family and others. Lauter and Myer (1992) argue that the consideration of such ideas is not extreme, but in today's debate, the issue is less about the right of a few severely and terminally ill human beings to take their own lives with or without assistance, and more about whether handicapped or 'socially useless or unproductive people' have the right to live. This, say these physicians from Germany, is where the slippery slope might end, and Hufeland's phrase that the doctor might become the 'most dangerous man in the state' will have come to fruition.

I fear seemingly altruistic language that speaks of letting or helping other people die. Consider the apparently very humane euthanasia advocates, such as Dr Jack Kevorkian, who makes media appeals that in essence say 'We would not let a dog suffer like that.' This must find an echo in us all, but it causes considerable concern in such organizations as the British Medical Association (Morris 1992). Recently I shared the experience of euphemistically 'putting to sleep' a dog who had shared our lives for more than fifteen years – the three-hour wait before the vet came will stay with us for the rest of our lives. I learned that rhetoric and reality were very different. Yes, I would not change the present system, which is based upon mutual trust of physician, nurse, patient and society.

Most people trust, almost completely, the average doctor and nurse who work alongside their patients, as we have confidence in their professional ethic, which puts the patient's interest first. But, consider an alternative scenario of the 'cost of success'.

David Lester (1993), an internationally eminent researcher, explored the effectiveness of suicide prevention centres over a decade. He was able to demonstrate that the overall suicide toll could be lowered, which coincides with the British Department of Health's view: not only can we reduce these preventable deaths, we should do so. However, there are two costs here: the expense of establishing, developing and running such centres, as clearly more resources would be needed; and the cost of the small, but fiscally significant, group of long-term mentally ill patients who live instead of dying, and who will probably need continued care with a concomitant rolling cost. After all, bearing in mind Thomas Szasz's assertion that 'mental illness is a myth' and such people are merely abdicating their responsibilities to life, why should society bear such a cost? Therefore, after, say, three 'episodes' of mental illness, would it not be kinder and more dignified to let them take their Kantian decision, and if they wished to die, to do so, in the name of 'citizen's choice'?

Let us attempt the finance officer's sums. Extrapolating from the United Kingdom 1992 suicide level, of 4,628 deaths, let us assume that 70 per cent had a 'mental disorder', which leaves us with a little more than 3,240 people, of whom say a half had been recurrent repeaters with a chronic mental illness, that is 1,620 people. In ten years there will be 16,200 'unit of care costs', at least requiring substantial long-term support, equalling a third of the current hospital beds. Can we afford it, should we afford it? Is such a calculation and question possible, even in the 'cold heart' of an accountant?

Is this an absurd situation? Not if the decision in the Supreme Court of Appeal in the Netherlands is a precursor of 'things to come'. A fifty-year-old social worker – inferred to be intelligent and able to make an informed consent – had experienced a number of depressions in a very tragic life: she lost one son from suicide and another from lung cancer, and suffered violence from her husband. Initially the psychiatrist treated her depression and tried to change her mind about suicide. She appealed to him for help because 'rope offers only a 70 per cent chance of success – and trains, I would resent the mess'. After consulting a number of other colleagues, the psychiatrist agreed to assist her suicide. The court decreed that the psychiatrist was not negligent and 'recognizes the rights of patients experiencing severe psychic pain to choose to die with dignity' (Toufexis 1994).

According to the Department of Health the frequency of 'affective psychosis' is estimated at 0.3 per cent of the general population, equivalent to about 173,000 people; a further 4.5 per cent have 'depressive disorder', approximately 2.5 million people. If we concentrate upon the 'affective psychotic' group, at least 1.9 per cent die by suicide, despite all our active efforts. What might the Netherlands court ruling do to the confidence that sufferer, family and fellow professionals have in the psychiatrist? This may be considered unfair, but hidden agendas could well develop hidden agendas. As there are potentially enormous savings, the temptation to let people die because of the direct and indirect costs to the rest of society might, in the world of book-keeping, find advocates who undoubtedly would wrap up the rationale in terms such as 'empowerment', 'patient choice' and the rest. This precedent from such an advanced country has led to acute consternation in the Royal College of Psychiatrists and the BMA and, rightly in our view, is said to be totally opposed by both organizations.

Such a future scenario might appear to be absurd, unthinkable, impossible. It is hoped so, and most people still trust the professional integrity of the 'human care professions' (teachers, doctors, nurses, social workers) because we all belong to a tradition of care that is individualistically based, enshrined in the United Nations Declaration of Human Rights and founded on the core Hippocratic concept of 'do thou no harm'. If there is a doubt, it emerges from those cash-responsible but *distanced* professionals, the hospital trust managers and finance officers, who are protected by their physical and therefore emotional distance from having to confront the 'disposable', 'useless' or 'burdensome' person's humanity, which would give them pause. Without that personal immediacy, it is easy to imagine just playing 'the numbers game' of 'units of care costs'.

The angry, self-righteous de Stogumber, in Shaw's *Saint Joan*, was appalled at the result of his previously detached approach to extreme action. This had inadvertently led him to great cruelty: he hadn't the imagination to see what the reality of 'burning the witch' really meant. It is similar in the decriminalization of 'humane euthanasia'. The chain of command in our caring institutions used to link the care and treatment professionals together: the matron, the hospital superintendent, the consultant, the ward sister or charge nurse, the social worker and the patient. Now we have largely non-care or treatment managers; or, if they were former patient-contact staff, their earlier professional values are treated as redundant, if not obstructive. These new 'rulers' have yet to *prove* that they truly are patient-centred, as they claim, and are not diverted by performance-related pay, which has seen the vast majority of nursing posts down-graded following staff changes. Thus unlike medicine, social work and nursing, whose rationale is the primacy of the patient above everything else (albeit never perfect), 'management' gives us little confidence that it will defend the defenceless, or take risks on behalf of an individual patient, as doctors, nurses and social workers do when they make palliative care decisions, which ensure a 'good death'. This is not being sophist, but very practical. There are grounds for our trust in the human care professionals, but the 'managers' have yet to earn it.

Critics will say that I am being extreme, that there has always been some form of rationing in the NHS, the only difference now being that there is public acknowledgement. This is true, except that the carefully sculptured public perception of ever-increasing health care costs is seen in terms of 'what we can afford' (Mrs Thatcher) and is just *not* true. We are spending *less* of our GDP on health than we were in the 1980s. Informed consent is a concept belonging to the professionals and, as Shaw warned, potentially professions are conspiracies against the laity. But whom would you trust with your life, to help, for *your* benefit, a 'good death'? Or, to borrow a phrase, 'Are you doing this for me, Doctor/Manager/Finance Officer, or am I doing it for you?'

Can we really trust an overly utilitarian society that makes *Homo economicus* its central player? The slippery slope is far too greasy, and the temptation to take an 'easy (cheaper) way out' with some chronic problems would be seductive. What might this mean in a future in which society did not have to wrestle with the consequences of long-term mental illness, disability and the like? There would be little impetus for research and treatment development, as it would be easier to resolve the problem indirectly with 'a bare bodkin'.

There can be no total or absolute position on euthanasia. It is *not* suggested that we should always 'officiously strive', but in the present situation, in which caring and dedicated staff ensure a 'good death', because of the ambiguity of the law, such staff are protected from Hufeland's hubris, and proper pain management is ensured, each individual situation being judged on its merits. This preserves citizens' faith in those who care for them when they are most vulnerable, and ensures that those professionals honourably merit such trust. The honourable argument for euthanasia is, in Litman's view, based upon 'an appeal to threatened personal values of dignity and autonomy. Altruistic motives are not stressed, although often, unfortunately, euthanasia would be an economic boon for families and the health system' (in Motto *et al.* 1992).

Euthanasia and its fellow traveller, assisted suicide, if released from tried and proved ethical constraints, might well prove to be society's ultimate rejection of the mentally ill.

CHAPTER 10

SYNTHESIS AND CONCLUSION

In our psycho-social study of suicide, we have tried to integrate three forms of knowledge. We have drawn upon the history, literature and poetry of our culture to seek an understanding that is psychologically authentic, to facilitate an empathetic response to people in distress. This has been juxtaposed with empirical research, which gives a degree, albeit imperfect, of greater focus and precision. Together these help us to understand the limits of our own backgrounds, and the limits of our current knowledge. They assist us in making person- and situation-specific judgements, to aid the primary objective, of confronting and preventing the personal and social despair that leads to suicidal behaviour – the ultimate rejection.

Practice knowledge, based ethically on a commitment to the pursuit of social justice, teaches us that we need to integrate our different sources of 'knowledge' so that we attain a balance between empathy and analysis. The *synthesis* of practice activity brings together the personal totality of the professional, who, although he or she is operating within a role and must always be conscious of his or her own humanity and fallibility, should also recognize his or her value to the client and the positive interventions that can be brought about.

All three kinds of knowledge are by themselves severely limited, but if we can successfully integrate the concepts into our professional mind-set, then each source enhances the others, to improve our understanding, awareness, empathy and ability to analyse, and to help us to maintain an open mind, which is crucial to the continued improvement of the service.

Based upon this tripartite approach to understanding suicidal behaviour, we came to identify the theme running through the phenomenon, which links both the personal and the socio-structural, that of rejection. The person, in response to intra-psychic distress, both psychiatric and stress-related, finds himself or herself either objectively or subjectively rejected. Such rejection has a reality, which is potentially deadly. The person then rejects the unresolved pain, rejects the immediate world, rejects the plethora of troubles, 'and by opposing end[s] them'.

Such rejection does not occur in a vacuum. The family around the person shares this ultimate rejection, because the person did not apparently value them sufficiently to want to live. Here is a rejection indeed, so that for the living the suicide is not an end but can be a disintegrative beginning.

A significant, and some would say the most reprehensible, kind of rejection is societal. For whatever reason, society's actions demonstrate to the person that he or she is one of the *Untermenschen*, the underclass, with a life and opinions that have no worth or esteem.

The personal experience of rejection is in a sense amoral because it is 'illness'-based: no one *intended* the hurt. And no one intended the stress-related hurt to kill, or the societal impact upon the citizen to destroy: the societal rejection was never personalized and therefore was passive. But we can no longer remain morally aloof by claiming either ignorance or no malevolent intent. Though no one intended the suicide, because of our knowledge of the *effect* of this psycho-socio-economic rejection, we are all potentially indicted because society and community do exist, not merely individuals. As a nation we have taken pride in our 'commitment' to human rights as enshrined in the United Nations Declaration of 1948.

We now live in a multi-cultural pluralistic society, and it is hoped that the review presented here of the historical responses to suicide helps us to understand the greater complexity confronting the front-line practitioner. It is vital to be culturally sensitive in any effective assessment and preventative intervention: account must be taken of age, ethnicity, gender, social class and any 'category' that might be used to de-individualize the citizen. This must be linked to a social and structural understanding of society, and how social and health policies evolve, because there is a constant danger of thinking of suicidal behaviour as essentially a personal, covert thing – ignoring the subtle social and cultural influences. Our review of other cultures should teach us about the relativity of our own, and of our own times. The data from the People's Republic of China not only demonstrated the value of an empirical approach, but in the unexpected finding demonstrated the limits of current knowledge. We need to revise our earlier understanding to include the demonstration that a culture may impose a sense of rejection or ill-worth from the day of birth, compounded further by socio-economic disadvantage, because the person is rural-based rather than urban-based. It was seen that the discrimination was mediated, rather as it is by social class in the West: for example, Chinese urban women had a lower suicide rate than rural men, in a society which normally has a higher female suicide rate; a Western industrialized corollary would be between the employed and the unemployed.

Another important feature emerging from the historico-social review was that, within our multi-cultural society, there are not only religious themes which differ (e.g. Christian, Hindu and Islamic) but also differing value systems reflecting gender, age and social class traditions. In any examination within a two-mile radius from the centre of any large British city, we would find all cultural, gender and age values systems mixed together. For example, there would be people who hold relatively traditional views about suicide and mental illness; these are more characteristic of Victorian England, because people maintain their young-adult value systems, so that a ninety-year-old person is in a sense living in a 'time capsule'. Conversely there will be those who are more similar to urban or rural Greece, India or Pakistan, or more typical of traditional Christian, Hindu or Islamic faiths or their 'liberal' versions, as well as many non-believing secularists. How easy it would be for a non-aware professional to reject, or be rejected by, such a pluralistic constituency.

Practice: prevention, control or care

Practice dilemmas, actual or potential, are legion. On the one hand it is easy to deny another's civil and political liberties by compulsory powers under the Mental Health Act 1983, even though this may be justified by an honourable intent. Conversely, we can deny people's rights by our reluctance to act or, because of inadequate resources or organization, deny the citizen the life-saving service.

The perennial difficulty for any service is that aspirations are always likely to outstrip our performance. While constructive criticism is essential, professionals working in the mental health field can find themselves being co-victimized – being blamed for shortcomings of either political will or social commitment. On the one hand we represent the 'positive' and 'progressive' aspect of societal conscience; on the other we face the classic dilemma of care versus control. Sanctions are laid upon us to protect society, while we try to reconcile the needs of individuals. It is believed that in the new millennium suicide will overtly become a paradoxical indicator of the cohesiveness of society, and suicide rates may well become politically sensitive. The temptation, therefore, if the rates do not fall, will be to blame the professionals or, even more worrying, to blame the victims, by a further excoriation of their value as people belonging to the under-class. However, there are real grounds for optimism: modern research indicates that for a substantial majority of sufferers, we can offer an effective preventative service.

Our review of current interdisciplinary research offers seven positive and encouraging messages.

First, an interdisciplinary *integrated* approach is, objectively, the optimal, and in any form of intervention or treatment, secondary support must include all aspects of the bio-psycho-social factors that contribute to the individual's particular predicament.

Second, mental illness, both psychiatric depression and the schizophrenias, can be effectively treated, and although substance abuse complicates any situation, sufferers can be helped if motivation can be engaged. While we need to keep a watchful eye on pharmacological treatment, the newer drugs, in conjunction with appropriate psycho-social therapy and support, show great promise. In respect of psychiatric depressions, the serotonin-based drugs are an exciting prospect, for at least a significant minority of sufferers.

Third, modern research has helped us to identify the contributing causes that lead to suicidal behaviour. The results are based upon aggregated data, demonstrating trends within groups of people, and tell us little about a specific individual, but they do assist us in assessing the potential intervention priorities, not least which area of 'stress' should first be addressed in order to reduce the accumulative stressors.

Fourth, and linked to what has gone before, we can with growing confidence make better informed predictions about the risks people experience, thus aiding better judgement about whether or not the 'crisis situation' is an 'emergency'. Ideally, by resolving the 'crisis', we can avoid the emergency.

Fifth, while there are overlapping elements between suicide and deliberate self-harm, there are important differences. This helps us to improve our assessment of risk levels. It also points to the need to maintain an open mind, lest we are over-sanguine and think that deliberate self-harm is 'only a cry for help', thus missing those vital clues that indicate a new risk of ultimate harm.

Sixth, the research has confirmed the importance and centrality of relationships to sufferers: with their immediate family and community, and with the professional. Without a positive rapport, the professional cannot communicate with the other person, and indicate that the sufferer need not feel or be rejected, thus making the ultimate appeal to the other's humanity.

Finally, bringing our sources of knowledge together in a new synthesis, we can confidently present to the potential victim that he or she need not be alone in the midst of personal despair. We can offer him or her a 'second chance' to avoid the ultimate rejection.

However, in respect of the potential victims of societal rejection, our appeal has to be directed elsewhere.

First, in the case of euthanasia, we warn of a slippery slope, which despite the honourable *intent* of the advocates of 'decriminalized' euthanasia, we deeply fear that the *effect* may be to undermine the core value society places upon the life of another person.

Second, in a world that is on the brink of seeing human beings only as *Homo economicus*, we marginalize and then dehumanize rejected citizens to the redundant category of the 'underclass'. We know that some of the 'underclass' may shake off their defensive apathy, and utilize an 'alternative market response' to their poverty by engaging in criminal activity. Others, however, are in danger of accepting the societal verdict of rejection, and engaging in self-damaging behaviour. But there is a dangerous combination in the inadvertent alliance of the euthanasia lobby with the rejecting makers of the underclass. Together they are in danger of shattering the central law of humanity, the veneration of human life.

Such an approach should be opposed at every level, recognizing that 'any man's death diminishes me'. Finally, we can point to considerable progress, but such development is not the end but only a beginning. To ensure that progress towards a fuller social justice continues, we must avoid the atrophy of personal, social and professional curiosity, which leads to rigidity of thinking and totalitarian thought. Thus the search for new knowledge and new understanding continues, eschewing all absolutist principles. We recognize with the poet Omar Khayyam:

> And this one thing I know.
> Whether the one true light shall kindle to love
> Or wrath, consume me quite.
> One glimpse of it within the tavern caught,
> Is better than in the temple lost outright.

BIBLIOGRAPHY

Abbar, M., Caer, Y. and Castelnau, D. (1993) Psychosocial stress factors and suicidal behaviour. *Enchaphale*, 19: 179–85.

Adams, D.M., Overholser, J.C. and Spirito, A. (1994) Stressful life events associated with adolescent suicide attempts. *Canadian Journal of Psychiatry*, 39(1): 43–8.

Agbayewa, M.O. (1993) Elderly suicide in British Columbia; an exploration of regional variation and related factors. *Canadian Journal of Public Health*, 84(4): 231–6.

AIMS (1986) Suicide attempts and suicides in India: cross-cultural aspects. *Acta Psychiatrica Scandinavia*, 32(2): 64–73.

Allebeck, P. (1988) Predictors of completed suicides in a cohort of young men: role of personality and deviant behaviour. *British Medical Journal*, 297: 176–8.

Allebeck, P. and Allgulander, C. (1990) Psychiatric diagnoses as predictors of suicide: a comparison of diagnoses at conscription and in psychiatric care in a cohort of 50,465 young men. *British Journal of Psychiatry*, 157: 339–44.

Allebeck, P. and Bolund, C. (1991) Suicides and suicide attempts in cancer patients. *Psychological Medicine*, 21(4): 979–84.

Allen, G. (1990) *Family Life*. Oxford: Blackwell.

Allgulander, C. and Fisher, L.D. (1990) Clinical predictors of completed and repeated self-poisoning in 8895 self-poisoning patients. *European Archives of Psychiatry and Neurological Science*, 239(4): 270–6.

Alvarez, A. (1971) *The Savage God: A study of suicide*. Harmondsworth: Penguin.

AMA (1990) Council on Scientific and Ethical and Judicial Affairs. *Journal of American Medical Association*, 263(3): 426–30.

Andreasson, S., Allebeck, P. and Rydberg, U. (1990) Schizophrenia in users and non-users of cannabis: a longitudinal study in Stockholm county. *Acta Psychiatrica Scandinavia*, 79(5): 505–10.

Angst, J., Scheidegger, P. and Stabl, M. (1993) Efficacy of moclobemide in different patient groups: results of new sub-scales of the Hamilton Depression Rating Scale. *Clinical Neuropharmacology*, 16 (Supplement 2): 55–62.

Appleby, J. and Desai, P.N. (1985) Documenting the relationship between homelessness and psychiatric hospitalisation. *Hospital and Community Psychiatry*, 36(7): 732–7.

Aquinas, T. (1963) *Summa Theologica*, T. Gilbly (ed.). London: Blackfriars.

Arato, M., Demeter, E. and Somogyi, E. (1988) Retrospective psychiatric assessment of 200 suicides in Budapest. *Acta Psychiatrica Scandinavia*, 77: 454–6.

Arato, M., Rihmer, Z. and Demeter, E. (1990) Suicide in subtypes of primary major depression. *Journal of Affective Disorders*, 18: 221–5.

Asguard, U. (1990) A psychiatric study of suicide among urban Swedish women. *Acta Psychiatrica Scandinavia*, 82(2): 115–24.

Aurelius, M. (1910) *Reflections: Marcus Aurelus Antoninus To Himself*, translated by G.H. Rendal. London: Macmillan.

Avery, D.H., Kahn, A. and Dager, S.R. (1990) Bright light treatment of winter depression: morning versus evening light. *Acta Psychiatrica Scandinavia*, 82(5): 335–8.

Bach, O. and Bach, C. (1993) Compulsory sterilisation and euthanasia: comments on the roots of a development that led to the Fascists' way of dealing with the mentally ill. *Deutsch Psychiatrisch Praxis*, 20(2): 78–81.

Baggott, R. (1994) *Health and Health Care in Britain*. Basingstoke: Macmillan.

Bagley, C. (1984) Adult mental health sequels of child sexual abuse, and physical neglect in maternally separated children. *Canadian Journal of Community Mental Health*, 3(1): 37–41.

Bailey, R. and Ward, D. (1994) *Consumer Views of Structured Probation Supervision*. Nottingham: Centre for Action Research, University of Nottingham.

Baker, F., Jodrey, D. and Straus, H. (1993) Community support services and functioning of the seriously mentally ill. *Community Mental Health*, 29(6): 321–31.

Baldwin, J. (1968) *Another Country*. London: Sphere.

Barker, P. (1993) Personal communication. Medical Director, Special Hospitals Authority.

Barraclough, B.M. (1990) The Bible suicides. *Acta Psychiatrica Scandinavia*, 86: 64–9.

Barraclough, B.M. and Hughes, J. (1987) *Suicide: Clinical and Epidemiological Studies*. London: Croom Helm.

Barraclough, B.M. and Shepherd, D.M. (1976) Public interest, private grief. *British Journal of Psychiatry*, 131: 400–4.

Barrett, T.W. and Scott, T.B. (1989) Development of the grief experience questionnaire. *Suicide and Life Threatening Behaviour*, 19(2): 201–15.

Barton, J. (1995) A review of *folie à deux*: implications for modern practice, M.Sc. Dissertation, Department of Social Work Studies, University of Southampton.

Bayatpour, M., Wells, R.D. and Holford, S. (1992) Physical and sexual abuse as predictors of substance use and suicide among pregnant teenagers. *Journal of Adolescent Health*, 13(2): 128–32.

Bean, P. (1986) *Mental Disorder and Social Control*. Chichester: Wiley.

Beck, A.T., Resnik, H.L. and Lettieri, D.J. (eds) (1974) *The Prediction of Suicide*. Bowie, MD: Charles Press.

Beck, A.T. (1987) *Depression: Clinical, Experimental and Theoretical Aspects*. New York: Harper and Row.

Beck, A.T. (1988) *Cognitive Therapy and Depression*, 2nd edn. Chichester: Wiley.

Beck, A.T. and Steer, R.A. (1989) Clinical predictors of eventual suicide: a 5–10 year prospective study of suicide attempters. *Journal of Affective Disorders*, 17: 203–9.

Beck, A.T. and Steer, R.A. (1991) Relationship between the Beck Anxiety Inventory and the Hamilton Rating Scale with anxious outpatients. *Journal of Anxiety Disorders*, 5(3): 213–23.

Beck, A.T., Steer, R.A. and Garrison, B. (1985) Hopelessness and eventual suicide: a 10 year prospective study of patients hospitalised for suicidal ideation. *American Journal of Psychiatry*, 142: 559–63.

Beck, A.T., Steer, R.A. and Brown, G. (1993b) Dysfunctional attitudes and suicidal ideation in psychiatric outpatients. *Suicide and Life Threatening Behaviour*, 23(1): 11–20.

Beck, A.T., Steer, R.A. and Newman, C.F. (1993a) Hopelessness, depression, suicidal ideation and clinical diagnosis of depression. *Suicide and Life Threatening Behaviour*, 23(2): 139–45.

Beck, A.T., Steer, R.A. and Skeie, T.M. (1990) Panic disorder and suicide ideation and behaviour: discrepant findings in psychiatric out-patients. *American Journal of Psychiatry*, 148(9): 1195–9.

Beecham, J., Cambridge, P. and Knapp, M. (1993) The costs of domus care. *International Journal of Geriatric Psychiatry*, 8(10): 827–31.

Bell, G., Hindley, N. and Reinstein, D.Z. (1991) Psychiatric screening of admissions to an accident and emergency ward. *British Journal of Psychiatry*, 158: 554–7.

Bellack, A.S. and Mueser, K.T. (1993) Psychosocial treatment for schizophrenia. *Schizophrenia Bulletin*, 19(2): 317–36.

Benatar, S.R. (1992) Dying and Euthanasia. *South African Medical Journal*, 82(1): 35–8.

Benezech, M. and Bourgeois, M. (1992) Homicide is strongly correlated with depression not mania. *Encephale*, 18 (Special Issue): 89–90.

Berrios, G.E. (1990) *Treatment of Depression*. Cambridge: Cambridge University Press.

Berrios, G.E. and Monaghan, M. (1990) Durkheim and French psychiatric views on suicide during the 19th century. *British Journal of Psychiatry*, 156: 1–9.

Biblarz, A., Brown, R.M. and Biblarz, D.N. (1991) Media influences on attitudes towards suicide. *Suicide and Life Threatening Behaviour*, 21(4): 374–84.

Birley, A. (1966) *Marcus Aurelius*. London: Eyre and Spottiswoode.

Black, D.W., Winokur, G. and Nasrallah, A. (1993) A multivariate analysis of the experience of 423 depressed inpatients treated with ECT. *Convulsive Therapy*, 9(2): 112–20.

Blackburn, I. (1981) The efficacy of cognitive therapy in depression. Treatment trial using cognitive therapy and pharmo-therapy, each alone and combined. *British Journal of Psychiatry*, 139: 181–9.

Bland, R.C., Newman, S.C. and Stebelsky, G. (1993) Epidemiology of gambling in Edmonton. *Canadian Journal of Psychiatry*, 38: 108–12.

Block, L. (1993) The employment connection: the application of an individual supported employment program for persons with chronic mental health problems. *Canadian Journal of Community Mental Health*, 11(2): 79–89.

BMA (1992) Euthanasia around the world, (editorial). *British Medical Journal*, 304: 32–8.

Bodmer, Sir Walter (1988) New approaches to the prevention and treatment of cancer, in J.M. Austyn (ed.) *New Prospects for Medicine*, 114–38. Oxford: Oxford University Press.

Bodmer, Sir Walter and McKie, R. (1994) *The Book of Man*. London: Little and Brown.

Bond, G.R. (1984) Economic analysis of psycho-social rehabilitation. *Hospital and Community Psychiatry*, 35(4): 181–9.

Borga, P., Stefansson, B. and Cullberg, J. (1992) Social conditions in a total population with long-term functional psychosis in three different areas of Stockholm. *Acta Psychiatrica Scandinavia*, 85: 465–73.

Bourgeois, M. (1991) Serotonin, impulsivity and suicide: a review. *Human Psychopharmacology*, 6 (Supplement): S31–S36.

Bourin, M. and Turpault. T. (1991) Pharmacology of a new specific serotonin re-uptake inhibitor: Paroxetine. *Psychological Medicine*, 23(9): 1079–94.

Box, S. (1988) *Recession, Crime and Punishment*. Basingstoke: Macmillan.

Brenner, M.H. (1983) Mortality and economic instability: detailed analysis for Britain and comparative analysis for selected countries. *International Journal of Health Services*, 13: 563–620.

Brent, D.A. (1989) The psychological autopsy: methodological considerations in the study of adolescent suicide. *Suicide and Life Threatening Behaviour*, 19(1): 43–57.

Brent, D.A., Perper, J.A. and Allmain, C.J. (1991) The presence and accessibility of firearms in the homes of adolescent suicides. *Journal of American Medical Association*, 266(21): 2989–95.

Brent, D.A., Perper, J.A. and Schweers, M.L. (1993) Stressful life events and adolescent suicide. *Suicide and Life Threatening Behaviour*, 23(3): 179–87.

Brindle, D. (1994) Compulsory treatment of the mentally ill. *Guardian*, 17 January: 2.

Brittlebank, A.D., Cole, A. and Hassanjay, F. (1990) Hostility, hopelessness and deliberate self-harm. A prospective follow-up. *Acta Psychiatrica Scandinavia*, 81(3): 280–3.

Bronisch, T. (1992) Does an attempted suicide actually have a cathartic effect? *Acta Psychiatrica Scandinavia*, 86(3): 228–32.

Brown, G.W. (1987) Social factors and the development and course of depression in women. *British Journal of Social Work*, Supplement: 17(6): 615–34.

Brown, G.W. and Harris, T.O. (1978) *The Social Origins of Depression*. London: Tavistock.

Brown, G.W., Bifulco, A. and Andrews, B. (1990) Self-esteem and depression II. Social correlates of self-esteem. *Social Psychiatry and Psychiatric Epidemiology*, 25(5): 225–34.

Brown, J.H., Henteleff, P. and Barakat, S. (1986) Is it normal for terminally ill patients to desire death? *American Journal of Psychiatry*, 143: 208–91.

Brown, L.K., Spirito, A. and Hemstreet, A. (1992) Adolescent coping behaviour when confronted with a friend with AIDS. *Journal of Adolescence*, 15(4): 467–77.

Brownstein, M. (1992) Contacting the family after suicide. *Canadian Journal of Psychiatry*, 37(3)1: 208–12.

Brudney, K. and Dobkin, J. (1991) Resurgent tuberculosis in New York City. Human immune deficiency virus, homelessness and the decline of tuberculosis programmes. *American Review of Respiratory Disease*, 144(4): 745–8.

Bunch, J. and Barraclough, B. (1971) The influence of parental death anniversaries upon suicide dates. *Social Psychiatry*, 6: 193–9.

Burton, Robert (1883) *The Anatomy of Melancholy*, (1621). London: Chatto and Windus.

Butler, A. and Pritchard, C. (1990) *Social Work and Mental Illness*. Basingstoke: Macmillan.

Cahill, C., Llewelyn, S.P. and Pearson, C. (1991) Long term aspects of sexual abuse which occurred in childhood: a review. *British Journal of Clinical Psychology*, 30: 117–30.

Canetto, S.S., Feldman, L.B. and Lupei, R.L. (1989) Suicidal persons and their partners: individual and interpersonal dynamics. *Suicide and Life Threatening Behaviour*, 19(3): 237–48.

Carey, T.G., Owens, J.M. and Horne, P. (1993) An analysis of new long-stay population. The need for mental hospitals. *Irish Journal of Psychological Medicine*, 10(2): 80–5.

Casey, P. (1991) Parasuicide and Personality Disorders, in S. Montgomery (ed.) *Current Approaches to Suicide and Attempted Suicide*, pp. 41–7. Southampton: Duphar Medical Publications.

Catalano, R., Dooley, D. and Novaco, R.W. (1993) Using the ECA survey data to examine the effect of job lay-offs on violent behaviour. *Hospital and Community Psychiatry*, 44(9): 874–9.

Central Statistical Office (1994) *Social Trends 1994*. London: CSO.

Chambers, D.R. and Harvey, J.G. (1988) Self inflicted death 1971–1985, in H.J. Moller and R. Schmidtke (eds) *Current Issues in Suicidology*, pp. 56–61. Berlin: Springer-Verlag.

Chambers, D.R. and Harvey, J.G. (1989) Inner urban and national suicide rates, a simple comparative study. *Medicine Science and Law*, 29(3): 182–5.

Chan, D.W. and Lau, B. (1993) Assessing psychopathology in Chinese psychiatric patients in Hong Kong using the Brief Psychiatric Rating Scale. *Acta Psychiatrica Scandinavia*, 87(1): 37–44.

Chaucer, G. (1986) *Canterbury Tales: Knight's and Nun's tales*. Oxford: Clarendon Press.

Cheetham, S.C., Katona, C.L.E. and Horton, R.W. (1991) Post-mortem studies of neurotransmitters in biochemistry in depression and suicide, in S.C. Cheetham (ed.) *Biological Aspects of Affective Disorders*. London: Academic Press.

Chen, E., Harrison, G. and Standen, P. (1991) Management of first episode of psychotic illness in Afro-Caribbean patients. *British Journal of Psychiatry*, 158: 517–22.

Cheng, K.K., Leung, C.M. and Lam, T.H. (1990) Risk factors of suicide amongst schizophrenics. *Acta Psychiatrica Scandinavia*, 81(3): 220–4.

Chiles, J. (1986) *Teenage Depression and Suicide*. New York: Chelsea House.

Clark, S.P., Delahunt, B. and Fernando, T.L.U. (1989) Suicide by band-saw. *American Journal of Forensic Medicine and Pathology*, 10(4): 332–4.

Clayton, P.J. (1982) Bereavement, in E.D. Paykel (ed.) *Handbook of Affective Disorders*. London: Churchill Livingstone.

Clough, A.H. (translator) (1957) *Plutarch's Lives*. London: Everyman Series, Dent and Sons.

Clough, A.H. *The Latest Decalogue*, in A.P. Wavell *Other Men's Flowers: An Anthology of Poetry, 1944*. London: Jonathan Cape.

Cohen, E., MacKenzie, R.G. and Yates, G.L. (1991) HEADASS, a psycho-social risk assessment instrument: implications for designing effective intervention programmes for runaway youth. *Journal of Adolescent Health*, 12(7): 539–44.

Cohen, L.J., Test, M.A. and Brown, R.L. (1990) Suicide and schizophrenia: data from a prospective community treatment study. *American Journal of Psychiatry*, 147(5)1: 602–7.

Cole, R.M. (1993) Communicating with people who request Euthanasia. *Palliative Medicine*, 7(2): 139–43.

Collins, T. (1990) *Open Verdict: An Account of 25 Mysterious Deaths in the Defence Industry*. London: Sphere Books.

Conway, A.S., Melzer, D. and Hale, A.S. (1993) The evidence of targeting community mental health services: evidence from West Lambeth schizophrenia cohort. *British Medical Journal*, 308: 627–30.

Cope, R. (1989) The compulsory detention of Afro-Caribbeans under the Mental Health Act. *New Community*, 15: 343–56.

Copeland, A.R. (1993) Suicide amongst AIDS patients. *Medicine Science and Law*, 33(1): 21–8.

Corney, H. and Clare, A.W. (1983) The effectiveness of attached social workers in the management of depressed women. *British Journal of Social Work*, 13(1): 57–74.

Cox, M. and Pritchard, C. (1995) Troubles come not singly but in battalions: the pursuit of social justice and probation practice, in M. Lacy and D. Ward (eds) *Current Issues in Probation and the Criminal Justice System*. Andover: Ashgate.

Crumley, F.E. (1990) Substance abuse and adolescent suicidal behaviour. *Journal of American Medical Association*, 263(22): 3051–6.

Cullberg, J., Wasserman, D. and Stefansson, C.G. (1988) Who commits suicide after a suicide attempt? *Acta Psychiatrica Scandinavia*, 77: 598–603.

Dalrymple, J. (1991) Death haunts millionaire author of suicide guide, *Sunday Times*, 13 October: 17.

Davies, M. (1994) *The Essential Social Worker*, 3rd edn. Andover: Ashgate.

Dawood, N.J. (translator) (1990) *The Koran*. Harmondsworth: Penguin.

Day, P.R. (1981) *Social Work and Social Control*. London: Tavistock.

Dean, C., Phillips, J. and Gadd, E.M. (1993) Comparison of community based service with hospital based service for people with acute severe psychiatric illness. *British Medical Journal*, 307: 473–6.

De Chateau, J. (1990) Mortality and aggressiveness in a 30-year follow-up study in child guidance clinics in Stockholm. *Acta Psychiatrica Scandinavia*, 147(6): 761–5.

De Man, A. and Labreche-Gauthier, L. (1991) Suicidal ideation and community support. An evaluation of two programmes. *Journal of Clinical Psychology*, 47(1): 57–60.

Department of Employment (1994) *Employment Gazette*, 102(3): March.

Department of Health (1992) *The Health of the Nation: A Strategy for England and Wales*. London: HMSO.

Department of Health (1993) *The Health and Social Care of People with HIV Infection*. London: HMSO.

Department of Health and Social Security (1984) *Management of Deliberate Self-Harm*, LA. SSL 84. London: HMSO.

Diekstra, R. (1991) Suicide and parasuicide: a global perspective, in S.A. Montgomery and L.M. Goeting (eds) *Suicide and Attempted Suicide Risk Factors, Management and Prevention*, pp. 1–22. Southampton, Duphar Medical Relations.

Di Maio, L., Squitieri, F. and Napolitano, G. (1993) Suicide risk in Huntington's Disease. *Journal of Medical Genetics*, 30(4): 293–5.

Doane, J.A. (1986) The impact of individual and family treatment on the affective climate of families of schizophrenics. *British Journal of Psychiatry*, 148: 279–87.

Dollimore, J. and Sinfield, A. (1985) *Political Shakespeare: New essays in cultural materialism.* Manchester: Manchester University Press.

Donne, J. (1988) *Biathanatos.* Harmondsworth: Penguin Classics.

Dooley, D., Catalano, R. and Serxner, S. (1989) Economic stress and suicide: multivariate analysis. Part 1. Aggregate time-series analysis of economic stress and suicide. Part 2. Cross-level analysis of economic stress and suicidal ideation. *Suicide and Life Threatening Behaviour*, 19(4): 321–36, 337–51.

Dooley, E. (1990) Prison suicide in England and Wales. *British Journal of Psychiatry*, 156: 40–5.

Duhressen, A. and Jorswieck, R. (1962) Towards a correction of Eysenck's report on psycho-analytical treatment results. *Acta Psychotherpiae*, 10: 329–42.

Dunne, E.J., McIntosh, J. and Dunne-Maxim, K. (eds) (1987) *Suicide and its Aftermath. Understanding and Counselling the Survivors.* New York: N.W. Norton.

Durkheim, E. (1888) *Suicide: A Study in Sociology*, translated by J.A. Spaulding and G. Simpson (1952). London: Routledge and Kegan Paul.

Dury, L. (1994) Eating disorder suicide took EXIT, *Guardian*, 6 January: 3.

Duster, T. (1994) Post-industrialism and youth unemployment: Afro-Americans as harbingers, in R. Lawson and W.J. Wilson (eds) *Poverty, Inequality and the Future of Social Policy.* New York: Russell Sage.

Eagleton, T. (1983) *Literary Theory: An Introduction.* Oxford: Blackwell.

Easteal, P. (1994) Homicide-suicide between adult sexual intimates: an Australian study. *Suicide and Life Threatening Behaviour*, 24(2): 140–51.

Egeland, B., Jacobwitz, D. and Papatola, K. (1987) Inter-generational continuity of parental abuse, in J. Lancaster and R. Gelles (eds) *Bio-Social Aspects of Child Abuse*, pp. 115–34. New York: Jossey-Bass.

El-Guebaly, A.M. (1990) Substance abuse and mental disorders: the Dual Diagnosis concept. *Canadian Journal of Psychiatry*, 35(3): 261–7.

Emerick, R.M. (1990) Self-help groups and former patients: relationships with mental health professionals. *Community Psychiatry*, 41(4): 401–7.

Eskin, M. (1993) Opinions about reactions to suicide amongst Turkish high school students. *International Journal of Social Psychiatry*, 38: 280–6.

Eudier, F. (1993) Interview with a psychiatrist after a suicide: interests and limits. *Française Psychologie du Medicine*, 25(5): 430–1.

Evans, G., Todd, S. and Beyer, S. (1994) Assessing the impact of the All-Wales Mental Handicap Strategy: a survey of four districts. *Journal of Intellectual Disability*, 38(2): 109–33.

Eysenck, J.H. (1952) The effects of psychotherapy: an evaluation. *Journal of Consulting Psychology*, 16: 38–44.

Faccincani, C., Mignolli, G. and Platt, S. (1990) Service utilisation, social support and psychiatric status in a cohort of patients with schizophrenia. A 7-year follow-up. *Schizophrenia Research*, 3(2): 139–46.

Falloon, I.R.H. (1985) *Family Care of Schizophrenia.* New York: Guildford Press.

Falloon, I.R.H. (1992) Early intervention for first episodes of schizophrenia. A preliminary exploration. *Psychiatry*, 55: 4–15.

Farberow, N.L., Gilewski, M. and Thompson, L. (1992) The role of social supports in the bereavement process of surviving spouses of suicide and natural death. *Suicide and Life Threatening Behaviour*, 22(2): 107–24.

Fenton, S. and Sadiq, A. (1991) *Asian Women and Depression.* London: Commission for Racial Equality.

Fernando, S. (1988) *Race and Culture in Psychiatry*. London: Routledge.

Ferriera de Castro, E., Pimenta, F. and Martins, I. (1988) Female independence in Portugal and the effect on suicide rates. *Acta Psychiatrica Scandinavia*, 48: 464–7.

Fine, S., Haley, G. and Forth, A. (1993) Self-images as a predictor of outcome in adolescent major depression. *Journal of Child Psychology and Psychiatry*, 34(8): 1399–408.

Finkel, K.C. (1987) Sexual abuse in children: an update. *Canadian Medical Association*, 136: 245–52.

Fischer, E.P., Comstock, G.W. and Spencer, D.J. (1993) Characteristics of completed suicide: implications of differences among methods. *Suicide and Life Threatening Behaviour*, 23(2): 91–100.

Floud, J. (1982) *Report of the Committee on Dangerous Offenders*. London: Home Office.

Ford, P., Pritchard, C. and Cox, M. (in press) Consumers' views of the Probation Service: towards a new understanding of 'Advise, Guide and Befriend'. *Howard Journal*.

Foucault, M. (1965) *Madness and Civilization*. New York: Random House.

Franc, R., Faisant, C. and Nacache, L. (1993) Old Folks Home: home for suicide or home for prevention? *Française Psychologie du Medicine*, 25(4): 316–19.

Frankenfield, D.L., Baker, S.P. and Lange, W.R. (1994) Fluoxetine and violent death in Maryland. *The Forensic Science Intern*, 64(2): 107–17.

Franklin, B. and Parton, N. (eds) (1990) *Social Work, the Media and Public Relations*. London: Routledge.

Frederick, J. (1991) *Positive Thinking for Mental Health*. London: The Black Mental Health Group.

Fremouw, W.J., Callahan, T. and Kashden, J. (1993) Adolescent suicidal risk: psychological problem solving and environmental factors. *Suicide and Life Threatening Behaviour*, 23(1): 46–54.

Fremouw, W.J., Perczel, M. and Ellis, T.E. (1990) *Suicide Risk: Assessment and Response Guidelines*. New York: Pergamon Press.

Freud, S. (1933) *Introductory Lectures to Psycho-analysis*. London: Hogarth Press.

Friedenberg, E.Z. (1973) *Laing*. London: Fontana.

Fromouth, F.E. (1988) The relationship of childhood sexual abuse with later psychological and sexual adjustment in a sample of college women. *Child Abuse and Neglect*, 10: 5–15.

Ganry, O., Zummer, K. and Ganry, C. (1992) Image and psychological repercussions of cancer among patients consulting a detection department. *Française Psychologie du Medicine*, 24(14): 1507–10.

Geddes, J.R., Black, R.J. and Eagles, J.M. (1993) Persistence of the decline in the diagnosis of schizophrenia among first admissions to Scottish hospitals 1969–1988. *British Journal of Psychiatry*, 163: 620–6.

Gelles, R.J. and Edfeldt, A.W. (1986) Violence towards children in the United States and Sweden. *Child Abuse and Neglect*, 10(4): 501–10.

Gibbons, J.L. (1983) *Clinical Psychiatry*. London: Heinemann Medical.

Gibbons, J.S. (1978) Evaluation of a social work service for self-poisoning patients. *British Journal of Psychiatry*, 133(8): 111–18.

Gibbons, J.S. (1987) Quality of life of 'new long stay' psychiatric in-patients, the effect of moving into a hostel. *British Journal of Psychiatry*, 151: 347–54.

Gibbons, J.S., Brown, R. and Powell, J. (1984) Schizophrenic patients and their families. *British Journal of Psychiatry*, 144: 70–7.

Gilberg, C.L. (1992) Autism and autistic-like conditions: sub-classes among disorders of empathy. *Journal of Child Psychology and Psychiatry*, 33: 813–42.

Gillon, R. (1988) Euthanasia: withholding life-prolonging treatment and the moral differences between killing and letting die. *Journal of Medical Ethics*, 24: 116–17.

Glover, D. (1984) *Causing Death and Saving Lives*. Harmondsworth: Penguin.

Glover, D. (1989) Why is there a high rate of schizophrenia in the British Afro-Caribbean? *British Journal of Hospital Medicine*, July: 42.

Goffman, I. (1961) *Asylums*. Harmondsworth: Penguin.

Goffman, I. (1968) *Stigma*. Harmondsworth: Penguin.

Golacre, M., Seagroat, V. and Hawton, K. (1993) Suicide after discharge from psychiatric inpatient care. *Lancet*, 342: 283–6.

Golden, R.N., Gilmore, J.H. and Corrigan, M.H.N. (1991) Serotonin, suicide and aggression: clinical studies. *Journal of Clinical Psychiatry*, 52(12) supplement: 61–9.

Goold, P. (1991) An investigation into the significance and employment of religious beliefs in schizophrenia, unpublished Ph.D. Thesis, University of Southampton.

Gordon, L. (1992) *Virgina Woolf: A Writer's Life*. Oxford: Oxford University Press.

Gottleib, B. (1983) *Social Support Strategies*. New York: Sage Publications.

Graetz, B. (1993) Health consequences of employment and unemployment: longitudinal evidence for men and women. *Social Science and Medicine*, 36(6): 715–24.

Graham, C. and Burvill, P.W. (1992) A study of coroners' records on suicide in young people 1986–1988 in Western Australia. *Australian and New Zealand Journal of Psychiatry*, 26(1): 30–9.

Green, C., Kendall, K. and Andre, G. (1993) A study of 133 suicides among Canadian federal prisoners. *Medicine Science and Law*, 33(2): 121–7.

Gunn, J., Maden, A. and Swinton, M. (1991) Treatment needs of prisoners with psychiatric disorders. *British Medical Journal*, 303: 338–41.

Gunnell, D. (1994) *The Potential for Preventing Suicide: a review of the literature on the effectiveness of the interventions aimed at preventing suicide*. Bristol: Health Care Evaluation Unit, University of Bristol.

Hachey, R. and Mercier, C. (1993) The impact of rehabilitation services on the quality of life of chronic mental patients. *Occupational Therapy and Mental Health*, 12(2): 1–25.

Haddad, P.M. and Benbow, S.M. (1993) ECT therapy – related psychiatric knowledge amongst British anaesthetists. *Convulsive Therapy*, 9(2): 101–7.

Hamilton, M. (1976) *Fish's Schizophrenia*. Bristol: John Wright and Sons.

Hammond, T. and Wallace, P. (1990) *Housing for People Who Are Severely Mentally Ill*. London: NFS Publications.

Harrison, G. (1988) Prospective study of mental disorder in Afro-Caribbean patients. *Psychological Medicine*, 18: 643–58.

Harrison, G., Mason, P. and Glazebrook, C. (1994) Residence of incident cohort of psychotic patients 13 years after follow-up. *British Medical Journal*, 308: 813–16.

Hawton, K. and Catalin, J. (1987) *Attempted Suicide*, 2nd edn. Oxford: Oxford University Press.

Hawton, K. and Fagg, J. (1988) Suicide and other causes of death following attempted suicide. *British Journal of Psychiatry*, 152: 359–66.

Hawton, K. and Roberts, J.C. (1985) Risk of abuse and attempted suicide. *British Journal of Psychiatry*, 146: 415–20.

Hawton, K., Fagg, J., Platt, S. and Hawkins, M. (1993) Factors associated with suicide after parasuicide in young people. *British Medical Journal*, 306: 1641–4.

Hawton, K., Kirk, J. and Clark, D.M. (1989) *Cognitive Behaviour Therapy for Psychiatric Problems*. Oxford: Oxford University Press.

Haycock, J. (1993) Comparative suicide rates in different types of involuntary confinement. *Medicine Science and Law*, 33(2): 128–36 .

Hazel, P. and Lewin, T. (1993) An evaluation of post-ventilation following adolescent suicide. *Suicide and Life Threatening Behaviour*, 23: 101–9.

Healey, D. (1993) Psychopharmacology and the ethics of resource allocation. *British Journal of Psychiatry*, 162: 23–9.

Heikkinen, M., Aro, H. and Lunquist, J. (1992) Recent life events and their role in suicide as seen by the spouses. *Acta Psychiatrica Scandinavia*, 86(6): 489–94.

Heim, N. and Lester, D. (1991) Factors affecting choice of method for suicide. *European Journal of Psychiatry*, 5(3): 161–5.

Hellema, H. (1992) Dutch euthanasia over-estimated. *British Medical Journal*, 304: 870.

Henderson, A.S. (1989) Editorial: psychiatric epidemiology and the elderly. *International Journal of Geriatric Psychiatry*. 4: 249–53.

Hendin, H. (1993) The suicide of Anne Sexton. *Suicide and Life Threatening Behaviour*, 23: 257–62.

Henry, J.A. (1993) Debits and credits in the management of depression. *British Journal of Psychiatry*, 163 (Supplement 20): 33–9.

Hewitt, P. (1993) *About Time: the Revolution in Work and Family Life*. London: Oran River Press.

Hibberd, R.A. and Zollinger, T.W. (1992) Medical evaluation and referral patterns for sexual abuse victims. *Child Abuse and Neglect*, 16(4): 533–40.

High, D.M. (1988) Foregoing life sustaining procedures: survey and analysis of Kentuckians' opinions. *Journal of the Kentucky Medical Association*, 86: 293–5.

Hills, G., Alexander, D.A. and Eagles, J.M. (1993) Premature termination of psychiatric contact. *International Journal of Social Psychiatry*, 39(2): 100–7.

Hirsch, S. and Leff, J. (1971) Parental abnormalities of verbal communication in the transmission of schizophrenia. *Psychological Medicine*, 1: 118–27.

HM Treasury (1993) *Financial Statement and Budget Report 1994/95*. London: HMSO.

HM Treasury (1994) *Financial Statement and Budget Report 1995/96*. London: HMSO.

Hogerty, G.E. (1986a) Family psycho-education, social skills training and maintenance chemotherapy in the after care of schizophrenics. *Archives of General Psychiatry*, 43: 633–42.

Hogerty, G.E. (1986b) Expressed emotion and schizophrenic relapse. Implications from the Pitsberg study, in M. Alpert (ed.) *Controversies in Schizophrenia*, pp. 123–45. New York: Guildford Press.

Holding, T.A. and Barraclough, B. (1978) Undetermined deaths – suicide or accident? *British Journal of Psychiatry*, 13: 542–9.

Holinger, P. (1987) *Violent Death in the United States*. New York: Guildford Press.

Holmes-Elber, P. and Riger, S. (1990) Hospitalisation and the composition of mental patients' social networks. *Schizophrenia Bulletin*, 16(1): 157–64.

Home Office (1993) *Digest of Criminal Statistics*. London: HMSO.

Horn, P.J. (1994) Therapists' psychological adaptation to client suicide: a review. *Psychotherapy*, 31(1): 190–5.

House of Commons (1988) *Select Committee for Health and Social Service Committee Report*. London: HMSO.

House of Commons (1990) *Select Committee for Health and Social Service Committee Report*. London: HMSO.

Howe, G.W., Feinstein, C. and Reiss, D. (1993) Adolescent adjustment to chronic physical disorders: comparing neurological and non-neurological conditions. *Journal of Child Psychology and Psychiatry*, 34(7): 1153–71.

Howse, C. (1993) The selfishness of self-slaughter – self-killing is wrong, *Daily Telegraph*, 19 September: 24.

Hudson, B., Cullen, R. and Roberts, C. (1993) *Training for Work with Mentally Disordered Offenders*. London: CCETSW.

Hughes, J. (1991) *An Outline of Modern Psychiatry*, 3rd edn. Chichester: Wiley.

Hulatt, I.P. (1992) Death making in the human services, M.Sc. Dissertation, Department of Social Work Studies, University of Southampton.

Huxley, P. and Kerfoot, M. (1993) Variations in requests to social service departments for assessment of compulsory admission. *Social Psychiatry and Psychiatric Epidemiology*, 28(2): 71–6.

Huyse, F.J. and Van Tilburg, W. (1993) Euthanasia policy in the Netherlands: the role of the consultant psychiatrist. *Hospital and Community Psychiatry*, 44(8): 733–8.

Illich, I. (1971) *Medical Nemesis: the Medical Expropriation of Health.* London: Calder and Boyer.

Isaacs, K.L., Gunn, J. and McMilkin, A. (1991) The concept of pre-death. *Lancet,* 341(8895): 734–7.

Isacsson, G., Boethius, G. and Bergman, U. (1992) Low level of anti-depressant prescription for people who later commit suicide: 15 years of experience from a population based drug database in Sweden. *Acta Psychiatrica Scandinavia,* 85: 444–8.

Isacsson, G., Holmgren, P. and Bergman, U. (1994) Use of antidepressants among people committing suicide in Sweden. *British Medical Journal,* 6297: 506–9.

Isometsa, E.T., Henriksson, M.M. and Aro, H.M. (1994) Suicide in major depression. *American Journal of Psychiatry,* 151(4): 530–6.

Jack, P.R. (1988) Personal networks, support mobilisation and unemployment. *Psychological Medicine,* 18: 397–404.

Janlert, U. and Hammarstrom, A. (1992) Alcohol consumption among unemployed youths: results from a prospective study. *British Journal of Addiction,* 87: 703–14.

Jenck, C. and Peterson, P. (eds) (1991) *The Urban Underclass.* Washington, DC: Brookings Institute.

Johnson, C., Smith, J. and Donovan, M. (1993) Suicide among forensic psychiatric patients. *Medicine Science and Law,* 33(2): 137–43.

Jones, K. (1959) *Social Policy and Mental Health.* London: Routledge and Kegan Paul.

Jones, S. (1994) *The Language of the Genes.* London: Flamingo.

Joseph, B.E. and Roman-Nay, H. (1990) The homeless intravenous drug abuser and the AIDS epidemic. *National Institute on Drug Abuse* (Research Monograph Series) 93: 210–53.

Josepho, S.A. and Plutchik, R. (1994) Stress, coping and suicide risk in psychiatric in-patients. *Suicide and Life Threatening Behaviour,* 24(1): 48–57.

Juvenal (1892) *Sixteen Satires,* translated by A. Leeper. London: Macmillan.

Kanner, L. (1943) Autistic disturbance of affective contact. *Nervous Children,* 2: 217–27.

Kaplan, M.L., Asnis, G.M. and Sanderson, W.C. (1994) Suicide assessment: clinical interview versus self-report. *Journal of Clinical Psychology,* 50(2): 294–8.

Kehoe, N.C. and Gutheil, T.G. (1994) Neglect of religious issues in scale-based assessment of suicidal patients. *Hospital and Community Psychiatry,* 45(4): 366–9.

Keitner, G.I., Ryan, C.E. and Miller, I.W. (1990) Family functioning, social adjustment and recurrence of suicidality. *Psychiatry,* 53(1): 17–30.

Kerfoot, M. (1984) Suicidal behaviour: adolescents and their families, in P. Wedge (ed.) *Social Work – Research into Practice.* London: BASW.

Kerfoot, M. and Butler, A. (1988) *Problems of Childhood and Adolescence.* Basingstoke, Macmillan.

Kesey, K. (1968) *One Flew Over the Cuckoo's Nest.* New York: Picador.

Kessler, R.C., Downey, G. and Milavsky, J.R. (1989) Network TV news stories about suicide and short-term changes in total US suicides. *Journal of Nervous Mental Disorders,* 177(9): 551–5.

King, C.A., Naylor, M.W. and Segal, H.G. (1993) Global self-worth, specific perceptions of competence and depression in adolescents. *Journal of American Academic Adolescent Psychiatry,* 32: 745–52.

King, K. and Barraclough, B. (1990) Violent death and mental illness. A study of a single catchment area over eight years. *British Journal of Psychiatry,* 156: 714–20.

Kingsbury, S. (1994) The psychological and social characteristics of Asian adolescent overdose. *Journal of Adolescence,* 17(6) 2: 131–5.

Kinzl, J. and Biebl, W. (1992) Long-term effect of incest: life events triggering mental disorders in female patients with sexual abuse in childhood. *Child Abuse and Neglect,* 16(4): 567–73.

Kleck, G. (1988) Miscounting suicides. *Suicide and Life Threatening Behaviour*, 18(3): 219–36.

Klerman, G. (1989) Depressive disorders: further evidence for increased medical morbidity and impairment of social functioning. *Archives of General Psychiatry*, 46: 856–8.

Kok, L.P. (1988) Race, religion and female suicide attempters in Singapore. *Social Psychiatry and Psychiatric Epidemiology*. 23(4): 236–9.

Kok, L.P. and Kok, A.W.S.C. (1992) Suicide in Singapore 1986. *Australian and New Zealand Journal of Psychiatry*, 26(4): 599–608.

Kolmos, L. and Bach, E. (1987) Sources of error in registering suicide. *Acta Psychiatrica Scandinavia*, 336: 23–43.

Kong, F., Perrucci, C.C. and Perrucci, R. (1993) The impact of unemployment and economic stress on social support. *Community Mental Health*, 29(3): 205–21.

Kosky, P., Silburn, S. and Zubrick, S.R. (1990) Are children and adolescents who have suicidal thoughts different from those who attempt suicide? *Journal of Mental Disorders*, 178: 38–43.

Kotler, M., Finkelstein, G. and Molcho, A. (1993) Correlates of suicide and violence risk in an inpatient population: coping styles and social support. *Psychiatry Research*, 473: 281–90.

Kreitman, N. (1978) *Parasuicide*. London: John Wiley and Sons.

Kreitman, N. (1988) Suicide, age and marital status. *Psychological Medicine*, 18: 121–8.

Kreitman, N. and Foster, J. (1991) The construction and selection of predictive scales with particular reference to parasuicide. *British Journal of Psychiatry*, 159: 185–92.

Kreitman, N. and Phillips, A.E. (1969) Parasuicide. *British Journal of Psychiatry*, 115: 746–7.

Kruks, G. (1991) Gay and lesbian homeless/street youth: special issues and concerns. *Journal of Adolescent Health*, 12(7): 515–18.

Kufeldt, K. (1992) Providing shelter for street youth: are we reaching those in need? *Child Abuse and Neglect*, 16(2): 187–99.

Kuhse, H. and Singer, P. (1986) For sometimes letting and helping die. *Law, Medicine and Health Care*, 3(4): 149–53.

Kuipers, L. (1987) Research in expressed emotion. *Social Psychiatry*, 22: 216–20.

Kushner, P. (1989) *Self-Destruction in the Promised Land: a Psycho-cultural Biology of American Suicide*. New Brunswick, NJ: Rutgers University Press.

Kyvik, K.O., Stenager, E.N. and Svendsen, A. (1994) Suicides in men with IDDM. *Diabetes Care*, 17(3): 210–12.

Lamb, H.R. (1993) Lessons learned from de-institutionalisation in the US. *British Journal of Psychiatry*, 162: 587–92.

Laurent, O. (1993) 'Fortunately, you were here'. Pessimistic remarks about a possible answer to a crisis situation in psychiatry. *Psychological Medicine*, 25(6): 511–12.

Lauter, H. and Meyer, J.F. (1992) The new discussion on euthanasia: a psychiatric approach. *Deutsch Fortschung Neurologie und Psychiatrisch*, 60(11): 441–8.

Lawrence, M. (1984) *The Anorexic Experience*. London: Women's Press.

Lawson, R. (1994) The challenge of the new poverty. Lessons from Europe and America. *Internationale Politik und Gesellschaft*, 2: 162–74.

Lazarus, A.A. (1985) *The Multi-Modal Casebook*. New York: Guildford Press.

Leenaars, A.A. (1989) Are young adult suicides psychologically different from those of other adults? *Suicide and Life Threatening Behaviour*, 19(3): 249–63.

Leff, J. and Vaughan, C. (1985) *Expressed Emotion in Families*. London: Guildford Press.

Lefley, H.P. and Johnson, D.L. (1990) *Families as Allies in the Treatment of the Mentally Ill*. New York: American Psychiatric Press.

Leonard, P. (1985) Introduction, in R. Banton [ed.] *The Politics of Mental Health*. Basingstoke: Macmillan.

Lester, D. (1993) The effectiveness of Suicide Prevention Centres. *Suicide and Life Threatening Behaviour*, 23(3): 263–7.

Lester, D. (1994) A comparison of 15 theories of suicide. *Suicide and Life Threatening Behaviour*, 24(1) 80–8.

Lettieri, D.J. (1974) Age, gender and the prediction of suicide, in A.T. Beck, H.L. Resnik and D.J. Lettieri (eds) *The Prediction of Suicide*, pp. 134–72. Bowie, MD: Charles Press.

Levav, I. and Aisenberg, E. (1989) Suicide in Israel: cross national comparisons. *Acta Psychiatrica Scandinavia*, 79(5): 468–73.

Linehan, M.M. (1985) The reasons for living inventory, in P. Keller and L. Ritt (eds) *Innovations in Clinical Practice: a source book*, pp. 321–30. Sarasota: Professional Resource Exchange.

Linehan, M.M. (1987a) Dialectical behaviour therapy: a cognitive approach to parasuicide. *Journal of Personality Assessment*, 1: 328–33.

Linehan, M.M. (1987b) Inter-personal problem-solving and parasuicide. *Cognitive Therapy Research*, 11: 1–12.

Linehan, M.M., Armstrong, H.E. and Heard, H.I. (1991) Behavioural treatment of chronically para-suicidal borderline patients. *Archives of General Psychiatry*, 48(12): 1060–4.

Linehan, M.M., Heard, H.L. and Armstrong, H.E. (1993) Naturalistic follow-up of a behavioural treatment for chronically para-suicidal borderline patients. *Archives of General Psychiatry*, 50: 971–4.

Linehan, M.M., Camper, P., Chiles, J.A., Strohsahl, K. and Shearin, E.N. (1987) Inter-personal problem-solving and parasuicide. *Cognitive Therapy Research*, 11: 1–12.

Lister, J. (1991) At the sharp end of care, in M. Page and R. Powell (eds) *Homelessness and Mental Illness: the Dark Side of Community Care*, pp. 26–30. London: Concern Publications.

Littlewood, R. and Lipsedge, M. (1982) *Aliens and Alienists*. Harmondsworth: Penguin.

Livesley, W.J., Jang, K.J. and Vernon, P.A. (1993) Genetic and environmental contributions to dimensions of personality disorder. *American Journal of Psychiatry*, 150(12): 1826–31.

Lowe, K., De Paiva, S. and Felce, D. (1993) Effects of a community-based service on adaptive and maladaptive behaviours. *Journal of Intellectual Disability*, 37(1): 3–22.

McCarthy, J. and Nelson, G. (1993) An evaluation of supportive housing: qualitative and quantitative perspectives. *Community Mental Health*, 12(1): 157–75.

McClure, G.M.S. (1987) Suicide in England and Wales 1975–84: mode of death. *British Journal of Psychiatry*, 150: 309–14.

MacFate, K., Lawson, R. and Wilson, D. (1994) *Poverty, Inequality and the Future of Social Policy*. Washington, DC: Joint Centre for Political and Economic Studies.

McGovern, D., Hemmings, P. and Lowerson, A. (1994) Long-term follow-up of young Afro-Caribbean Britons and white Britons with a first admission diagnosis of schizophrenia. *Social Psychiatry and Psychiatric Epidemiology*, 29(1): 8–19.

McIntosh, J.L. (1993) Control group studies of suicide survivors: a review and critique. *Suicide and Life Threatening Behaviour*, 23(2) 146–61.

McIntosh, J.L. and Wrobleski, A. (1988) Grief reactions among suicide survivors: an exploratory comparison of relationships. *Death Studies*, 12: 21–9.

Macleod, A.K., Williams, J.M.G. and Linehan, M.M. (1993) New developments in the understanding and treatment of suicidal behaviour. *Behavioural Psychotherapy*, 20: 193–218.

Madge, N. (1983) Unemployment and its effects upon children. *Journal of Child Psychology and Psychiatry*, 24: 311–20.

Madianos, M.G. and Economou, M. (1994) Schizophrenia and family rituals: measuring family rituals amongst schizophrenics and 'normals'. *European Psychiatry*, 9(1): 45–51.

Madianos, M.G. and Stefanis, C.N. (1994) Symptoms of depression, suicidal behaviour and use of substances in Greece. A nationwide general population survey. *Acta Psychiatrica Scandinavia*, 89(3): 159–66.

Maguire, P., Hopwood, P. and Tarrier, N. (1985) Treatment of depression in cancer patients. *Acta Psychiatrica Scandinavia*, 72: 81–4.

Mahy, G. (1993) Suicide behaviour in the Caribbean. *International Review of Psychiatry*, 5: 261–9.

Males, M. (1991) Teen suicide and changing cause-of-death certification. *Suicide and Life Threatening Behaviour*, 21(3): 245–59.

Mann, J.J. and Arango, V. (1992) Integration of neurobiology and psychopathology in a unified model of suicidal behaviour. *Journal of Clinical Psychopharmacology*, 12(2) Supplement: 2S–7S.

Maris, R.W., Berman, A.L. and Yufit, R.I. (eds) (1992) *Assessment and Prediction of Suicide*. New York: Guildford Press.

Marshall, P.E. and Reed, J.L. (1992) Psychiatric morbidity in homeless women. *British Journal of Psychiatry*, 160: 761–8.

Martin, J.P. (1984) *Hospitals in Trouble: an Analysis of Hospital Inquiry Reports*. London: Routledge and Kegan Paul.

Marttunen, M.J., Aro, H.M. and Henriksson, M.M. (1994a) Anti-social behaviour in adolescent suicide. *Acta Psychiatrica Scandinavia*, 89(3): 167–73.

Marttunen, M.J., Aro, H.M. and Lunquist, J.K. (1991) Mental disorders in adolescent suicide: DSM III-R Axes I and II diagnoses in suicides among 13–19 year olds in Finland. *Archives of General Psychiatry*, 48: 834–9.

Marttunen, M.J., Aro, H.M. and Lunquist, J.K. (1994b) Psycho-social stresses more common in adolescent suicides with alcohol abuse compared with depressive adolescent suicides. *Journal of American Academic Child Psychiatry*, 33(4): 490–7.

Marzuk, P.M., Tierny, H. and Tardiff, K. (1988) Increased risk of suicide in persons with AIDS. *Journal of American Medical Association*, 259(9): 1333–7.

Mascro, J. (1962) *The Bhagavad Gita*, translated by J. Mascro. Harmondsworth: Penguin.

Masson, J. (1990) *The Assault on Truth: Freud's Suppression of the Seduction Theory*. Harmondsworth: Penguin.

Mechanic, D. (1968) *Medical Sociology*. New York: Free Press.

Mendleson, G. (1981) Electrotherapy and placebo electrotherapy: a review. *Medical Journal of Australia*, 213: 125–8.

Mendleson, W.B. and Rich, C.L. (1993) Sedatives and suicide: the San Diego study. *Acta Psychiatrica Scandinavia*, 88(5): 337–41.

Mercier, C., Renaud, C. and King, S. (1994) A thirty year retrospective study of hospitalisation among severely mentally ill patients. *Canadian Journal of Psychiatry*, 39(2): 95–102.

Mermelstein, H.T. and Lesko, L. (1992) Depression in patients with cancer. *Psycho-Oncology*, 1(3): 199–215.

Merrill, J., Milner, G., Vale, A. and Owens, T.D. (1992) Alcohol and attempted suicide. *British Journal of Addiction*, 87(1): 83–9.

Meyer, J.C. (1988) The fate of the mentally ill in Germany during the Third Reich. *Psychological Medicine*, 18: 575–81.

Michel, K., Arestegui, G. and Spuhler, T. (1994) Suicide with psychotropic drugs in Switzerland. *Pharmacology and psychiatry*, 27(3): 114–18.

Middlebrook, D.W. (1992) *Anne Sexton: A Biography*. New York: Vintage Books.

Micklowitz, G. (1984) International correlates of expressed emotion in the families of schizophrenics. *British Journal of Psychiatry*, 144: 482–7.

Miles, A. (1991) *Women, Health and Medicine*. Buckingham: Open University Press.

Miller, N.S., Mahler, J.C. and Gold, M.S. (1991) Suicide risk associated with drug and alcohol dependency. *Journal of Addiction Disorders*, 10(3): 49–61.

Millett, K. (1991) *The Loony Bin Trip*. London: Virago Press.

Milliband, R. (1969) *The State in Capitalist Society*. London: Merlin Press.

Milroy, C.M. (1993) Homicide followed by suicide (dyadic death) in Yorkshire and Humberside. *Medicine Science and Law*, 33(2): 167–71.

Milton, J. (1958) *The Complete Poems*. London: Everyman Series, Dent and Sons.

MIND (1974) *Coordination or Chaos? The Run-down of Psychiatric Hospitals.* London: MIND Publications.

Modestein, J. and Schwarzenbach, F. (1992) Effect of psycho-pharmacotherapy on suicide risk in discharged psychiatric patients. *Acta Psychiatrica Scandinavia,* 85: 173–5.

Moller, H.J. and Steinmeyer, E.M. (1994) Are serotonin re-uptake inhibitors more potent in reducing suicidality? An empirical study on paroxetine. *European Neuro-Psychopharmacology,* 4(1): 55–9.

Montaigne, M. (1988) *Essays.* Translated by J.M. Cohen. Harmondsworth: Penguin Classics.

Montgomery, S.A. (1993) Suicide prevention and serotinergic drugs. *Clinical Psychopharmacology,* 8/Supplement (2): 83–5.

Morgan, H.G. and Owen, J.H. (1993) Secondary prevention of non-fatal deliberate self harm: the Green Card study. *British Journal of Psychiatry,* 163: 111–12.

Morris, D. (1992) Dr Death faces a grand jury. *British Medical Journal,* 304: 102.

Morton, M.J. (1993) Prediction of repetition of parasuicide: with special reference to unemployment. *International Journal of Social Psychiatry,* 39(2): 87–99.

Moscicki, E.K., O'Carroll, P. and Regier, D.A. (1988) Suicide attempts in the epidemiological catchment area study. *Yale Journal of Biology and Medicine,* 61: 259–68.

Motto, A.A. (1985) Preliminary field-testing of a risk estimator for suicide. A clinical model approach. *Suicide and Life Threatening Behaviour,* 15: 139–50.

Motto, A.A., Maris, R., Litman, R.E., Battin, M.P. and Richman, J. (1992) Review of D. Humphry, *Final Exit: the Practicalities of Self-Deliverance and Assisted Suicide for the Dying. Suicide and Life Threatening Behaviour,* 22: 513–24.

Muller, M.T., Van der Wahl, G. and Ribbe, M.W. (1994) Voluntary active euthanasia and physician assisted suicide in Dutch nursing homes: are the requirements for prudent practice properly met? *Journal of the American Geriatric Society,* 42(6): 624–9.

Murphy, G.E. and Wetzel, R.D. (1990) The life-time risk of suicide in alcoholism. *Archives of General Psychiatry,* 47(4): 383–93.

Mzraz, W. and Runco, M.A. (1994) Suicide ideation and problem-solving. *Suicide and Life Threatening Behaviour,* 24: 38–47.

Neimeyer, R. and Pfeiffer, A.M. (1994) Evaluation of suicide intervention effectiveness. *Death Studies,* 18(2): 131–66.

Newberger, E.H. (1983) The helping hand strikes again: the unintended consequences of child abuse reporting. *Journal of Clinical Child Psychology,* 12(3): 307–11.

Noakes, P. (1967) *The Professional Task in Welfare Practice.* London: Routledge and Kegan Paul.

Nordstrom, P., Samuelsson, M. and Asberg, M. (1994) CSF 5 -HIAA predicts suicide risk after attempted suicide. *Suicide and Life Threatening Behaviour,* 24: 1–9.

Obafunwa, J.O. and Busuttil, A. (1994a) A review of completed suicide in the Lothian and Border region of Scotland. *Social Psychiatry and Psychiatric Epidemiology,* 29(2): 100–6.

Obafunwa, J.O. and Busuttil, A. (1994b) Clinical contact preceding suicide. *Postgraduate Medical Journal,* 70: 428–32.

O'Carroll, P.W. (1989) Validity and reliability of suicide mortality data. *Suicide and Life Threatening Behaviour,* 19: 1–16.

O'Carroll, P.W. (1993) Suicide causation. *Suicide and Life Threatening Behaviour,* 23: 27–36.

O'Donnell, I. (1994) Epidemiology of suicide on the London underground. *Social Science and Medicine,* 38: 409–18.

Oliver, J.E. (1988) Successive generations of child maltreatment. *British Journal of Psychiatry,* 153: 543–53.

Olkin, R.L. and Pearsall, D. (1993) Patients' perception of the quality of their life 11 years after discharge from a state hospital. *Hospital and Community Psychiatry,* 44(3): 236–40.

Owen, C., Tennant, C. and Jones, M. (1992) Suicide and euthanasia: patient attitudes in the context of cancer. *Psycho-Oncology*, 1: 79–88.

Owen, C., Tennant, C. and Jones, M. (1994) Cancer patients' attitude to final events in life: wish for death, attitudes to cessation of treatment, suicide and euthanasia. *Psycho-Oncology*, 3(1): 1–9.

Pallis, D.J., Gibbons, J.S. and Pierce, D.W. (1984) Estimating suicide risk among attempted suicides: II Efficiency of predictive scales after the attempt. *British Journal of Psychiatry*, 141: 37–44.

Paraskavias, E., Kitchener, H.C. and Walker, L.G. (1993) Doctor–patient communication and subsequent mental health in women with gynaecological cancer. *Psycho-oncology*, 1: 195–200.

Parkes, M.C. (1986) *Bereavement Studies of Grief in Adult Life*. London: Routledge.

Parry, G. and Shapiro, D.A. (1986) Social supports and life events in working class women. *Archives of General Psychiatry*, 43: 315–23.

Patmore, C. (1987) *Living After Mental Illness: Innovations in Services*. Chichester: Croom Helm.

Patton, M.Q. (1991) *Family Sexual Abuse: Front-line Research and Evaluation*. New York: Sage Publications.

Paykel, E.S., Prusoff, B.A. and Meyers, J.K. (1975) Suicide attempts and recent life events. *Archives of General Psychiatry*, 32: 327–33.

Pearson, G. (1983) *Hooliganism: the Study of Respectable Fears*. Basingstoke: Macmillan.

Pearson, G., Treseder, J. and Yelloly, M. (eds) (1988) *Social Work and the Legacy of Freud*. Basingstoke: Macmillan.

Peng, K.L. and Choo, A.S. (1990) Suicide and parasuicide in Singapore. *Medicine Science and Law*, 30(3): 225–33.

Pennebaker, J.W. and O'Heeron, R.C. (1984) Confiding in others and illness rates amongst spouses of suicide and accidental death victims. *Journal of Abnormal Psychology*, 93: 473–6.

Perkins, R.E. and Moodley, P. (1993) Perception of problems in psychiatric inpatients: denial, race and service usage. *Social Psychiatry and Psychiatric Epidemiology*, 28(4): 189–93.

Peterson, L.G. and Bonger, B. (1990) Repetitive suicidal crises: characteristics of repeating and non-repeating suicidal visitors to a psychiatric emergency service. *Psychopathology*, 23(3): 136–45.

Pfeiffer, C.R., Klerman, G.L. and Siefker, C.A. (1991) Suicidal children grown-up: demographic and clinical risk factors for suicidal attempts. *Journal of American Academy of Child and Adolescent Psychiatry*, 30(4): 609–16.

Pilgrim, D. and Rogers, A. (1993) *A Sociology of Mental Health and Illness*. Buckingham: Open University Press.

Plant, M. (1989) The epidemiology of illicit drug misuse in Britain, in S. MacGregor (ed.) *Drugs and British Society*, pp. 52–63. Basingstoke: Macmillan.

Plant, R. (1968) *Casework and Moral Theory*. London: Routledge and Kegan Paul.

Plath, S. (1981) *Collected Poems: Poems 1956–1963*. London: Faber and Faber.

Platt, S. (1984) Unemployment and suicidal behaviour: a review. *Social Science and Medicine*, 19: 93–115.

Platt, S. (1988) Social construction of causal ascription: distinguishing suicide from un-determined deaths. *Social Psychiatry*, 23(4): 217–21.

Platt, S. and Kreitman, N. (1985) Parasuicide and unemployment among men in Edin-burgh 1968–82. *Psychological Medicine*, 15: 113–23.

Platt, S. and Robinson, A. (1991) Parasuicide and alcohol: a 20 year survey of admissions to a regional poisoning treatment centre. *International Journal of Psychiatry*, 37(3): 159–72.

Platt, S., Bille-Brahe, U. and Kerkhof, A. (1992) Parasuicide in Europe: the WHO

EURO multi-centre study on parasuicide. I. Introduction and preliminary analysis for · 1989. *Acta Psychiatrica Scandinavia*, 85: 97–104.

Porter, R. (ed.) (1992) *The Faber Book of Madness*. London: Faber and Faber.

Power, C. and Manor, O. (1992) Explaining social class differences in psychological health among young adults: a longitudinal perspective. *Social Psychiatry and Psychiatric Epidemiology*, 27(6): 284–91.

Powers, A.L., Eckenrode, J. and Jaklitsch, B. (1990) Maltreatment among runaway and homeless youth. *Child Abuse and Neglect*, 14: 87–98.

Prasad, A.J. and Kumar, N. (1988) Suicidal behaviour in hospitalised schizophrenics. *Suicide and Life Threatening Behaviour*, 18: 265–9.

Prins, H.P. (1992) The diversion of the mentally ill: some problems for criminal justice, penology and health care. *Journal of Forensic Psychiatry*, 13: 431–43.

Prins Report (1994) *The Report of the Enquiry into In-patient Deaths in Special Hospitals*. London: Special Hospital Health Authority.

Pritchard, C. (1971) A consumer's approach to child mental health. *Medical Officer*, 125(1): 3–8.

Pritchard, C. (1986) European peace movements 1958/65 and 1978/85: hopes for the future and lessons to be learned, in L. Pauling (ed.) *World Encyclopedia of Peace Studies*, pp. 228–30, 297–301. Oxford: Pergamon Press.

Pritchard, C. (1987) *Maintaining Morale Through Staff Development and Training*. Norwich: University of East Anglia, Social Work Monographs.

Pritchard, C. (1990) Suicide, unemployment and gender variations in the Western World 1964–1986: are women in Anglophone countries protected from suicide? *Social Psychiatry and Psychiatric Epidemiology*, 25: 1–8.

Pritchard, C. (1991) Levels of risk and psycho-social problems of families on the 'At Risk' register: indicators of outcome two years after case closure. *Research Policy and Planning*, 9(2): 19–26.

Pritchard, C. (1992a) Is there a link between suicide in young men and unemployment? A comparison of the UK with other European Community countries. *British Journal of Psychiatry*, 160: 750–6.

Pritchard, C. (1992b) Changes in elderly suicides in the USA and the developed world 1974–87: comparison with current homicide. *International Journal of Geriatric Psychiatry*, 7: 125–34.

Pritchard, C. (1992c) What can we afford for the NHS? An analysis of Government expenditure 1974–1992. *Social Policy and Administration*, 26(1): 40–54.

Pritchard, C. (1993a) A comparison of youth suicide in Hong Kong, the developed world and the People's Republic of China. *Hong Kong Journal of Mental Health*, 22(1): 6–16.

Pritchard, C. (1993b) Re-analyzing children's homicide and undetermined deaths as an indication of improved child protection: a reply to Creighton. *British Journal of Social Work*, 23(6): 645–52.

Pritchard, C. (1993c) Kindestotungen: die extremeste Form der Kindesmisshandlung: Ein internationaler Vergleich zwischen Baby/Kleinkind und Kindestotungen als ein Indikator fur den Schutzen dieser Gruppen. *Nachrichten Dienst*, 72(3): 65–72.

Pritchard, C. (1994a) Psycho-socio-economic factors in suicide, in P. Mathias and M. Thompson (eds) *Mental Health and Disorder*, 2nd edn., pp. 69–117. London: Baillière Tindall.

Pritchard, C. (1994b) Sudden-infant-death-syndrome, children's homicide and child malignancies: connections or coincidences? Towards a new approach to child protection. *Social Work and Social Science Review*, 5(3): 195–227.

Pritchard, C. (1995a) Psychiatric targets in 'Health of the Nation': regional suicide 1974–1990 in Britain by age and gender and changes in regional unemployment prospects 1990–1994 – precursors of failure? *British Journal of Social Work*.

Pritchard, C. (1995b) Changes in patterns of suicide by age and gender in the United

Kingdom and Western industrial nations 1974–1991: suicide a paradoxical indicator of effective psychiatric services. *Social Psychiatry and Psychiatric Epidemiology.*

Pritchard, C. (1995c) Cultural influences upon suicide. Lessons from a comparative study of the People's Republic of China the and the western world. *Acta Psychiatrica Scandinavia.*

Pritchard, C. and Clooney, D. (1994) *Single Homelessness – Fractured Lives and Fragmented Policies,* Report to Department of the Environment. Bournemouth: Bournemouth Churches Housing Association.

Pritchard, C. and Taylor, R. (1978) *Social Work: Reform or Revolution?* London: Routledge and Kegan Paul.

Pritchard, C., Cotton, A. and Cox, M. (1992) Truancy, illegal drug use and knowledge of HIV infection in 932 14–16 year old adolescents. *Journal of Adolescence,* 15: 1–17.

Pritchard, C., Olivetti, S. and Coleman, P. (in press) An international comparison of Italian suicide rates reveal neglect of the elderly. *Psychiatrica Italica.*

Pritchard, C., Cotton, A., Bowen, D. and Williams, R. (1995a) *Consumer Survey of an Educational Welfare Service: Views of Children and Parents,* Report to Dorset Education Partnership. Dorchester: Dorset.

Pritchard, C., Cotton, A., Cox, M., Godsen, D. and Weeks, S. (1993) Mental illness, drug and alcohol misuse and HIV risk behaviour in 214 young adult (18–35 yrs) probation clients: implications for policy, practice and training. *Social Work and Social Science Review,* 3(2): 150–62.

Pritchard, R.A.H. (1989) Women and the valuing of work. A comparison between gender in a Northern and Southern City, unpublished dissertation, University of London, RHBNC.

Pyke, J. and Steers, M.J. (1992) Suicide in a community-based case-management service. *Canadian Journal of Community Mental Health,* 28(6): 483–90.

Quinton, D. and Rutter, M. (1988) *Parenting Break-down: the Making and Breaking of Inter-generational Links.* Aldershot: Avebury.

Rack, P. (1982) *Race, Culture and Mental Disorder.* London: Tavistock.

Rahe, R.H. and Holmes, D. (1980) Measuring stress: study of illness and illness patterns. *Journal of Psychosomatic Research,* 13: 355–79.

Reed, M.D. (1993) Sudden death and bereavement outcomes: impact of resources on grief symptomatology and detachment. *Suicide and Life Threatening Behaviour* 23: 204–20.

Reker, T. and Eikelmann, B. (1993) Current practice in psychiatric vocational rehabilitation. *Deutsch Psychiatrica Praxis,* 20(3): 95–101.

Rende, P.D., Plomin, R. and Hetherington, E.M. (1993) Genetic and environmental influences on depressive symptomatology in adolescence: individual differences and extreme scores. *Journal of Child Psychology and Psychiatry,* 34(8): 1387–98.

Rich, C.L., Fowler, R.C. and Young, D. (1989) Substance abuse and suicide. The San Diego study. *Annals of Clinical Psychiatry,* 1(2): 79–85.

Rockett, I.R.H. and Smith, G.S. (1993) Covert suicide among elderly Japanese females: questioning unintentional drowning. *Social Science and Medicine,* 36(11): 1467–72.

Rosenhan, D.L. (1973) On being sane in insane places. *Science,* 179: 250–8.

Rosenthal, D. and Kelty, S.S. (1978) *Genetics and Mental Illness.* Oxford: Pergamon Press.

Rotheram-Borus, M.J., Piacentini, J. and Miller, S. (1994) A brief cognitive behavioural treatment for adolescent suicide attempters and their families. *Journal of American Academic Adolescent Psychiatry,* 33(4): 508–17.

Roy, A. (1986) Suicide in Schizophrenia, in A. Roy (ed.) *Suicide,* pp. 97–112. Baltimore: Wilkins & Wilkins.

Runeson, B.S. (1992) Youth suicides unknown to psychiatric care providers. *Suicide and Life Threatening Behaviour,* 22: 494–503.

Rutter, M. and Gillier, R. (1984) *The Challenge of Juvenile Delinquency.* London: Heinemann.

Rutter, M., Bailey, A. and Le Couteur, A. (1994) Autism and known medical conditions: myth and substance. *Journal of Child Psychology and Psychiatry,* 35: 311–22.

Sahfi, M., Carrigan, S. and Derrick, A. (1985) Psychological autopsy of completed suicide · in children and adolescents. *American Journal of Psychiatry*, 142: 1061–4.

Sainsbury, P. (1983) Validity and reliability of trends in suicide statistics. *World Health Statistics Quarterly*, 36: 339–48.

St Aubyn, G.A. (1993) *Queen Victoria: a Portrait*. London: Sceptre Press.

Scheff, T.J. (1984) *Being Mentally Ill: a Sociological Theory*, 2nd edn. Hawthorne: Aldine.

Schene, A.H., Van Wijngaarden, B. and Gersons, B.P.R. (1993) The Utrecht comparative study on psychiatric day and inpatient treatment. *Acta Psychiatrica Scandinavia*, 87(6): 427–36.

Schmitt, L., Oliver, F. and Pereson, G. (1992) Distress in hospitals after a suicide. *Française Psychologie du Medicine*, 24(10): 1035–7.

Schneideman, E.S. (1985) *Definition of Suicide*. New York: Wiley Inter-Science.

Schneider, S.G., Farberow, N.L. and Kruks, G.N. (1989) Suicidal behaviour in adolescent and young adult gay men. *Suicide and Life Threatening Behaviour*, 19: 381–94.

Schneider, S.G., Taylor, S.E. and Hammen, C. (1991) AIDS-related factors predictive of suicidal ideation of low and high intent among gay and bisexual men. *Suicide and Life Threatening Behaviour*, 21: 313–28.

Schreber, D.P. (1955) *Memoirs of My Nervous Illness*. London: Dawsons.

Schwarzenbach, F. and Modestin, J. (1993) Influence of therapy variables on suicide of discharged psychiatric inpatients: results of a controlled investigation. *Nervenart*, 64(3): 181–6.

Scott, J. (1993) Homelessness and mental illness. *British Journal of Psychiatry*, 162: 314–24.

Scott, M.P. and Stradling, S.G. (1991) The cognitive behavioural approach with depressed clients. *British Journal of Social Work*, 21(5): 533–44.

Sedgwick, P. (1982) *Psycho Politics*. London: Pluto Press.

Seneca, L.A. (1948) *Morals and Essays*. London: Everyman.

Sexton, A. (1977) *The Awful Roaring Toward God*. London: Chatto and Windus.

Shakespeare, W. (1980) *The Complete Works of William Shakespeare*, Symmons edition. London: Atlantis.

Shaw, G.B. (1934) *Complete Plays*. London: Helmsley Press.

Shenon, P. (1994) Lonely Chinese face uphill search for Ms Right, *Guardian*, 17 August: 18.

Shepherd, D.M. and Barraclough, B.M. (1976) The aftermath of parental suicide for children. *British Journal of Psychiatry*, 129: 267–76.

Shepherd, D.M. and Barraclough, B.M. (1978) Suicide reporting: information or entertainment? *British Journal of Psychiatry*, 132: 283–7.

Sherin, E.N. and Linehan, M.M. (1994) Patient–therapist ratings and relationship to progress in dialectical behaviour therapy for borderline personality disorder. *Behaviour Therapy*, 23(4): 730–41.

Shilling, C. (1993) *The Body and Social Theory*. London: Sage.

Sibeon, R. (1992) Sociological reflections on welfare politics and social work. *Social Work and Social Science Review*, 3: 184–203.

Simpson, C.J., Seager, C.P. and Robertson, J.A. (1993) Home-based care and standard hospital care for patients with severe mental illness: a randomised controlled trial. *British Journal of Psychiatry*, 162: 239–43.

Soni Raleigh, V., Bulusu, A. and Balarajan, R. (1990) Suicides among immigrants from the Indian sub-continent. *British Journal of Psychiatry*, 156: 46–50.

Sorenson, S.B. and Golding, J.M. (1988) Suicidal ideation and attempts in Hispanic and non-Hispanic whites: demographic and psychiatric disorder issues. *Suicide and Life Threatening Behaviour*, 18: 205–18.

Sournia, J.C. (1990) *The History of Alcoholism*. Oxford: Blackwell.

Speechy, M. and Stavarky, K.M. (1991) The adequacy of suicide statistics for use in epidemiology and public health. *Canadian Journal of Public Health*, 82(1): 38–42.

Spiegel, D. (1991) Psychosocial aspects of cancer. *Current Opinions in Psychiatry*, 4: 889–97.

Stack, S. (1992) The effect of the media on suicide: the Great Depression. *Suicide and Life Threatening Behaviour*, 22: 255–67.

Stack, S. (1993) The media and suicide: a non-additive model 1968–1980. *Suicide and Life Threatening Behaviour*, 23: 63–6.

Stein, A., Forrest, G.C. and Baum, J. (1989) Life threatening illnesses and hospice care. *Archives of Diseases of Childhood*, 64: 697–702.

Steinberg, L.D., Catalano, R. and Dooley, J. (1982) Economic antecedents of child abuse and neglect. *Child Development*, 52: 975–85.

Stensman, R. and Lundquist-Stensman, U. (1988) Physical disease and disability amongst 416 suicide cases in Sweden. *Scandinavian Journal of Social Medicine*, 16(3) 149–153.

Stevenson, R.L. (1936) *The Suicide Club*. London: Everyman.

Stewart, D.A., Stein, A. and Clark, D.M. (1991) Psychosocial adjustment in siblings of children with chronic life-threatening illnesses. *Journal of Child Psychology and Psychiatry*, 33(4): 779–84.

Stewart, D.J. and Stewart, M. (1993) *Social Backgrounds of Young Offenders*. London: Association of Chief Probation Officers.

Stiefel, F., Volkenandt, M. and Breitbart, W. (1989) Suizid und Krebserkrankung. *Schweizer Medizin Wochenschreiber*, 119: 891–5.

Stiffman, A.R. (1989) Suicide attempts in runaway youths. *Suicide and Life Threatening Behaviour*, 19: 147–59.

Stockley, D. and Stockley, M. (1993) *Young People on the Move*. Guildford, University of Surrey: Rowntree Foundation.

Stone, N. (1993) Parental abuse as a precursor of childhood onset of depression and suicide. *Child Psychiatry and Human Development*, 11: 34–41.

Strosahl, K., Chiles, J.A. and Linehan, M.M. (1992) Prediction of suicide intent in hospitalised parasuicide: reasons for living, hopelessness and depression. *Comprehensive Psychiatry*, 33(6): 366–73.

Szasz, T. (1960) The myth of mental illness. *American Psychologist*, 15: 113–18.

Tacitus (1866) *The Annals Vols 1 and 2*. London: Bell and Daldy.

Takahashi, Y. (1989) Suicidal Asian patients: recommendations for treatment. *Suicide and Life Threatening Behaviour*, 193: 305–13.

Taylor, R.K.S. and Pritchard, C. (1982) *The Protest Makers: the British Anti-Nuclear Movement 1958–65 Twenty Years On*. Oxford: Pergamon Press.

Thomas, C.S., Stone, K. and Osborn, M. (1993) Psychiatric morbidity and compulsory admission among UK born Afro-Caribbean and Asians in Central Manchester. *British Journal of Psychiatry*, 163: 91–9.

Thornicroft, G., Margolius, O. and Jones, D. (1992) The TAPS project 6: new long-stay psychiatric patients and social deprivation. *British Journal of Psychiatry*, 161: 621–4.

Toufexis, A. (1994) Killing the psychic pain. *Time*, 4 July: 71.

Toynbee, P. (1987) Unnecessary surgical deaths?, *Guardian*, 26 February: 17.

Toynbee, P. (1993) Rage at the dying of the light, *Guardian*, 24 September: 28.

Tubi, N., Calev, A. and Nigel, D. (1993) Subjective symptoms in depression during the course of ECT. *Neuropsychiatry, Neurophysiology and Behaviourial Neurology*, 6(3): 187–92.

Turner, B.S. (1992) *Regulating Bodies: Essays in Medical Sociology*. London: Routledge.

Tweedie, J. (1993) *Eating Children*. Harmondsworth: Penguin.

US DHHS (1993) *Health of the United States 1992*. Hyattsville, MA: Department of Health and Human Services.

Usher, J. (1991) *Women and Madness*. Aldershot: Harvester Wheatsheaf.

Van der Maas, P.J., Van Delden, J.J. and Looman, C.W.N. (1991) Euthanasia and other medical decisions concerning the end of life. *Lancet*, 338: 669–74.

Van der Wahl, G., Muller, M.T. and Christ, L.M. (1994) Voluntary active euthanasia and physician assisted suicide in Dutch nursing homes: requests and administration. *Journal of the American Geriatric Society*, 42(6): 620–3.

Van Dongen, C.J. (1990) Agonizing questions: experiences of survivors of suicide victims. *Nursing Research*, 39(4): 224–9.

Van Egmond, M.J. and Jonker, D. (1988) Sexual and physical abuse: suicide risk factors for women? The results of an empirical study amongst 158 female attempters. *Tijdschrift und Psychiatrie*, 30(1): 21–38.

Van Praag, H.M. and Lecrubier, Y. (1992) New perspectives on the treatment of depression. *Drugs Supplement*, 43, 1–57.

Vega, W.A., Gil, A. and Zimmerman, R. (1993) The relationship of drug use to suicide ideation and attempts among African-American, Hispanic and white non-Hispanic male adolescents. *Suicide and Life Threatening Behaviour*, 23: 110–19.

Vernon, M. and Phillipe, A. (1988) Suicidal pathology in migrants. *Psychiatric Psychobiology*, 3: 115–23.

Vigderhaus, G. and Fishman, G. (1979) The impact of unemployment and family integration on the changing suicide rates in the USA 1920–1969. *Social Psychiatry*, 13: 239–48.

Vogel, R. and Wolfersdorf, M. (1989) Suicide and mental illness in the elderly. *Psychopathology*, 22: 202–7.

Wagner, A.W. and Linehan, M.M. (1994) Relationship between childhood sexual abuse and topography of parasuicide among women with borderline personality disorder. *Journal of Personality Disorder*, 8(1): 1–9.

Wagner-Martin, L.W. (1991) *Sylvia Plath: A Biography*. London: Cardinal Books.

Wahl, O.F. (1993) Community impact of group homes for mentally ill adults. *Community Mental Health*, 29(3): 247–59.

Walton, R. (1976) *The Modern Social Worker*. London: Routledge and Kegan Paul.

Warr, P. (1987) *Work, Unemployment and Mental Health*. Oxford: Oxford University Press.

Warr, P. and Jackson, P. (1988) Adapting to the unemployed role: a longitudinal investigation. *Social Science and Medicine*, 25(1)1: 1219–24.

Wasserman, D., Varnik, A. and Eklund, G. (1994) Male suicides and alcohol consumption in the former USSR. *Acta Psychiatrica Scandinavia*, 89: 306–13.

Wasylenki, D.A., Goering, P.N. and Lemire, D. (1993) The hostel out-reach program: assertive case management for homeless mentally ill people. *Hospital and Community Psychiatry*, 44(9): 848–53.

Weisbrod, B.A., Test, M.A. and Stein, M.L. (1980) Alternative to mental hospital: economic cost and benefits. *Archives of General Psychiatry*, 37: 398–400.

Weisman, M. (1981) Depressed patients. Results after one year treatment with drugs, and/or inter-personal psychotherapy. *Archives of General Psychiatry*, 37: 401–5.

Weisman, M. and Klerman, G. (1990) Inter-personal psychotherapy and its derivatives in the treatment of depression, in D. Manning and A. Francis (eds) *Pharmacotherapy and Psychotherapy for Depression*, pp. 115–32. Washington, DC: APA Press.

Westfield, J.S., Cardin, D. and Deaton, W.L. (1992) Development of the College Student Reasons for Living Inventory. *Suicide and Life Threatening Behaviour*, 22: 442–52.

Wertheimer, A. (1991) *A Special Scar: the Experiences of People Bereaved by Suicide*. London: Routledge.

White, G.L. and Mullen, P.E. (1989) *Jealousy: Theory, Research and Clinical Strategies*. New York: Guild Press.

Whitehead, M. (1990) *The Health Divide: Inequalities in Health in the 1980s*. Harmondsworth: Penguin.

Wiedenmann, A. and Weyerer, S. (1994) The impact of availability, attraction and lethality of suicide methods on suicide rates in Germany. *Acta Psychiatrica Scandinavia*, 88: 364–8.

Wild, N.J. (1988) Suicide of perpetrators after disclosure of child sexual abuse. *Child Abuse and Neglect*, 12: 112–16.

Williams, R., Pritchard, C. and Bowen, D. (1996) Engaging the client: truant adolescent and parental perspectives of education social workers. *British Journal of Social Work*.

Wilson, M. and Daly, M. (1994) Spousal homicide risk and estrangement. *Violence Victims*, 8(1): 3–16.

Wing, L. (1981) Asperger's Syndrome: a clinical account. *Psychological Medicine*, 11: 115–29.

Wing, L. (1988) The continuum of autistic characteristics, in E. Schopler and G.B. Mesibov (eds) *Diagnosis and assessment in autism*. New York: Plenum Press.

Winokur, G., Coryell, W. and Maser, J.D. (1994) Recurrently situational (reactive) depression. A study of course, phenomenology and familial psychopathology. *Journal of Affective Disorders*, 31(3): 203–10.

World Health Organization (1973–1994) *World Health Statistics Annual*. Geneva: WHO.

Wymer, R. (1986) *Suicide and Despair in the Jacobean Drama*. Brighton: Harvester Press.

Yates, G.L., Mackenzie, R.G. and Swofford, A. (1991) A risk profile of homeless youth involved in prostitution and homeless youth not involved. *Journal of Adolescent Health*, 12(7): 545–8.

Yeo, H.M. and Yeo, W.W. (1993) Repeat deliberate-self-harm: a link with childhood sexual abuse? *Archives of Emergency Medicine*, 10(3): 161–6.

Young, M.A. and Fogg, L.F. (1994) Interactions of risk factors in predicting suicide, *American Journal of Psychiatry*, 151(3): 439–40.

Zhang Xianliang (1989) *Half of Man is Woman*. Harmondsworth: Penguin.

INDEX

A SOCIOLOGY OF MENTAL HEALTH AND ILLNESS

David Pilgrim and Anne Rogers

This new textbook provides a critical introduction to literature on mental health and illness of relevance and interest to undergraduate sociologists. The sociological analysis offered of this material will also be of particular relevance to mental health professionals from a wide variety of disciplines. Questions of race, age and gender are addressed, along with explorations of work on psychiatric treatment, the mental health professions, the organization of mental health work, legalism and service users. The book begins with an examination of the competing perspectives about mental health and illness, which have contributed to multiple understandings and terminologies, both inside and outside of sociology. A recognition of these diverse perspectives informs the way in which subsequent chapter topics are explored.

> . . . the book provides a useful, critical introduction to the literature of mental health and illness . . . An extremely well-referenced book providing excellent background reading for any professional worker in the community or caring services.
>
> *Journal of the Institute of Health Education*

Contents
Perspectives on mental health and illness − Gender − Race and ethnicity − Age − The mental health professions − Questions of treatment − The organization of psychiatry − Psychiatry and legal control − Users of mental health services − References − Index.

208pp   0 335 19013 8 (Paperback)   0 335 19014 6 (Hardback)

THE DEVELOPMENT OF SOCIAL WELFARE IN BRITAIN

Eric Midwinter

This textbook is aimed at undergraduate and diploma students across a wide range of the social sciences, with particular reference to those preparing for or involved in careers in social and public administration. It provides, in compact and accessible form, the story of social provision from medieval times to the present day, systematically examining major themes of:

- the relief of poverty and social care,
- healthcare and housing,
- crime and policing,
- education.

With the rise of the welfare state, and its current questioning as a chief focus, the book sets out to analyse how the state has responded to the social problems that have beset it. Consideration is given to comparative elements in Europe, North America and elsewhere, together with specific reference to issues of race, ethnicity and gender. A specially prepared glossary completes what is a well-packaged review and description of the growth and present disposition of the full range of social and public services in Britain.

Contents
Preface: How best to use this book − Introduction: Social casualty and political response − Medieval life and welfare − The nation-state and the money-economy − Industrialism's impact and the initial response − Piecemeal collectivism: Precursors of the welfare state − The silent revolution of the 1940s − The Butskellite consensus (c.1951−1973/9) − The questioning of the welfare state − General advice on further reading − Glossary of terms − Index.

208pp   0 335 19104 5 (Paperback)   0 335 19105 3 (Hardback)